WITHDRAWN

D0387838

3 1215 00017 1329

HENRY VII

THE FIRST TUDOR KING

By the same author:

NOVELS
THE AMAZING SANDERS
DEAR ENGLAND
A LADY OF NO LEISURE
FRIENDLY ELEVEN
THE WHISTLE BLEW

HISTORICAL
LORD OF LONDON
THE DEVIL OF THE VAULT
INTO UNKNOWN WATERS
THE QUEEN AND THE REBEL
THE REIGN OF EDWARD IV

FOR YOUNG PEOPLE
THE STORY OF METALS

Eric N. Simons

HENRY VII

THE FIRST TUDOR KING

FREDERICK MULLER

First published in Great Britain 1968
by Frederick Muller Ltd., Fleet Street, London, E.C.4

Printed and bound by The Garden City Press Limited
Letchworth, Hertfordshire

To Audrey
my darling daughter

Contents

Illustrations

Preface

THE LATE HENRY FORD once shocked the mandarins severely. 'History,' he said, 'is bunk.' Earlier it had been termed 'philosophy teaching by examples', 'the essence of innumerable biographies', 'the true poetry', 'a distillation of rumour', and by Gibbon 'the register of the crimes, follies and misfortunes of mankind'. To Helps it was 'the chart and compass for national endeavour', while long before Ford, Sir Robert Walpole dismissed it roundly as 'false'. Two even more cynical modern definitions are: 'the assassination of the romantic by the pedantic' and 'the pursuit of the unknowable by the unreadable'—to both of which there are many many exceptions, but of both of which there are outstanding examples.

The excuses for writing history are, first, a consuming interest in tracing the route—however devious, broken and difficult—by which a people has achieved its position in the world. Like a mountaineer one goes step by step over an ancient, dangerous, half-forgotten and overgrown track. Secondly, one has a wish to demonstrate that history is exciting and enjoyable.

For some years now I have been looking at medieval England with close attention. In doing so the conviction has steadily grown that Henry VII has been grossly neglected and underrated. He was a much more vigorous and arresting personality than I had been led to believe. Far from being mean, dull and miserly, a narrow autocrat, his reign tepid and flat, he was civilized, intelligent, and to me in many ways attractive. True, he was neither as warlike, handsome, jovial nor amorous as his predecessor, Edward IV, nor as ambitious, efficient and merciless as the 'hunchback' Richard III. Nevertheless he was immensely able, wiser and more humane than most of his era, passionate, sensitive, his reign a kaleidoscope of fascinating events and personages.

Less spectacular physically, less dramatic by temperament, than the Plantagenets, he was both calmer and deeper. His passions were statecraft, religion, music and jewellery, his major weaknesses not mistresses or Malmsey wine, but money; not brutality and barbarism, but bigotry; not cruelty and conceit but sometimes excessive caution. Neither poltroonery nor pettiness marred his normal behaviour. He was above all a monarch dedicated to his kingdom.

This story of his reign begins with a man running for his life into the wild mountains of Wales, and the soft glances of a royal widow. It ends with the burial of a mourned sovereign. In between comes the life of the first Tudor king. As a child Henry was tossed from pillar to post, became an exile in a foreign land, had on occasion to fly from pursuers, broke the power of Richard III in battle, but in the end took a blood-stained, half-ruined, backward and war-weary island and transformed it over the years into a thriving, peaceful, solid and enduring nation, out of which Elizabethan magnificence was to grow.

Let me stress that I have written primarily for those like myself who find the past absorbing and of inestimable value in judging the present. I have tried to be accurate, but contemporary accounts of the period are few, and these not always trustworthy, while there are also discrepancies between them. Later writers, such as Lord Bacon, are often controversial and far from authentic. In consequence I have resuscitated many traditions and quoted many legends and stories not because they are necessarily true or proven, but because they are amusing and entertaining in themselves and because they indicate what was believed at the time or came to be believed in later ages.

The events of the reign are told largely as seen through English eyes alone. I have not devoted page after wearisome page to minute details of the rivalries and scheming of the foreign powers of the period, ever seeking to preserve an uneasy balance of power among themselves, to grab territory, or to outmanoeuvre and thrust back the newly pertinacious invading Turks. These matters loom up darkly on the horizon of the story like battleships, fire a broadside or two, then disappear again for a period. This, it seems to me, is how they would have impinged upon the minds of ordinary men and women of the time.

As some recompense I have lightly sketched in the more important European potentates and personages with whom Henry had to grapple. The reader wishing to know the intimate details of their national and personal history may pursue them to his heart's content in more specialized and longer works.

I have also refrained from adopting a common practice and cutting up the reign without regard for chronological order into chunks headed 'Ireland', 'France', 'Spain', 'Parliament', 'Church', 'Economy', and so on, each taken separately, then dismissed. Instead, I have as far as possible told the story as it occurred, taking each year in turn, and only running ahead occasionally to wind up a point or dismiss a person. This to my mind gives an effect of immediacy the other method does not. Essentially I have sought to make the reader see the reign not as a god surveying it from above, but as a contemporary man or woman, watching it unfold before him from day to day, from year to year.

To get the story into the compass of an economically viable book, I have refrained from quoting long passages of little interest from the records and have had at times to telescope explanations, events, discussions and descriptions. Consequently this is an outline rather than an exhaustive and exhausting study. Nevertheless I believe the essentials are here, and the story may be none the worse because at moments it lingers on some scene or event that kindled my imagination.

My thanks are due to Mr. Geoffrey C. Piper, Editorial Director of Frederick Muller Ltd., for his consistent help and encouragement, and to his colleague, Mr. L. V. Archer, a Director of the same company, whose expert knowledge of heraldry and weapons of war has been generously placed at my disposal. I also thank Mr. Norman of the Wallace Collection for valuable advice on the arms and armour of the period, and my wife for reading the proofs and generally giving shrewd feminine advice.

ERIC N. SIMONS

Westham, Sussex
1966

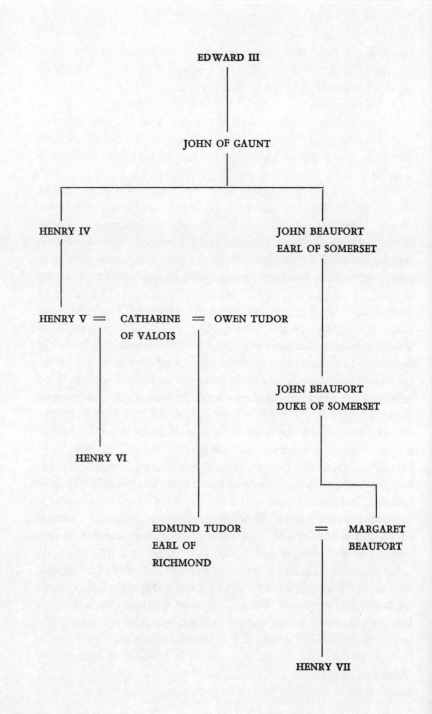

EDWARD III

JOHN OF GAUNT

HENRY IV

JOHN BEAUFORT
EARL OF SOMERSET

HENRY V = CATHARINE = OWEN TUDOR
OF VALOIS

JOHN BEAUFORT
DUKE OF SOMERSET

HENRY VI

EDMUND TUDOR
EARL OF
RICHMOND

= MARGARET
BEAUFORT

HENRY VII

CHAPTER ONE

The Welsh Refugee

[1]

A FORMER BREWER of Beaumaris in Anglesey, a man of little worth, his total income said to have been not £40 a year, was travelling fast into the rough and barbarous mountains of Wales around Snowdon to escape justice. He had killed a man in a quarrel, and the King's men were seeking him. His name was Meredydd ap Tudor, and he was the great-grandfather of Henry VII, steward or 'scutifer' (originally shield bearer, but probably messenger) of the Bishop of Bangor's establishment. At one time his task in this capacity had been to take possession as 'escheator' of whatever property fell to his master, the feudal lord, when any man died intestate. He now found safety and refuge in this wild country and settled down at Plas Pen-y-Mynydd, 'beside Anglesey', on the Tetford road to Bangor, where his son, Owen ab Meredydd ab Tewdr ab Gronw ab Tewdr, was born. We now call him 'Owen Tudor'. They still show the two-storied house of his birth, with four rooms to a floor, all low and small, claiming it to be as it was in his day, but although some part of the 3 ft. thick hewn stone chimney and gateway may be authentic, the rest it is certain has been rebuilt.

Of the early life of Owen Tudor little is known, but he fought bravely for Henry V in France, and seems to have been appointed to that King's personal bodyguard, coming back with him to England. He was a handsome young man, who claimed to have the blood of old Welsh kings in his veins and was said by George Borrow to have had 'the most beautiful of heads', yet at the outset of his career at Court he was ridiculed as 'the dumb Welchman', his knowledge of the English language being so small.

One fine day at Windsor, however, early in the reign of Henry VI, the bright eyes of Shakespeare's 'Sweet Kate'—Catharine of Valois, widowed Queen of Henry V, only twenty-one when her husband died—fell upon this dark-haired, vivacious young man, and she lost her heart. The story told in Wales is that one day, when Owen was on guard in Windsor Castle, he was suddenly invited to dance in the Queen Dowager's presence. One version says that he attempted a too ambitious pirouette, and stumbling, collapsed into Catharine's lap. The manner in which she pardoned him for his clumsiness and unanticipated use of her person is said to have revealed her emotions to her waiting-maids, who whispered among themselves that she greatly demeaned herself by doing such honour to one of low origin, member of a race of barbarous Welsh tribesmen, and meaner than the poorest yeoman.

The young widow, overhearing these comments, remarked that as she was a Frenchwoman, she did not know there were such great racial distinctions in England.

Another version is that when the Welshman was dancing with the Queen Dowager, his knee accidentally touched hers, whereupon he stooped and tied a ribbon round it.

'Why do you use that ribbon, sir?' the lady asked.

'Please, your grace, to avoid touching you.'

'Perhaps you may touch me in another part,' she made answer.

Whichever version is correct, if either, the fair Catharine set to work to discover the true origins of her new favourite. One story is that she sent privately to Anglesey to find out what she could. Knowing of this, Owen sent his own messengers post-haste to notify his mother beforehand of the visit she could expect. The Queen Dowager's men arrived to find her dining on a dish of potatoes, the dish resting on her knee. When questioned, she told them 'I feed upon roast and boiled, and would not take £100 for my table' (her knees). 'I keep six male and six female servants constantly under arms for my defence.' (These were her goats.) Since potatoes were not then known in Europe, this particular legend is almost certainly apocryphal.

The more likely story is that either as an excuse for seeing him again or to ascertain the truth, Catharine herself questioned him closely regarding his origins, and was told that he was one of a line of ancient princes. This tale is embroidered by the addition that when asked to bring some of these illustrious persons to the Court, he sent for two of his cousins, John ap Meredydd and Howell ap Llewellyn, neither of whom could speak a word of English. Their stature and bearing were, however, such that Catharine described them as 'the goodliest dumb creatures I ever saw'.

She soon found opportunity to appoint the young man, known as 'the Rose of Anglesey', to the household of the infant Henry VI, and he became in due course her own Clerk of the Wardrobe, guarding her jewels, receiving her instructions regarding the style of new gowns, and on her behalf buying the material for them. Catharine was a Parisian, daughter of Charles VI of France and the licentious Isabel of Bavaria. It soon became common knowledge that these two young people were enamoured of each other, and indeed, in 1428 or 1429 they threw their bonnets over the windmill and fled the Court, living together as man and wife. Historians have argued for generations concerning whether or not they were ever legally wed, for the facts are few, no document having been found that records their marriage. When their escape was known, Duke Humphrey of Gloucester rushed an Act through Parliament expressly to prevent Catharine from remarrying without the sanction of the King's Council. By this law both she and Owen became liable to severe penalties.

Nevertheless, there is reason to believe that they had secretly married, either before the Act or in its despite. By their religion, to live together unwed would have been a sin. There was no true impediment to marriage, since both were free. Moreover, any children of their union would have been 'bastards', a dishonourable label to leave them. In any event the Act in itself would have compelled them to keep their marriage secret. It is said to have been deleted at a later date from the records. Perhaps the lovers can be given the benefit of the doubt.

Certainly they withdrew from public life. Some believe they resided in Wales, but for a time at least they had a home in the rural districts of England. They appear to have been happy, for Catharine gave Owen three sons, Edmund, Jasper and Owen, and at least one daughter (some say two). The daughter, Margaret, is said to have lived but a few days. Through their mother, all were half-brothers of Henry VI, and also distantly related to him through John of Gaunt.

The year 1436 saw their happiness disrupted. Duke Humphrey's power in the land was increasing, and he was popular. He now extended a cruel hand towards Owen, whom he peremptorily summoned to Court and lodged in Newgate jail. The distressed and ailing Catharine, now thirty-five, was immured in Bermondsey Abbey, her children being snatched from her and put in the care of the Abbess. She died there on the 3rd January, 1437, less than a year after her admission, and was buried first in the Lady Chapel of Westminster, then in the tomb of Henry V. The epitaph placed there by Henry VI made no mention of Owen, but Henry VII removed it and introduced another, which named his grandfather.

Owen, still in Newgate when she died, now escaped and took sanctuary in Daventry, which he refused to leave, though invited to 'disport himself' in the capital. Weary of inactivity, however, he eventually came to London under a safe-conduct, obtained before he would move, and defended himself before the Privy Council so well that the King allowed him his liberty. This time he went home to his native Wales, but Gloucester had not done with him. Medieval statesmen were ruthless and unforgiving. By his orders Lord Beaumont seized him and whisked him back to London, where he was once more thrown into Newgate.

Resourceful and daring, however, he escaped a second time with his servant and his chaplain 'after foully wounding their jailer', and made his way first to Wallingford, then back once more to Wales, where it is believed he was shielded and assisted by the Duke of Bedford.

Owen always maintained that he was descended from Cadwallader, King of North Wales in the seventh century. In this connection it is worthy of note that soon after Henry VII had ascended the throne, he appointed a Commission headed by Sir John Leiaf, Father Guttun Owen, a priest, and others, to trace his ancestry. These learned persons sat down with the Welsh Chronicles in front of them and *proved*, they said, that he was 'lineally descended from Brutus, grandson of Aeneas the Trojan'!

Owen's first-born son was Edmund, followed by Jasper. The third, Owen, took up a monastic life at Westminster Abbey, dying soon afterwards. There was also a natural son, Dafydd, eventually knighted by Henry VI, who married Mary, daughter of John Bohun of Midhurst, and was brought a great inheritance. Owen Tudor became respectable, and in 1459–60, because of his good services, was summoned to London and granted the sum of £40, his sons being declared legitimate. He was also made Keeper of Parks in the lordship of Denbigh, and Woodward of the same lordship, receiving in addition £100 a year from the revenues of the Kentish manors of Falkston, Walton and Bensted.

Though he was an old man in 1460, this did not prevent him from fighting bravely in the Wars of the Roses at the head of the men of Morgannoc. Captured by the young Edward, Earl of March, later Edward IV, on his way to the battle of Mortimer's Cross, he was imprisoned in the Castle of Usk. The chieftains of his clan, led by John ap Meredydd, a kinsman, came to rescue him, but on their way were attacked in a field beside Caerleon by a greatly superior force. There were but a hundred of them. John ordered one son from each family to the rear, so that one member at least of each should have a chance of escape, but made his own sons charge with him in the front rank. They swept the superior force from the field, and in revenge for this defeat Owen was taken to Hereford market place and beheaded on the 4th February, 1460, his head being set up on the cross there. He was buried in the chapel of the church of the Grey Friars.

[2]

Owen's eldest son, Edmund, had been born in 1430 in a manor house belonging to his mother at Hadham in Hertfordshire. He and his brothers were strictly supervised and trained by the Abbess of Barking, Catharine de la Pole, daughter of the Earl of Suffolk. A petition dated 1440 records the payment of money to her for this purpose. The account was probably presented because when Edmund was ten, the King himself accepted responsibility for Owen's sons.

Evidently a sympathetic personality, Edmund was honoured by a knighthood, and in the year 1453 was made Earl of Richmond, his status being inferior to that of a Duke alone. Moreover, his legitimacy had been, as stated, formally established by Act of Parliament. About the same time, his brother Jasper was created Earl of Pembroke. Whether the King and his Council were now convinced that his parents had been truly married at their birth, or whether they considered it politically advisable to remove the stigma of bastardy from the royal half-brothers, cannot be said.

Edmund continued to find favour. A bride was found for him in Lady Margaret Beaufort, born in 1433, daughter of John Beaufort, Earl of Somerset, and lineal heiress of the great John of Gaunt, head of the House of Lancaster. She was for her time an unusually intelligent woman, well-versed in French, so that she even translated a religious work in that language, and having a smattering of Latin. The Earl of Somerset himself was technically a bastard, since Catharine Swynford did not become Gaunt's wife until after he was born. However, Somerset was legitimized by Act of Parliament during the reign of Richard II.

John of Gaunt had already had two wives before he married Catharine, but neither had produced a male heir, and he may deliberately have delayed marrying her until certain she had given him one. The children of Edmund and Margaret were his legitimate descendants, which was important, because if anything happened to Henry VI, they would then have some claim to the succession.

In consequence, when Edmund died at the early age of twenty-six, leaving Margaret more than six months pregnant, much depended on the sex of her coming child. It was a boy, Henry, who inherited his father's title of Earl of Richmond, and was born on the 28th January, 1457, the feast of St. Agnes the Second (not St. Anne, as many years later his mother wrote in error). Margaret Beaufort is said to have been twenty-four when, with her adored infant, she lay on the first floor of what is now known as 'Henry VII's Tower' in Pembroke Castle. The small room in which the child was born, and which was restored in 1929, was on the north wall of the outer ward, close to the Keep, and came to be known as 'The Queen's Nursery'. In later years, according to Leland, it contained 'a chymmeney as new made with the arms and badges of King Henry VII'. The chimney is still there, but although the fireplace also exists, the mantel over it has disappeared, as has the coat of arms and badges, set on an oblong shield. They are believed to have been destroyed when Pembroke Castle was besieged by Oliver Cromwell's men, though one writer claims to have seen traces of them during the nineteenth century.

The room was one of the best and quietest of the castle, and passages led from it to the dwelling chambers of the gatehouse and the rooms in other towers, so that whatever help or comfort the Countess of Richmond required could readily be brought to her. It is only right to mention, however, another theory—that Henry was born in the castle chapel, but this is not now considered likely, though the chapel had, in fact, been richly furnished for the Countess's use.

Pembroke Castle belonged to Jasper Tudor, the child's uncle. A strong, handsome fortification, built on a 'hard' rock close to the town walls and the decayed west gate, it contained when Henry was born a splendid dining hall, from one end of which a winding circular stone staircase led and still leads into an underground chamber known as 'the Wogan', measuring about 80×30 ft. By way of this a man could easily escape through an enormous arched opening above the river, known as 'Hoyle's Mouth'. The Wogan was used as a storage place for boats, and taking one of these whenever danger threatened he could slip down to the river, reach the harbour of Pembroke town, and from there ride or sail to Tenby and take ship to Brittany or France.

In his early manhood, Henry was known in England as 'Henry Tydder'. As he grew up, he surveyed from the castle battlements the old town of Pembroke lying within stout stone walls, parts of which can still be seen. Little more than a village, it consisted of ramshackle dwellings lining the one refuse-littered 'street', just wide enough to merit the name; opposite stood the strongly built dominant tower of St. Mary's Church. The river waters to the north had been dammed to drive a large mill, and westwards, Monckton Priory, a home of Benedictine monks, raised its head.

There Jasper Tudor shielded both mother and son from the bitter Wars of the Roses, which raged beyond this far western outpost. Their peace was not disturbed till, in 1460, the Yorkists came to power. Nevertheless, the Yorkist hold on the kingdom was far from secure, for the Lancastrians held many fortresses in Wales as refuges, rallying points and defence posts. During the next few years, Jasper himself played a part in the struggle between these two Houses. He had already fought for Henry VI at St. Albans in 1455, and two years later, authorized the strengthening, for better defence, of Tenby's town walls, badly built and in disrepair, at the plea of the Mayor, Thomas White, whose portrait, complete with 'liripop' or 'liripipe' (the long tail of his hood slung over his left shoulder), can be seen in the fifteenth-century 'Merchant's House' in Tenby. He has a monument in the same small town.

In 1459 Henry Tudor's mother, the Countess of Richmond, was married again to Henry, Lord Stafford, Steward of Edward IV's household, younger son of the second Duke of Buckingham, and went away to live with him. The boy Tudor is said to have been entrusted thereafter to a Welsh foster-mother.

In the following year Jasper captured Denbigh and its castle from the Yorkists, and was joined there by the fugitive Queen Margaret of Anjou, wife of Henry VI, who had been deposed by the victorious Earl of March after a heavy Lancastrian defeat at Mortimer's Cross. Jasper, who had fought bravely in that battle, did the same at the battle of Towton, but escaped the holocaust that followed that shattering Yorkist victory. He sought refuge in North Wales, crossed to Ireland, and was presently attainted by Edward IV's Parliament. In 1462 he returned to England and helped to defend Bamburgh Castle when besieged. After its capitulation, crossing into Scotland at Christmas, he joined the escaped Queen Margaret in exile in St. Mighel in Barrois, France, where she kept her Court.

One fortress alone held out in Wales against the Yorkist King for eight years, defeating every attempt to capture it—Harlech. Landing in Wales in 1468, Jasper tried to raise the siege, but was defeated by a powerful force under William, Lord Herbert, one of Edward's best generals. Like his grandfather, Meredydd, Jasper hid in 'wild Wales' for a time, then making his way to Pembroke, shut himself up in the castle. Herbert promptly besieged it, his men taking it by storm so swiftly that Jasper had barely time to escape, probably by way of the Wogan, and return to France.

Henry seems to have been sheltering in Harlech Castle when, in 1468, Herbert at last obtained its surrender. He was now nearly twelve, and Comines has said that from the age of five he had been compelled to hide in one Welsh castle after another. By royal command Herbert took Jasper's title of 'Earl of Richmond', and accepted guardianship of the boy, whose future now depended entirely on his benevolence or otherwise. Henry was taken to Herbert's new home, Raglan Castle, the ruins of which are carefully maintained, and brought up for a brief period by Anne Devereux, Lady Herbert.

The powers of a medieval guardian were great. He could, if he wished, make the life of his ward a misery. None save the King could say him nay, and not always he. To the credit of the Herberts, and particularly of Anne, the boy was treated as their own son. He had been a weakly infant, and this possibly rendered his guardians sympathetic, but there may have been another reason. The new Earl had an only daughter, Maud, and evidently contemplated a match between her and the boy, for his will of the 16th July, 1468, declared: 'I will that Maud, my daughter, be wedded to the Lord Henry of Richmond.'

When the rising of Robin of Redesdale broke out in the following year, however, the Earl was killed at the battle of Danesmoor, Edward IV fled the country, and the Lancastrians once more took control of all England. Jasper came back with the great Earl of Warwick, who had dethroned Edward IV, and a Welsh bard predicted, it is said, that

> Jasper will build for us a dragon,
> of the fortunate blood of Brutus he,
> a Bull of Anglesey to achieve,
> He is the hope of our race.

Throughout these years Anne Devereux continued to treat Henry as her son, appointing as his tutors Andreas Scotus and the Dean of Warwick. Scotus thought highly of his native abilities.

However, it was time, Jasper Tudor thought, for his nephew to be removed from Yorkist hands, however gentle, and taking him from Raglan, he brought him to the King's Court. The marriage with Maud never took place, for Maud eventually became the wife of Henry Percy, fourth Earl of Northumberland. Jasper, having resumed possession of Pembroke Castle as well as his original title, presented Henry to his own early benefactor, King Henry VI, and tradition has it that that simple, pathetic monarch greeted Jasper with the words 'Welcome, for thou has taken good care of thy nephew', and struck by the intelligence of his young half-nephew, said: 'Lo, surely this is he to whom both we and our adversaries shall hereafter give place.' This, however, is an improbable story, and in any event the King was a poor judge of men.

Then, dramatically, the boy's world was once more brought down in ruins about him. That daring, brilliant and lucky warrior, Edward IV, invaded England and regained his kingdom.

[3]

Jasper Tudor greeted Margaret of Anjou, the wife of Henry VI, when she landed with a force in England to set her husband on the throne again, then left her and set off for Wales to raise a Welsh army. She and her military commander, the Duke of Somerset, marched towards the river Severn, meaning to cross it and link up with him. However, Edward, following hard on her heels, defeated her at Tewkesbury and eventually took her prisoner. The Lancastrian cause was lost for good and all, for shortly afterwards the King died in the Tower, by Richard of Gloucester's hand, it was asserted. Henry VI's only son, Prince Edward, having been killed in or after the battle, Jasper now saw that in the person of his nephew he had the sole heir to the House of Lancaster and a possible future King of England. He took the boy to Chepstow Castle, where he was nearly captured by Vaughan and the people of Chepstow, then to Pembroke Castle, where he was again besieged by Morgan ap Thomas, but the fortress was relieved by Morgan's brother, David. Uncle and nephew hastened to Tenby, being given warm hospitality by John Griffith White, the Mayor, though his robes doubtless offended their nostrils, being regularly kept in the latrine of his house, since men of his station had no wardrobes. (The ammoniacal effluvia were held to protect them from the moth.) The Mayor was later rewarded by being granted the lease of all the crown lands about Tenby.

Henry had been attainted by Edward's Parliament, together with his uncle. George, Duke of Clarence, Edward IV's younger brother, vainly sought the title of Earl of Richmond. Under the Yorkists

England was no place for either of the Tudors, and a chronicler asserts that their departure from Tenby to France was on the advice of Henry VI himself, given just before his death.

Crossing the Channel was no easy matter in medieval times. The tiny ships were never more than a couple of hundred tons burden and at the mercy of every gale. A storm blew the refugees right off course on to the shores of Brittany, where they were taken prisoner. Comines, the French historian, claims to have witnessed this latter event.

Brittany was then no part of the Kingdom of France, but an independent Dukedom, ruled by Francis II. She had her own standing army, her own system of taxation, and a perpetual and increasing need to hold her own against Louis XI, the French King, who secretly coveted her to round off his dominions.

Jasper's request to the Duke for asylum was willingly granted, not from pure benevolence, but because Francis saw in these two Lancastrians a possible bond between his Duchy and the still powerful forces of their House in England which might prove useful should he need an ally to resist French encroachment. Henry's mother, no longer a widow and not with them, approved of their escape, knowing that while ever Henry remained in England or Wales he would be in peril. A pious, strong-willed martinet of a woman, strict in her attention to the commands of her church, she too saw in Henry the head of the House of Lancaster. As such he would, she knew, always represent a threat to the shrewd and able Edward IV.

To Edward's credit he did not humiliate her nor limit her freedom. On the contrary, he gave her estates in Devonshire from which she drew an adequate income. Most of her days were spent in that remote county. When Lord Stafford died in 1482, she took a third husband in Thomas, Lord Stanley, Steward of Edward's household, on condition that he respected her chastity. Whether he kept his promise is a matter of opinion. She held the Queen's train at the Coronation of Richard III, and her re-marriage was a great factor in bringing the immensely rich and powerful Stanley to look favourably upon young Henry.

Uncle Jasper and his nephew settled down at the Breton Court, and with every year that passed, Henry Tudor became more popular with his host, the Duke of Brittany. Nevertheless, Edward IV had by no means forgotten him, and presently Francis was asked to return him to England on the pretext that the King wished to marry him to a daughter of his own. Edward insisted he had no intention of holding or harming the young man.

The policy of medieval princes was largely that of balancing opposing forces, and indeed it can almost be said that the notion of a balance of power dates from this period. In the ultimate decisions they reached, individuals were unimportant or expendable. To Francis, the now well-established Yorkist king was a bird in the hand worth far more than a Lancastrian youth in the bush. Accordingly he agreed to Edward's request. An English embassy came over to receive the fugitive and conduct him to England, and without more ado the Duke handed him to them. Rejoicing in their success, the envoys carried Henry to the walled citadel and port of St. Malo, where a ship for England awaited them. By this time, however, the boy was old enough to understand his danger. He could not believe that Edward would leave any Lancastrian member of the blood royal alive. Once in England, he was as good as dead.

Whether he genuinely fell ill or feigned illness as a pretext we do not know. The chronicle says: 'For very pensiveness and inward thought he fell into a fervant and sore ague', so that he was unable to travel. The English ambassadors had to wait until he had recovered. Possibly they appreciated that if he died during the voyage home they would be accused of murdering him.

Meantime, a Breton admiral, Jean de Quelenec, jealous for the honour of his ruler and his country, and ashamed that a young man who had trusted himself to them should be betrayed, pleaded so well with Francis for his rescue that the Duke, repenting, sent his treasurer post-haste to cancel the order for his surrender. This emissary, Pierre Landois, with a band of followers rode into St. Malo, sought admission to the English envoys' lodging and kept them talking. Meanwhile, his men surreptitiously snatched Henry from his sick bed and clapped him into the nearest sanctuary, where he could not be touched.

[4]

Sanctuary, mention of which will recur throughout this book, was of great importance in the medieval years. It was of two kinds—'general' and 'peculiar'. 'General' sanctuary meant that a felon could go into any church and be sure that he would not be forcibly removed. Within a period of forty days he had to confess his crime before a representative of the crown and take an oath to leave the kingdom for good. He forfeited his property, but was given time to depart, setting forth with a cross of wood on his shoulder, wearing a white gown, and travelling by the royal highway and no other route. He could stay no more than a couple of nights under any roof, and had to board his ship in the shortest possible time.

In 'peculiar' sanctuary, the rules were different. Only a limited number of churches—about thirty in all in England at this period— could by charter from the King shelter the refugee. It lasted as long as the man or woman concerned remained within the sanctuary walls. The grave offences of those who claimed shelter here occasionally led to their refuge being violated and themselves hurried off to execution, but by and large, sanctuary was respected. On the other hand, great abuses of the privilege existed, especially during the reign to be described.

When Henry's escape was known, Landois stormed hypocritic- ally at the English, telling them it was their own fault for guarding him so badly, and as the Duke would never commit sacrilege by violating sanctuary, they would have to go home empty-handed. However, he solemnly promised that the young Earl of Richmond should not leave the sanctuary church except to be held in strict custody.

In the event, Henry never left Brittany during the lifetime of Edward IV, and was always carefully watched, but when the Yorkist monarch died in 1482, he became free to follow his own inclinations again.

In his will, Edward bequeathed to Henry, curiously enough, a new horse with trappings of velvet. The gloomy Richard of Gloucester seized the throne, which he had long coveted, and took up the reins of government as Richard III. He was, and by the majority still is, believed to have been responsible for the murder in the Tower, shortly afterwards, of Edward's two young sons, Edward V and Prince Richard of York.

A man of different stamp altogether from his genial, dissolute, pleasure-loving, avaricious, but popular brother, Richard III knew better than Henry himself the legitimacy of the Tudor claim to the throne. He became especially apprehensive when a proposal was mooted that the young man should marry Anne of Brittany, eldest daughter of Duke Francis. Possibly the nervous Francis was again insuring himself in case Henry should one day occupy the throne of England. Richard had no reason to believe that Henry fully understood his rights of reversion to the crown given by Act of Parliament referred to, for Edward and his Parliament had indeed taken good care to omit all reference to these rights in the Act of Henry's Attainder and all later documents.

Nevertheless, the new King saw that if a cunning Lancastrian noble should persuade the young man to assert a claim and foster his ambitions, that claim could be legitimately founded on his descent from Catharine of Valois, once Queen of England.

Such an adherent appeared, in fact, in the person of the second Duke of Buckingham, of the Stafford line, who had married a Woodville, and was therefore of the same family as the still living Dowager Queen Elizabeth, widow of Edward IV. Buckingham was 'neither unlearned and of nature marvellously well-spoken', had held high office under and enjoyed the confidence of Edward IV. Nevertheless, he had aided Richard's usurpation of the throne. Though Lancastrian by birth, he was Yorkist in sympathy, but Richard, who trusted him as far as he trusted anyone, had given him important offices, such as that of High Constable of England. The Duke was greedy and claimed in addition the lands of the Earl of Hereford, which had, he told Morton, Bishop of Ely, been unfairly taken from him by Edward IV. Richard refused to restore them, reproaching him fiercely for his presumption, the Hereford lands being 'interlaced with the title to the crown', while he also took away his office of High Constable. Enraged, Buckingham determined on revenge.

On Edward's death the Countess of Richmond, Henry's mother, daughter-in-law of the 1st Duke of Buckingham by her second marriage to his son, Henry, Lord Stafford, in 1459, had seen an opportunity to bring her beloved Henry home from Brittany. She tried to persuade her former father-in-law through his influence with the new King to achieve this, but Buckingham knew full well that any such proposal would be like the hiss of a serpent in Richard's ears. Though Buckingham nursed his private resentments, he ignored the Countess's pleas, in which she was joined by his son, Henry, and set off for Bridgnorth through Shrewsbury, leaving her to make her way to Worcester.

Tradition has it that Buckingham himself, being of royal blood, aspired to the crown. As his horse's hooves sent the mud flying he suddenly realized that the Earl of Richmond stood between him and all aspiration to kingship—stood, in fact, 'as both bulwarcke and portecolis betwene me and the gate to entre into the majestie royal and gettynge of the crowne'. There and then the notion of using the Tudor across the Channel to wreak his revenge upon Richard came to him like a flash of lightning.

It is an improbable story, for medieval nobles would never have abandoned their ambitions for a comparatively unknown youth. Moreover, not Henry but his mother stood next in succession to the throne should the King die. It is more probable that Buckingham meant to make Henry his tool, with the support of the Lancastrians, and supplant him when he had served his purpose.

At the same time, the bloody murders of the two princes in the Tower had turned his stomach, for he shared the popular belief in Richard's guilt. His own royal lineage made him also a potential menace to his sovereign, so that at any moment that cold glittering royal eye might light upon him and the shadow of the executioner fall across his path. It would be folly, he felt, to wait supinely for assassination or death by the axe.

His first step was to correspond secretly with Henry Tudor, who almost certainly did not know, and was not told, that his birth had been legitimized by Act of Parliament. Buckingham may have thought it better not to reveal the full strength of his protégé's position. He also persuaded the Marquis of Dorset, who had taken sanctuary to escape Richard's clutches, to come out and muster a large force in Yorkshire.

John Morton, Bishop of Ely, who had incurred the King's

displeasure, being suspected of plotting against him, was lying under arrest in the Tower, to which he had been sent by the Council on the 13th June, 1483. There is a tradition that when he was walking in his garden with Richard III just before his arrest, the King jested with him about the strawberries he prided himself on growing at Holborn in his episcopal garden.

The King was prevailed upon by Buckingham to transfer Morton to his (Buckingham's) castle at Brecknock and on the pretext of interrogating his prisoner, the Duke took horse and went via Shrewsbury to the castle. It is said that the Ely Tower was the scene of their discussions. He conveyed to the prelate his readiness to dethrone the grim and ruthless King. (On the other hand, some historians claim that Morton was the instigator of the conspiracy.)

However this may be, his suggestion was that the crown should be offered to the young Earl of Richmond on one condition, that he would solemnly vow before witnesses to take as his Queen Elizabeth of York, eldest daughter of Edward IV. The admirable good sense of this suggestion lay in the promise it held out of healing the terrible wounds inflicted on the aristocracy by the Wars of the Roses. The coming together of these two young people in holy matrimony would end the rivalry between York and Lancaster, and seat on the throne a royal pair who could legitimately claim the support of both great Houses. The astute and able lawyer–ecclesiastic saw at once the advantage of the proposal. Overjoyed at such unexpected ducal support he threw himself passionately into the conspiracy, and advised taking into their confidence Henry's mother, the Countess of Richmond, and in addition her servant, Reginald Bray, a Worcestershire man, steward of her household and receiver-general of her second husband, Henry, Lord Stafford.

Bray was at once invited to Brecknock Castle, and came posting there from the Stafford residence in Lancashire. Told of the plan, he was instructed to report to the Countess, his patroness, who, if she agreed, was to crave audience with Elizabeth Woodville, Edward's widowed Queen, living in sanctuary in Westminster Abbey, confide the proposals to her, and gain her consent to the eventual marriage of her daughter to the exiled Henry. If she agreed, the Countess must at once send a secret messenger to her son and insist that the crown lay within his reach if he would give the required undertaking as regards the marriage.

Bray carried out his orders, and the Countess, her eyes sparkling with delight, reminded the conspirators that Elizabeth of York had once before been proposed as a wife for her son, saying that she herself would accept her as a daughter-in-law even if she came with only a penny. She quickly sought an interview with the Queen Dowager by means of Dr. Lewes, Elizabeth's physician, and on learning that the Queen would see her, made her way to Westminster.

The Queen Dowager, living under guard with her five daughters in a small room, virtually a prisoner lest she should escape overseas, received her and was in full agreement with the proposal. The question now arose: Whom should they send to Henry as their accredited secret messenger?

Father Christopher Urswick, a priest in the Countess's household, though relatively new to her employ, had already impressed her as trustworthy and intelligent. After deliberation, however, she decided instead upon Hugh Conway, a respected, capable member of her staff, who would probably be more welcome to Henry than a prelate. He was instructed to convey her message, obtain a reply, and return at once to Wales. Sympathetic Lancastrians there would aid him if required.

Conway promptly rode to Plymouth, found a ship for Brittany, landed, and journeyed swiftly to the Court of Francis II. At this period, it is said, despatches could be carried one hundred miles in a day, horsemen being posted at intervals of twenty miles for the purpose. In fifteenth-century England, however, messengers by land or sea risked their lives, so the Countess duplicated her despatches, sending off a second member of her establishment, Thomas Ramme, with the same instructions, who sailed from *Kent* to Calais, and arrived in the Breton Court but an hour after Conway.

The tradition is that at the monastery at Rennes Conway handed the Earl of Richmond a ring and a letter procured from Elizabeth of York. Henry, wearing a black surcoat, fell to his knees, kissed the ring, and read the letter.

Either then or later Buckingham decided that his prisoner,

Morton, would be Henry's best adviser if the young man agreed to their conditions. Understandably, however, the Duke was nervous. He could not openly release the Bishop, so laying himself under suspicion, nor could he go to Brittany himself without royal leave. It was equally impossible to send the Countess, while Bray, though a good and loyal servant, had neither Morton's prestige nor his abilities. Finally, the Duke found an old solution. Morton should 'escape' from Brecknock.

One dark night, therefore, the priest shed his garments, slid into a disguise, and broke out of the castle. Before many days he had ridden across England to his old headquarters at Ely, where he speedily linked up with Lancastrian partisans, who gave him funds and a ship. He set sail for Flanders, and on arrival made his way at once to Henry's abode.

[5]

The proposal from England excited the Earl, quick to see that Richard was becoming increasingly unpopular in England. The crown was far more enticing to Henry than the daughter of Duke Francis. He let three weeks go by, probably taking soundings, then coolly and decisively abandoned the notion of marrying Anne, and vowed to take Elizabeth to wife if he overthrew the King. The messengers were sent back to their mistress so that the conspirators might set to work without delay on his behalf.

Perhaps when they had gone this young man of twenty-six paused to look at his shield, carrying the arms of England and France, 'quartered within a border azure and charged alternately with fleurs de lys and marteleted or', while dreaming of a glittering future.

What is certain is that he had never set eyes on the Princess he had pledged himself to marry. Did a little uneasiness assail him as he made his vow? Was he pledging himself to some plain Jane, some scraggy or obese young girl whom he would come to loathe?

CHAPTER TWO

The Affair at Poole

[1]

AWAY IN ENGLAND the brooding Richard had not forgotten the refugee youth still sheltering under the wing of the Duke of Brittany. A subtle and audacious ruler, the King had taken chances throughout his life, standing by the consequences without flinching. His brother, King Edward IV, had trusted even if he had not loved him, and for him Richard had fought bravely and well. He had not always agreed with his policies, as, for example, at Picquigny in France, when Edward allowed himself to be bought off by the French King for a pension and took home a splendid army without striking a blow. Nor had he shared his brother's intemperance and dissolute habits. Quietly he had gone about his work, a good general, a capable administrator, popular enough at one time with the people, who knew and respected him for his fearlessness in battle.

When he wished, he could be captivating and diplomatic, yet was inwardly corroded by the knowledge that in seizing the crown from the rightful heir, the boy Edward V, he had betrayed his brother's trust. Whether or not he was responsible for the murder of the two princes in the Tower, the old Roman saying *Cui bono* lingered in the minds of his subjects. The King more than any other man had benefited from these two bloody deaths, and all knew it.

Overnight his popularity vanished. 'For which cause King Richard lost the hearts of the people', the chronicler says. This barbarous deed wrought in the dark silence of the Tower threatened England with a new plunge into internecine warfare. The Yorkists were infuriated and the Lancastrians themselves sickened by the deed, as Buckingham had been. The entire kingdom was weary of

3—H VII

bloodshed. Edward had given them a few precious, precarious years of unity and peace. They had begun to breathe freely again, to build up their shattered homes and fortunes. But now . . .

The King perceived his decline in public goodwill, and his naturally suspicious character reacted sharply. He studied closely every man at his Court, listening to and weighing their words, observing their gestures and expressions, putting out sensitive antennae in search of plot and intrigue, yet he failed to detect the conspiracy centring on the young Tudor Earl. All he knew was that while ever Henry of Richmond was alive and free he was a potential threat. The King was too intelligent to leave that threat in being. Somehow he had to get the Tudor into his own hands.

He tried diplomacy, for invasion of Brittany was out of the question, being unjustifiable by any excuse to his people. Instead, he whipped up a team of skilled negotiators and packed them off to the Breton Court on the pretext that urgent matters of trade needed discussion. His true motive was, however, to persuade Duke Francis to send the young refugee back to England. By doing so he would win the friendship of the King of England. If not, he must place Henry in some fortress where he could be watched and prevented from any rash escapade, or at least undertake never to let his ports and harbours become jumping-off points for a rebel invasion.

The King did not know any such attack impended, and was merely from common sense seeking to forestall and defeat his enemies. He did not suspect Buckingham, and in consequence his negotiators were handicapped, for Francis, a wily and far-seeing man, had evidently been trusted with some part at least of the secret, and had promised the conspirators every possible help.

While returning soft answers to Richard's ambassadors, he did not commit himself. The ambassadors came back to England with shiploads of apparent goodwill, not knowing that their contents were worthless, while Richard, if disappointed, remained unalarmed.

[2]

The days passed and Buckingham presently fixed a date for Henry's landing in England, writing in his own hand on the 24th

September, 1483, to urge him to land as near to the 18th October as the weather would allow. Lord Stafford had died in the previous year and his widow, the Countess of Richmond, had married again, Thomas, Lord Stanley. He himself, he explained, would assemble and march with forces from Brecknock on that same date, and this would be the signal for other uprisings throughout the south of England.

In confirmation of this Edward and Piers Courtenay, two Devonshire brothers, together with the Bishop of Exeter, mustered their men in Cornwall and Devon. Sir Richard Guildford and other squires called up their levies in Kent. The plan was that these forces with the dissidents of Wiltshire and Berkshire as well as those of East Anglia, should link up at four focal points—Exeter, Salisbury, Newbury and Maidstone—as soon as Henry disembarked in Wales.

[3]

Richard III was no simpleton, and his administrative machine efficient. Learning at last from spies of the stirrings in the counties and Wales, he is said to have summoned Buckingham to his Court, but the Duke, divining what was intended, assembled his Welsh followers and marched them through the border lands of Wales to bring out all his tenants. True to his word he then raised his standard at Brecknock and advanced through the Forest of Dean, but was furious when Lord Stanley, the most powerful of the northern nobles, instead of joining him, remained neutral.

Richard countered at once by a proclamation issued on the 23rd October denouncing Buckingham and offering a big reward for his head. John Paston was ordered by the Duke of Norfolk to bring with him to the assembly point for the royal forces such company of 'tall men as ye may goodly make at my cost and charge . . . ordeyne them jakets of my livery'. Orders were given to guard all the shores of the country. Then, marching out from his castle of Middleham in Yorkshire, the King moved towards Coventry, meaning to interpose his army between that of Buckingham and those of his supporters from the rest of the kingdom.

Three days later the storm broke, both literally and metaphorically, for on the one hand Buckingham moved south and on the other a great gale sprang up in the Channel, rain poured down incessantly, and an overflow of the Wye and Severn rivers caused heavy loss of animals and human life. It lasted at least six days, though some say ten. The tributaries gorging the rivers flooded the country. Sheep were washed away from the lower pastures. Struggling cattle were snatched from the meadows, trees uprooted, buildings overthrown, while a surging torrent raced over a vast waste of agitated waters, imperilling or destroying whatever opposed it. Children went screaming down the swirling river, some of the infants afloat on their wooden cradles.

Buckingham could not cross the Severn, especially as every remaining ford was held against him, while Norfolk successfully prevented the rebels of Surrey and Kent from combining at Gravesend with those from farther north.

Meanwhile, on the 12th October, Henry, allowing six days for the voyage to Wales, sailed from Brittany, taking with him a force estimated at about 5,000, which seems an exaggeration, since he had only fifteen small ships provided by the Duke of Brittany. When they met the gale, his tiny ships were scattered and tossed hither and thither about the sea until, fleeing before the wind, some took refuge in the ports of Normandy, others in their own Breton harbours.

Buckingham and his army made towards Gloucester, meaning to cross the Severn by the bridge there and unite with the Courtenays, but this proved impossible. Learning that by forced marches the King had already reached Salisbury, many Welshmen, short of pay, money and food, and heedless of their commander's promises and threats, slipped away. Buckingham was also continually harassed by local bands under the Earl of Devon. By the time he had moved back into Weobley in Herefordshire, home of Lord Ferrers, his numbers had greatly diminished and despair overcame him. The Marquis of Dorset now fled.

Meantime, Henry's ship had lost contact with the rest of his fleet. Either her skipper's navigation was better or Henry's own will stronger than that of his vanished Admiral, for his ship, holding fairly well to her course, sighted at last the southern coast of England. Even now Richard did not know that an invasion fleet had sailed, for his proclamation of the 23rd October made no allusion whatsoever to Henry Tudor.

The invaders drew in close enough to recognize the Hampshire harbour of Poole (some say Plymouth). Since in such dreadful weather it was no longer possible to reach Wales, and in any event their stocks of food would not have sufficed for a return voyage should they have failed to land on that coast, they made their way inshore. To their dismay the shores and sea banks bristled with men-at-arms, silently watching and waiting. No cheering crowds greeted their slow glide into the harbour, yet not an arrow or gun was fired, and no howls of rage betokened resistance. Perhaps these armed men were friends after all, gathered to receive and reinforce the returning exile.

Nevertheless, scenting danger, Henry dropped anchor, sending a boat ashore to discover whether they were hostile, or if not, their numbers and strength. Meantime he forbade all landings unless the rest of his fleet came in.

The little boat, oars dipping and gleaming, pulled away, a mark of interrogation on the dimpled water. . . .

[4]

His position now hopeless, Buckingham tamely surrendered to reality. Putting on peasant clothes under 'an old piled black cloak', he hid in a hut in a small plantation of fruit trees close to a house— Lacon Hall, near Wem in Shropshire—belonging to Ralph Bannister, one of his own retainers. The price put on Buckingham's head induced this man to betray him. It is said in another version of the story that his presence was revealed by the exceptional quantities of food taken into the hut. The county Sheriff, Sir John Mitton, seized him and carried him off to the King. His principal commanders had already dispersed and made their way by sea to the Continent. With characteristic speed and ruthlessness, Richard came through Wiltshire, entered Salisbury, and after the Duke had been tried by Sir Ralph Assheton, ordered his immediate execution. The Duke was taken to the market square of Salisbury (Hutton says 'the top of Price Hill') and having confessed, was beheaded on the 2nd November on a new scaffold. Bannister received the manor of Yalding as his reward.

Though none of these happenings were known to the young Earl, waiting for his little boat to come back from Poole, he had correctly interpreted what he had already seen. The ease and assurance with which the armed men moved and looked out to sea, the absence of Buckingham's standard or the standards of his Lancastrian supporters, warned him to be cautious. He had arrived not with an army, but with a ship badly battered by the storm and containing at most a few hundred men. Some writers have suggested that he was cowardly in not landing, but clearly he would have been mad to do so without some sign of enthusiastic welcome and without the bulk of his forces.

On its return the boat brought messages from the port. Those gathered there in arms claimed to be adherents of Buckingham, who, they said, was in camp near-by with a great force. Henry was urged to come in and land. Nevertheless the conclusions he had already reached, and perhaps something in the wording of the message or the bearing of the messenger, convinced him this was a ruse. His storm-scattered fleet showed no sign of arriving, so he ordered the anchor to be raised and sail hoisted. His tiny ship put about and made off to sea again. This time she had a strong following wind, made good headway and was able to reach a convenient harbour in Normandy, where Henry rested for three days, heartening his disappointed men.

This is the more widely accepted account, based on Holinshed, and probably true, but in Wales there is a strong tradition, supported by many details, that Henry did, in fact, reach Wales, and took refuge at Tre-Mostyn, where a band of the King's men, hot in pursuit, arrived just as he was sitting down to dinner. He had barely time to jump out of a rear window and escape to safety through a secret opening now known as 'The King's'. His host, the Lord of Mostyn, was Richard ap Howel. There is a charming legend that long afterwards hundreds came to see a bush bearing both red and white roses that was growing at this place.

Henry is also said to have had a similar narrow escape from Richard's men at Cors-y-gedol in Ardudwy, but shaking off his pursuers, reached the little port of Barmouth. The 'White House' there, built by the Vaughans of Cors-y-gedol, is said to have been his lodging before he departed for Brittany.

Normandy was at this time an appanage of the French King, Charles VIII, whose sanction was necessary before the Earl could travel safely back through the territory to Brittany. Accordingly Henry despatched a messenger to the French Court, probably as a courtesy and a formality, for he did not wait for the royal permit. However, the bad luck that had greeted his first attempt had won him a degree of sympathy in France, and no objection was raised.

Having already dismissed his seamen and their craft and sent them off to their Breton home ports, he moved slowly until overtaken by the returning messenger. Charles not only sent him a safe-conduct, but also some badly-needed cash to cover his immediate needs. He then quickened pace, arriving in the little fishing harbour of Paimpol, off the coast of Brittany, on the 30th October.

Francis II generously lent him a considerable sum of money (10,000 gold crowns), and Henry sat down to await news of Buckingham's rising in England. His first accurate tidings came from those supporters who, on the collapse of the rebellion, had fled the country and come to join him. At their head was Thomas Grey, Marquis of Dorset, who went on to Paris, the two Courtenays from Devonshire, Lord Welles, Sir Giles Daubeney, Sir John Bourchier, Sir Thomas Arundel, Sir John Cheyney, Sir William Berkeley, Sir Richard Edgecombe and Sir Edward Poynings, as well as Bishop Morton and other members of their families. These had all come to Vannes, a Breton town near Morbihan, and some of their names will recur in this account.

From these men and their messengers the aspirant to the throne learned that not only was Buckingham dead, but also Thomas Ramme, the Countess of Richmond's trusted messenger, and Sir Thomas St. Leger, the King's own brother-in-law, who had been beheaded at Exeter. Like Morton, Father Urswick had escaped and was now in Flanders.

Seeing that this nucleus of his adherents remained, and that neither Brittany nor France had deserted him, the Earl of Richmond, who might otherwise have been cast down by his misfortunes, took fresh heart. With the gold of Brittany and France clinking in his coffers, he called his friends to meet him in Rennes, the Breton capital, on a day appointed. There it was decided that a second attempt should be made when conditions were once more favourable.

[5]

In England Richard was striving with might and main to make himself and his crown secure. Calling a Parliament in January, 1484, he obtained the outlawry of the Earl of Richmond and the Countess of Richmond, his mother. Henry was labelled a 'bastard' with neither a legitimate claim to the throne nor a following. There is little doubt what his fate would have been had he been taken at Poole.

The Countess was a different kettle of fish altogether. In Lord Stanley she had now a rich and powerful husband whom the King dared not antagonize. Consequently she was neither imprisoned nor abused. Her death, unless demonstrably natural, would have added to the sombre rumours already gathering like dark clouds about Richard's head. However, her husband was ordered to keep her close and prevent her from acting rashly—a severe task for even a lordly husband. Her estates also were transferred to Lord Stanley's management.

Although Richard had punished the leaders of the conspiracy, he was less drastic with the rank and file, pardoning those whom he feigned to regard as misled and not their own masters. Anxious to present himself to his people in a favourable light, he swore in the presence of the Mayor, Aldermen and Councillors of the city of London that he would not harm the Queen Dowager and her children, but would shield them from all danger. Meantime, knowing she was weary of life in sanctuary, he proposed in March that she should trust his oath, emerge with her daughters, and take her rightful place at Court.

Elizabeth Woodville was also given to understand that if she agreed, the King would marry her daughters to suitable husbands, and set aside for each the annual sum of 200 marks. The Queen Dowager, alarmed, no doubt, by the swift suppression of the revolt, was afraid of what might happen to her and her children if she refused. Accordingly she left her refuge, and at the King's instigation wrote to the Marquis of Dorset, still a refugee, begging him to return to his own country, where he would receive a full pardon from the King and great advancement.

Nothing loth, the Marquis, still in Paris, slipped away in haste and stealth, and set out on the long ride to Flanders, meaning to take the first possible ship for England.

By now Richard had discovered the importance of Edward IV's eldest daughter, the Princess Elizabeth of York, to the plans of Henry Tudor and his supporters, but her mother, the Queen Dowager, had put her person and life in his hands, and in this way, he conceived, the Earl's guns had been spiked, or, as was said: his 'chiefe combe had been clerely cut'.

[6]

In Brittany, Henry's Council at Rennes concurred with him in believing that in his second attempt at invasion he should land, as originally intended, on a friendly rather than a hostile shore, that of Wales, and nowhere else. Christmas was approaching and there was need for a solemn, binding agreement among the Richmond party. On Christmas Day 1483 all repaired, therefore, to the old Cathedral of the town, destroyed centuries later by fire. There all his followers swore allegiance to him, he in turn swearing—with secret misgivings, perhaps—to marry Elizabeth of York if he seized the crown. Henry was now treated by his followers with reverence and respect 'as though he had bene that tyme the crowned kynge and anoynted prince'.

Told of these vows, Francis of Brittany was asked for help, for which he should be repaid if all went well.

The Duke undertook to support the attempt, but had to be cautious, since he would badly need England's aid if the covetous French attacked him. He was seriously disturbed, therefore, to receive at this juncture an envoy from Richard of England instructed to insist on the surrender of the Earl of Richmond to his lawful sovereign. Richard was indeed perpetually 'pricked and tortured by . . . dread of the earl's return'. So much so, in fact, that he had had the castles of Pembroke, Tenby and Haverfordwest specially warned to look out for 'Henry Tydder', while a fleet of warships was posted at Southampton to beat off any hostile fleet.

The worldly Richard had coupled a bribe with his urgent demand, namely the return to Brittany of the Earldom of Richmond, to which it had formerly belonged. Either the mental stress now imposed upon Francis was too great or his previous nervous breakdown had developed into a more serious and lasting disturbance, for he now lost his reason and was unable to transact state business. It is, on the other hand, possible that this illness was an old and tried diplomatic trick to evade the issue. However, the task of receiving and negotiating with the English envoy fell once more upon his principal minister, Pierre Landois.

Landois was in a dilemma. His instinct as a man of spirit was to refuse Richard's harsh request and spurn his bribe, but as a statesman he knew the weakness of his country's position. He was already being strongly criticized by factions at home, and should the powerful pincers of England and France close upon the Bretons as a result of his actions, his country's and his own downfall would be certain. Reluctantly, therefore, he agreed to have Henry seized and handed over.

Somehow or other there was a 'leak', genuine or contrived. Even Bishop John Morton, still living in Flanders, learned of the impending arrest of the Earl. Perhaps the 'leak' came through Landois himself. At all events, Morton, summoning Father Urswick, ordered him to obtain a safe-conduct for Henry from the French and ride at top speed to warn him. The safe-conduct speedily forthcoming, Urswick hurried into Brittany and met the Earl at Vannes, where he was then living.

Henry had always envisaged that at any moment he might have to fly for his life. In consequence he had earlier familiarized himself with all the available routes from Vannes to the French border. To his followers he now propounded a scheme designed to frustrate Landois and his emissaries. Francis II had been taken to the frontier region of Brittany to recuperate. It would be courteous and entirely logical for Jasper Tudor, Henry's uncle, to take the main body of the Richmond party to the Duke's abode, pay their respects to him and inquire as to his progress towards recovery. Once there, however, Jasper would quietly lead the party by the quickest path into Anjou, a province of France.

This was done without delay or mishap. No suspicion was aroused by the departure of these Englishmen from Vannes on a polite visit to their infirm protector. Indeed, their absence may have been welcomed, for it left the Earl of Richmond entirely without protection. Henry waited a couple of days, making no attempt to escape until he could safely assume that all was well with Jasper and his company. On the third day, however, keeping his intentions to himself, he mounted his horse as if to ride in the country. The few hundred English left in the town were not only unaware that he was going, but ignorant of when and where he had gone.

Accompanied by a servitor and a handful of men he rode about five miles, then, coming into a thick wood, he and the servitor changed clothes, Henry becoming the servant and the servant the Earl, a well-known but often effective ruse. His carefully acquired knowledge of the least frequented forest routes now proved its worth, for he and his party threaded an erratic way towards France, throwing possible pursuers off the track, and came safely and without incident to Angers on the river Maine, with its castle, beautiful stained-glass windows and rich tapestries. It was now the end of October, 1484.

[7]

Having returned to Rennes, Landois was assembling armed men to seize Henry in Vannes. They were ostensibly to be his 'protectors', but at the opportune moment were to hand him over to Richard's emissaries. In due course they arrived in the town, only to find Henry gone. Landois sent them scouring the countryside on horseback in search of him, and tradition has it that they reached the French frontier but an hour after Henry had crossed it. They could not follow him, for to send armed men riding across the border would have constituted an act of war.

When he recovered his wits, Francis II was or appeared to be annoyed with Landois for breaching the laws of hospitality. After severely censuring him, he summoned Admiral Sir Edward Woodville and Sir Edward Poynings, two of the Earl's friends, and furnished them with the funds and supplies they needed to rejoin their master in Anjou. In consequence, between three hundred and five hundred of the remaining English crossed into France, presumably by permission, to support their leader.

It seems peculiar, to say the least, that Landois should not have known of Henry's escape. The entire affair reeks of collusion and prearrangement. Was the Duke's sudden illness feigned? Did Landois, while undertaking to arrest Henry, deliberately and secretly delay his capture long enough to ensure that he got away undetected? Did Henry, privately warned, know he could safely wait two days in Vannes without fear of capture? Did Landois stage-manage matters so cleverly that his soldiers were only a dramatic hour too late to catch their man? Was it coincidence, too, that once the refugees were safely in France, Francis recovered sufficiently to return to Rennes and berate his chief minister? The reader must form his own conclusions. Incidentally, Landois was responsible for bringing Louis of Orleans to Nantes with a promise that he should marry the Duke's daughter, Anne. (Landois was hanged in 1485.)

The French King, Charles VIII, at that time in Langeais, a village on the right bank of the Loire where he had a large château in which some years later he was married, was only fourteen years old and not legally of age. France was being governed, therefore, by a Council under a Regent, Anne de Beaujeu. Henry repaired at once to the French Court, partly to thank the Regent for her previous help, and partly to ask support for his forthcoming adventure. When the Court moved to Montargis in central France, Henry moved with it, having been already assured by both Regent and Council that the oppression of the English people by Richard and his harsh and brutal rule were detested and they would look with favour on his efforts to remove the 'Crookback'. Learning of the escape of the Marquis of Dorset, they allowed English horsemen under Sir John Cheyney to pursue him at Henry's request. The Marquis was overtaken at a point near Compiègne on the Oise in northern France, arrested, and either persuaded to return or forcibly brought back to Paris. If he was persuaded, it was with difficulty.

[8]

Disturbing news now came from England. On the 10th March, 1485, Anne Neville, Richard III's Queen, died, making him a widower. Anne, a daughter of the great Earl of Warwick, had brought him a considerable inheritance, as well as the enmity of his ill-fated brother, George, Duke of Clarence, who had disapproved of the match. She had also given him a son, who had died in the April of the previous year. Possibly her death was hastened by grief at this loss. The fact remained that the King had now no heir, and although there is a strong tradition that he had an illegitimate son, whom on the eve of Bosworth he promised to recognize, it is much more likely that he determined to marry again and beget a legitimate one.

He had not overlooked Henry's solemn declaration that if he won the crown he would marry Elizabeth of York. The rumour now ran round London that the King intended to forestall his rival by marrying Elizabeth himself. As she was his unprotected niece, this caused great popular indignation. The unpopularity already won for him by previous rumours and by the work of some of his ministers was heightened. It has not been proved that he did in fact plan to marry the Princess, but the story spread far and wide. Possibly he said something to this effect as a sop to those Yorkists won over by Henry's vow to marry the Princess, but of this we cannot be sure. He may have promised to unite the two Houses by the marriage and so rob Henry of reluctant support. This achieved, he could later repudiate the promise, for having declared Edward's children illegitimate, he could hardly make one of them his Queen.

However, the story, reaching Elizabeth of York herself, appalled her. She is reputed to have said, 'I will not thus be married, but unhappy creature that I am, will rather suffer all the torments which St. Catherine is said to have endured for the love of Christ than be united with a man who is the enemy of my family.' Probably she spoke more tersely and violently even than this, for she was by all accounts an intelligent and attractive girl with a sense of her own worth. Who would blame her for refusing to marry an uncle not only thirty-three years old, but also with a withered arm and believed to have murdered her darling brothers?

This storm of collective protest alarmed Richard. In a public pronouncement he denied any such designs on his niece. Nonetheless the rumour crossed the Channel and reached Henry, who was 'nypped at the verie stomacke' and believed it. Although he had no feeling for his prospective bride, he saw at once that Richard could rob him of his strongest card. At that moment he was supervising the preparation of an invasion fleet in the great French port and city of Rouen, to sail before many days had passed from the little Norman port of Harfleur. If, as now seemed possible, the Yorkist princess would be denied him, he had better cast about for a different spouse who would also bring him useful support. One such young woman was a sister of Sir Walter Herbert of the great Herbert family, his original guardians. An alliance with her would win over the Welsh, of whose aid he was otherwise far from sure.

In pursuance of this plan he sent friends in secret to the Earl of Northumberland, brother-in-law of the maiden in question, but it is suggested that these envoys failed to land, perhaps because of a storm at sea. By the time they returned to France, Henry had learned of Richard's public repudiation of the rumour, and the Herbert match was abandoned.

It being now widely known in England that an invasion fleet was almost ready in Normandy, those Englishmen, hostile to Richard, who had sought shelter in France flocked to the Tudor's standard. They included men of considerable distinction, such as a scholarly priest, Richard Fox of Lincolnshire, son of a yeoman, but at that time residing in Paris, who greatly impressed the Earl. Others who joined Henry were Sir John Fortescue, the 'Porter' of Calais, then an English possession; the Earl of Oxford; and Sir James Blount, Captain of Calais.

Oxford, a turbulent character of the earlier reigns, had been imprisoned in the Tower, had fought for the Earl of Warwick, fled to France, landed a force against Edward IV, captured St. Michael's Mount in Cornwall, and held it for several months before being forced to surrender. A prisoner in Hammes Castle for ten years thereafter, he had once been found half-drowned in the moat, possibly attempting to escape. Getting away at last, by the connivance of Blount and Fortescue, he had joined Henry's army. At this period he was about forty-three.

Blount, the commander of Hammes who set Oxford free, had since placed the fortress itself at Henry's disposal.

Henry welcomed Oxford 'with an incredible gladness', tempered by the later news that Richard's men in Calais had since laid siege to Hammes and obtained its capitulation, though on honourable terms.

A large number of young English students at the University of Paris also joined the Earl, while the French allotted him a small sum to offset the cost of his fleet. As security for this loan, however, they politely requested that he should leave in their hands Sir John Bourchier and the Marquis of Dorset. In addition to money, they provided him with a body of men under Philibert de Shaunde, later very well-rewarded. Nevertheless, in number and power, Henry's new fleet was but a shadow of the first.

Before setting off for England a second time, Henry sent letters hither and yon stigmatizing the usurper King of England as 'that homicide and unnatural tyrant', signing himself 'Henricus Rex' and referring to himself as a 'poor exiled friend'.

Richard retorted by shrieking that Henry and his followers were 'open murderers and extortioners', and, imputing dishonour to his grandmother, Henry himself a bastard of both families, an accusation of which his countrymen must by now have been growing weary. The King, knowing that an invasion was being prepared, reacted energetically, and profiting by the lessons learned in the field with that great warrior, his brother Edward IV, not only posted troops in all those areas where the Tudor fleet might land, but also raised a considerable army, mustered at Nottingham. The money to pay for it was extracted from those with the funds available. To keep Elizabeth of York well away from trouble, he had her escorted to Sheriff Hutston (Hutton) Castle in Yorkshire, a property of the Nevilles. The reprieved Princess was probably glad to escape the miseries of impending civil war.

[9]

In Harfleur the standard of the Earl of Richmond could now be seen beside that of his uncle, the middle-aged Jasper Tudor, showing the royal arms of England and France. It had been already decided to land in southern Wales, for a diligent lawyer, John Morgan of Kidwelly, had indicated by letter that two well-known and courageous soldiers there were prepared to arm in his cause the moment he landed—Rhys ap Thomas and Sir John Savage.

Rhys ap Thomas's grandfather had fought, like Owen Tudor, at the battle of Mortimer's Cross, but unlike Owen, had been killed. Rhys's own father had earlier been murdered. Rhys himself was brought up at the Court of Philip of Burgundy, where his father was stationed, and received a knightly training. He had secretly plotted with Buckingham. His two brothers, older than himself, having been killed in the Wars of the Roses, he inherited the Lordship of the greater part of Carmarthenshire, and was Richard III's deputy in Wales, to which he had returned in 1470, living at Derwydd. To ensure his fidelity, Richard had sent commissioners to Carmarthen Castle to demand his son and heir as a hostage, and to insist that he swear an oath of fidelity. Against his inclination Rhys took the oath of allegiance, but would not give up his four-year-old boy. Eventually he was persuaded by the Abbot of Talley and the Bishop of St. David's to join Henry when he landed, the Bishop promising to absolve him from his oath to the King. When one of Henry's letters appealing for support reached him, it turned the scale. Rhys promptly set to work to raise a force. 1,900 tenants were bound to join him at short notice and altogether he could muster from 4,000 to 5,000 men. It was this news that now reached Richmond.

Rhys would be an extremely important accession because of his military training, connections, administrative ability and learning, and his possession of twenty castles. Savage was a member of the once powerful Woodville family.

Instead of sending out his Southampton-based, strengthened warships to sweep the English Channel and intercept any approaching fleet, Richard let it sit idle, a blunder he had cause to regret, yet he was intelligent enough to have signallers posted on the hills around Milford Haven to warn of any approach by sea.

So the two men, each on his own side of a narrow strip of water, awaited the day that should bring them to grips with one another. On the 1st August, 1485, the Earl of Richmond transferred to

Harfleur and boarded his flagship with a force not exceeding 2,000 men, and possibly fewer. It was a pocket-size army, whose success would depend on wind, weather and the response of the Welsh to the united call of the Earl and his uncle Jasper, the former Earl of Pembroke, for their original loyalty and allegiance, as well as on the support of the disaffected and the non-Plantagenet Yorkists.

The ordinary man finds it difficult to conceive the emotions of the would-be king as he surveyed his handful of ships, his savage-looking bearded men, his captains and confederates. Did he truly believe he had a fair chance of winning a whole kingdom with this pitiful array? It seems to the observer from this distance of time that he must have been gloomy, filled with foreboding, half-inclined to abandon the attempt. Yet he could not have been. His spirit had two great supports, a belief in his royal blood and his rights, and trust in that God who, he felt, had singled him out to be the ruler of England.

The weather was fair, the wind blew this time from the right quarter, and the voyage was altogether more pleasant and successful than the first. All spirits rose, and the men remembered a prophecy that Henry would land at Milford Haven. In fact, his ships let go their anchors east of the headland in Mill Bay, close to what was then the tiny hamlet of Milford, or Aber-dan-Gleddan. Richmond himself came ashore at a village named Dale, and tradition has it that the moment his feet touched Welsh soil he knelt, crossed himself and kissed the ground, a histrionic gesture such as the makers of legend are fond of attaching to kings. His followers chanted the Psalm *Judica me Deus et decerne causam meam* (God judge me and decide my cause—by battle).

An amusing legend has it that after swearing fidelity to Richard III, Rhys ap Thomas added to his oath the words 'whoever ill affected to the state shall dare to land in these parts of Wales where I have any employment under your Majestie, must make entrance only over my bellie'. Rhys was there to meet his new master, and to ensure that he was not forsworn, flung himself to the ground face upwards, allowing the Tudor to stride over him. A Welsh poet makes him say 'To make my mockery complete, as I did with the tyrant treat, Ere press your feet on British grass you first shall o'er my body pass? When down he laid him on the sand, And o'er him passed the Earl to land.' Another version says that Rhys crouched under Mulock bridge as Henry passed over it.

To hearten and reward his followers and in earnest of the prizes victory would bring them, Henry ordered a few of them to kneel and receive the accolade of knighthood. Then, with resolute heart and smiling face, he commanded the assembled force to march forward in the name of God and St. George. In the words Shakespeare was later to put in the mouth of his predecessor, Henry V, 'the game' was 'afoot'.

CHAPTER THREE

The Battle of Bosworth

[1]

THE FRENCH HISTORIAN, Comines, wrote of the army mustered by Henry for this invasion that it was unworthy of the name of soldiery, being the dregs of jails, hospitals and streets. This may have been true of the French contingent, for Comines, one would think, must have known his own countrymen, but there is no proof that it applied to the English, the Bretons or the Welsh. In any event the statement is of little worth. Soldiers are to be judged by their performance in battle, not by niceties of speech, moral character, origins or elegance of dress. Comines, a courtier, had little understanding of the rough English and Welsh soldiery of the time, or of the common people from whom they sprang. These men had yet to be proved in war, but proved in due course they would be and were.

More to the point is the kind of man they had as their leader. As far as is known, no painting of Henry at this period exists. The much later portrait by Michael Sitium in the National Gallery, dated 1505, is no true guide to the appearance of the young man who, ten years before it was painted, landed at Milford Haven. According to Holinshed he was at this time grey-eyed, golden-haired, cheerful in appearance, quick in speech and repartee, but sober and temperate in demeanour. Of greater importance than his looks, however, was his character, and of this there are indications.

In the first place, he had known hardship, fear, little comfort, and all the dangers and disadvantages of exile. Throughout his life he had been chivvied from pillar to post. After her second marriage his mother had virtually abandoned him, and he had been dependent on the goodwill of strangers and foreigners. Only his uncle Jasper had given him intermittently in adolescence the counsel and support he would normally have had from a father. From boyhood onwards he had had to cultivate the arts of tact and diplomacy. In consequence he had learned not only how to manage men and gain their trust and friendship, but also to see into their minds. His illusions had all been quickly rubbed away by the joint frictions of flight and homelessness, and he had acquired as a result a hard realistic outlook on life and humanity which was to prove of exceptional value throughout his career.

He had learned to detect the mainspring of men's actions and judge them critically while preserving an appearance of unbroken amity. He could control his impulses, conceal his thoughts, keep his own counsel and avoid treading on the toes of those around him. He had enormous patience and rarely allowed his desires to outrun his capacity to fulfil them. In short, he presented the greatest possible contrast to the gay, easy-going, swashbuckling young Edward who had won the crown for York.

For the rest he was about 5 ft. 9 in. in height, handsome, dignified in carriage, and although of no great age by the standards of today, possessed what the youthful Edward IV had always lacked, a seemliness of moral and social behaviour befitting one who meant to be king. He was serious, unassuming and trustworthy, and if he had vices, these were never paraded nor made public.

Either before or during his voyage to Wales he had written letters to his mother, her third husband Lord Stanley and his brother, Sir William Stanley, Sir Gilbert Talbot and other potential supporters, including, as we have seen, Rhys ap Thomas. These letters indicated his impending arrival and his intention to cross the Severn at Tewkesbury and make for London. He urged them to join him with every man they could arm and raise. It is hardly likely that the letters were written in the short interval between the landing and the beginning of his march. More probably they were written beforehand, but left unsigned until he arrived, then sent by messengers. He also transmitted more formal and authoritative orders to the chieftains of the Welsh country to muster and join him. His claim to the crown was just, he asserted, and would be proved in battle. He meant to dethrone the usurper.

[2]

The Welsh bards had for decades been declaiming that one day a Welsh King would arise and become Lord of all England. Henry was a Welshman by birth. Consequently a whole area of Wales was already prepared to welcome him with fervour and flock to his standard. All west Wales, including the areas between Pembroke and Harlech, Harlech and Anglesey, and on to the border, was his in sympathy, but the north of Wales, where the Stanleys held sway, was uncommitted.

After the landing Rhys ap Thomas is said to have entertained Henry at both Derwydd and Carew Castles. A room in the latter castle showing the royal arms is claimed to be where 'the hope of England' slept.

Dawn came, and after their brief rest the army broke camp and advanced toward Haverfordwest, a distance of some ten miles. In this region the natural sympathies of the population were beyond doubt with their hereditary prince, whom they greeted enthusiastically with cries of 'King Henry! King Henry! Down with the bragging white boar!', an allusion to Richard's emblem.

This was encouraging, but at the same time disturbing reports were coming in. Sir John Savage, a relative of the Stanleys, was said to be marching with his men to join the King, and some hinted that despite his warm welcome, Rhys would also take his men to Richard. If so, this would be a grievous blow to Tudor hopes. Nevertheless, Henry refused to be discouraged, and returning from Carew Castle to Pembroke, the town of his birth, of which he was 'natural and immediate lord', he again received an enthusiastic welcome. From there he advanced to Cardigan, where his first encouraging success came, for two Welsh chieftains, John Morgan and Richard Griffith, came riding in at the head of their men to join his standard, their banners with the red dragon of Wales flying in the breeze.

Thenceforward his progress was rapid. Carmarthen offered no opposition, and the Prior there at a later date made a new lodging to shelter him and his son if they ever came back to these parts. Castle after castle in Wales surrendered to him with little or no resistance. The Welsh associated him with the House of Lancaster, to which they were attached, and were therefore sympathetic, but not only on this account. More important was that they believed him kin to the ancient kings of Wessex.

There exists a letter headed 'By the King', in which, summoning John ap Meredyth, a relative, to join him, Henry refers to his loving and true subjects, and calls Richard 'the odious tyrant, usurper of our said right'.

So this little army of mingled races, increasing in confidence and strength with the passing of each day, advanced towards Shrewsbury.

They moved along the shores of Cardigan Bay, through Aberayron, Aberystwyth and Machynlleth, through Llwyn Dafydd and Llanbadarn. Then the force divided, one part moving up the Severn Valley to Cevn Digoll, near Welshpool, and the other swinging northwards by Mallwyd and Llanvylin and on also to Cevn Digoll. Both arrived in Welshpool on the 13th August.

Wales is a flower-bed of legends concerning Henry's march. Thus, he is said to have presented a drinking horn, mounted in silver and known as the 'Hilas Horn', to Dafydd ap Ieuan, who was his host at Llwyn Dafydd. This was for many years kept at Stackpole Court and may still, it is said, be seen at Golden Grove, Carmarthenshire, the seat of Earl Cawdor. It was handed down to the Lloyds of Llanllas, and came by the marriage of Bridget Lloyd to Richard Vaughan, Earl of Carbery. It may, however, have been Dafydd's christening gift to his grandson, born nine months after Henry's visit, and as his mother was Dafydd's daughter, malicious tongues were quick to hint that Tudor blood ran in the infant's veins.

At Solva, the stone of St. David is said to have helped Henry to mount his horse. At Cardigan, in a narrow winding lane near the big dark gate by the bridge, is an inn known as 'The Three Mariners', where Henry is reputed to have slept. But perhaps the best attested of these stories relates to the old farmhouse at Wern Newydd near Llanarth in Cardiganshire, once an old mansion. Here the Earl of Richmond is said to have been the guest of Einon, son of David Lloyd. In one of the bedrooms is a wall carrying a tablet with an inscription in Welsh recording that Henry slept here on his way to Bosworth field. The actual bedstead is reputed to be preserved there in a loft. It should be noted, however, that another village of the same name in the Teivi Valley disputes this claim to have sheltered the Earl.

There is a well-known legend that when Henry's supporters in the field met any body of men whose allegiance they did not know, they pulled up a wild hyacinth, a daffodil, a leek, an onion, any white root available—even that of a blade of grass—and the others, if Richmond men, did the same. Hence, the leek became the symbol of the Welsh until 1911, when a daffodil was substituted.

The Stanleys had given as yet no hint of their designs, but were arming their men in North Wales, Cheshire and Lancashire. These two nobles constituted a large and dangerous 'third force' hovering on his left flank and capable of overwhelming him should they take the opposing side.

Real progress came at last when Rhys ap Thomas on his war-horse 'Grey Fetterlocks' came riding into Welshpool to join him with 'a great baulk of soldiers' and flaunting his banner showing the raven. This not only relieved one of Henry's greatest anxieties, but also greatly strengthened his army. Rhys had branched off from his home in Carew Castle at Haverfordwest, and made his own way to Welshpool via Carmarthen and Brecon, moving well to the east of Henry. He brought the Salusburies of Ystrad Clewydd, the men of Ardudwy and Eivionydd, Lleyn and Arvon, the stalwarts of Monmouth and many other districts. At Peytyngwyn there is said to be a tenement known as 'Standel', where Rich-mond's flag was unfurled as Rhys and his men marched through on their way to Shrewsbury.

Sir Walter Herbert seems to have remained in Raglan Castle, though this has been denied. 1,600 miners and colliers came in, however, from Flintshire under Richard ap Howell, Lord of Mostyn.

Tradition has it that a half-timbered house at Myle Cop, Shrewsbury, was the resting place of Richmond on the night of the 14th. If one believed all Welsh legends, one would have to endow Henry with as many beds to his credit in Wales as to Elizabeth I's in England.

[3]

Surprisingly, it was not until the 11th August that Richard, still in Nottingham Castle, of which he was extremely fond, and to which he had added a tower known as the 'Castle of Care', learned that his espionage and system of signals had failed him for once, his rival having come ashore undetected in Wales and being already in Shrewsbury. He believed Henry had landed at Nangle, near Milford, but was wrong. Alarmed, he ordered Lord Stanley to join him at once in Nottingham with his men, or if not ready to march at once, his son George, Lord Strange, eldest child of Stanley's first wife, Eleanor Neville, must come to explain the delay. Stanley, pretending illness as his reason for not setting out at once, had no option but to despatch the youth to Richard, knowing that if he himself openly declared for the Tudor, with whom his sympathies lay, Strange would certainly be put to death. For his son's sake, therefore, he did not commit himself to Henry Tudor's cause, but quietly went on with his military preparations. Within a few days he had raised a sizeable and well-armed force to be used as events dictated. Meantime, he sat warily on the fence.

When the King knew that Shrewsbury had fallen, he was convinced Sir William, Lord Stanley's brother, had connived at this. He learned also of the defection of Rhys ap Thomas and Savage, and at once declared both men traitors. When Lord Strange reached Nottingham, Richard demanded to know why his father had not come himself at the head of his soldiers. Strange explained that his parent was ill, but this excuse served only to infuriate the King, who threatened him so fiercely that in the end, while insisting that his father's fidelity was unchanged and that he fully intended to bring his men to Nottingham, the youth admitted that letters had been exchanged between the Stanleys and Henry Tudor. Richard immediately placed him under arrest as a hostage for his father, whom he strongly suspected of treachery.

Militarily the King had been caught napping and knew it. Now, days late, he assembled his forces, but although ready to march on the 15th August, would not do so because this was the day of the Assumption of Our Lady. Once midnight had struck, however, he proceeded to Mansfield, in whose market square his men paused and rested. Before the day was well launched they resumed their march, some footslogging, some riding, and covered the twenty-five miles between Mansfield and Leicester well before nightfall.

The discipline and strength of the royal army would have been plain to any experienced observer. It was divided into three separate bodies. In ranks of five the vanguard of infantry plodded steadily forward over relatively dry ground, for the weather had been good for some days. Behind came munitions, stores and baggage in springless carts, whose wheels grumbled, grated and squeaked over the rough roads. Next, leading the main body, came Richard himself in resplendent armour, probably of the slender, elongated, Gothic type, riding on a huge vigorous white horse, also armoured and richly caparisoned. Beside and behind him rode stalwart armed guards. This force also marched in ranks of five. That the King was worried was shown, a chronicler says, by his strained features and silently moving lips as he translated his bitter angry thoughts into unuttered and perhaps unutterable words.

The horsemen, entirely separate from the footsoldiers, followed this main body. The army as a whole covered a total stretch of about three miles of road.

They passed through the gates of Leicester with all the panache of a well-equipped, well-trained, soldierly army, but it was growing dark, and few watched them enter. A room had been pre-empted for the King by his 'harbiger' in the 'Old Blue Boar', a tavern close to Blubber Lane. The army's baggage included Richard's bedstead, a big timber construction, highly gilded, whose base had a false bottom secreting from £200 to £300 of gold coinage. In effect, therefore, the King slept on his own war treasury. This royal bedstead had a remarkable career.

In the time of Queen Elizabeth I, the Blue Boar inn passed into the possession of a Mr. Clarke, whose wife, when making the bed one day, saw a gold piece fall from the wooden base. Investigation revealed the royal hoard. Clarke and his wife made full use of their windfall, and eventually having amassed considerable wealth, became Mayor and Mayoress of Leicester. After Clarke's death, however, the Mayoress was murdered for her money by a female servant and her lover, both of whom were caught and put to death after trial. Whether true or not, the story is a good one.

The bed itself is said to have been still in existence in Leicester in 1685, and what was claimed to be the same bed was inspected at the home of W. P. Herrick in 1850 or thereabouts by members of the Archaeological Society. Herrick had bought it from its owners, the Babingtons, who had themselves obtained it from the Drake family. They found the bed stock possibly authentic, but otherwise the greater part was Elizabethan.

After a good night's rest, Richard, hearing that Henry was in Lichfield, advanced eleven miles along the old road, through Peckleton and Kirkby Mallory to the village of Elmthorpe. There is a story that as he was leaving Leicester by the southern gate, his foot struck a projecting piece of wood. A blind beggar stationed on the bridge cried out: 'His head shall strike that very pile as he returns.' (See p. 57.) There his soldiers slept wherever they could find shelter, the King and his officers putting up in the church. Next day, passing through Atherstone, the King pitched camp in a field known as 'the Royal Meadow'. He had expected to encounter his rival at Hinckley, but this little town was quiet when he came through it. Consequently, on the 18th August he advanced, moving along an old trackway which crossed Ambien Hill by way of a marshy stream, to Sandeford and Shenton, covering a further six miles to Stapleton. 'No jollity was observed in his march.' Here he camped and on the following day occupied high ground called 'The Bradshaws', where he ordered the construction of a breastwork three hundred yards long by about fifty wide to defend his rear, which task occupied his sappers for three days. His tents were set in two rows, probably on the crest of Willerington hill, a mile and a half east of Bosworth Field and two miles from the summit of 'Amyon' (Ambien) Hill, a key point of the actual battlefield. 'Ambien', originally Anglo-Saxon, means in effect 'one tree'. From this position he could survey the ground below. Tactically it was a sound choice, for no opposing force could now approach him undetected. Here the King made his stand, awaiting his enemy. It was the 21st August.

[4]

Henry, having left Shrewsbury, camped for the night of the 16th on a minor eminence near Newport, Salop, with its old market cross. Here another useful man, Sir Gilbert Talbot, joined him with about five hundred men. As each day passed more and more came in singing their ballad:

> Richmond, sprung from British race
> From out this land the boar shall chase.

His pause next day was at Stafford. Sir William Stanley, who, like his brother, was hesitating to throw in his lot openly with Richmond, was moving with his men from Holt Castle on the borders of Denbighshire on a course parallel to Richmond's, and made contact with his brother's force at Lichfield. He is said to have left his army at Stone so as to confer with Henry. After the meeting he returned to his camp. Thomas, Lord Stanley, had marched to Lichfield, and learning that the Earl was approaching the town, withdrew with all his forces towards Leicester. Henry spent an entire day resting his men, passing the hours of darkness outside the town in an unwalled camp. When day broke on the 19th, he entered Lichfield and was received with joy, so that the 'Gonnes in Lichefyld craked'.

From this town as dusk was approaching he marched towards Tamworth, six miles off, and on the way welcomed two important new allies in Sir Walter Hungerford and Sir Thomas Bourchier, who had deserted Richard just beyond Stony Stratford and now came to Henry's standard. On the following day Sir John Savage, his followers wearing hoods and Welsh flannel coats of white, Sandford, Digby and other men of rank, came in. Savage was placed in command of Henry's left wing. The vanguard of the army reached Tamworth before Richmond himself.

In explanation of this is a story, not too authentic, that Richmond, worried because he had not received a positive promise of support from the Stanleys, did not join his men on their night march, but loitered 'as a man disconsolate, musynge and ymagenynge what was best to be done'. In the pitch-black darkness he lost track of them, and on the 20th put up for the night *incognito* at a small hamlet halfway between Lichfield and Tamworth. At dawn he rode back into the camp explaining that he had not missed his way, but had stayed behind to meet a messenger from some unnamed friends who would join him as soon as they safely could. Possibly these were the Stanleys.

Shortly afterwards he again left his men, this time before they were ready to march, and made his way to 'the Three Tuns', an inn at Atherstone, nine miles distant, a handful of bodyguards accompanying him. There he met Lord Stanley in a room believed to have been at Hall Close, in the rear of the 'Three Tuns'. The two men are said to have agreed that both Stanleys should come to Bosworth Field before Henry had pitched his tents, and declare for him at the earliest possible moment, launching their men against the King.

A feature of this coming conflict was that neither contestant used outriders nor advanced scouting parties. They appear to have relied upon individual spies for news of each other's movements. Under the impression that Richard was close at hand Henry decided to intercept him on Watling Street, a mere mile or so beyond Hinckley. His men, moving with style and bravura, passed through Barwell and took the road to the village of Stapleton in Leicestershire. They then diverged along a track that brought them out on to the Ashby-de-la-Zouch road, roughly two miles north of Hinckley, and made camp near Merevale Abbey, Atherstone, on the 21st. The townsfolk of Hinckley came out to the camp either to sell food and wares to the men-at-arms, or to gratify their own curiosity, or both.

Henry perceived from reports on Richard's movements that to continue along Watling Street would be to miss him altogether. His object being to seek battle, he changed course, moving northeast and leaving Atherstone on his left, crossed over Wetherley Bridge, and travelled along the Fen Lanes to a point below Stoke Golding and Shenton. Thence he continued leftwards by the Coleshill road to where the Ashby-de-la-Zouch canal now runs, and crossed the bridge over a stream, the Tweed, camping on the 22nd about a mile from the summit of Ambien Hill (Holinshed calls it 'Anne Beame') in a field on the left known as White Moors, near Shenton, beside the trackway. He was now but three miles from the King and half a mile from Sir William Stanley and his men.

[5]

The Stanleys had already moved up. Thomas, having come through Lindley, Higham and Stoke, posted his men on a hill about a mile away south of Bosworth Church, known as Gamble's Close, near Darlington, well to Richard's rear and slightly to his left. The Tweed furnished both camps with water. Between the armies of Stanley and the King lay the breastwork constructed by the royalists, and the reason for making and strengthening this may have been to prevent a surprise attack by the Lancastrian barons, of whose loyalty the King was by no means sure.

Meantime, Sir William Stanley had marched through Shenton and come up to Bosworth Field from the west, two miles north of Ambien Hill, possibly at Nether Cotton, opposite to his brother.

The four armies were in full sight of one another throughout the day as they rested, not more than a couple of miles separating any of them. The area of battle was not then named Bosworth, but 'Redmoor' from its reddish soil. On a modern road map it is shown as an open space bounded on the north by Market Bosworth, by Cadeby on the east, on the south-east by Sutton Cheyney and on the west by the road between Market Bosworth and Shenton. The actual battle was fought within an elliptical space about two miles wide by one deep, covering about 1,500 acres. A fence surrounded the entire area, while the surface was irregular, being a blend of tilled soil, marshland and grass. About the length of a cricket pitch beyond a plantation of trees was a spring, known as Dick's Well, because tradition claims that Richard quenched his thirst there during the battle. (It was rediscovered in 1813 by Dr. S. Parr, who erected a stone pyramid still to be seen on the spot.)

This spring trickled slowly into the Tweed, making part of the field swampy and difficult to cross. Virtually in the centre stood Ambien Hill, the highest point, sloping sharply on both northern and southern flanks, the steeper being the northern. At its foot were the stream and the marsh. The flat stretches below were occupied by three of the four resting armies, which virtually formed the four corners of a square. Today this area is crossed by both the railway and a canal, and harbours a couple of farms and their buildings, being cut up into separate fields criss-crossed by hedges, etc. Where once the marsh stood is now a plantation of trees. In 1485, however, it was entirely open. The Tudor camp lay about three hundred yards from the Tweed, which shielded Henry's left and rear, while his right could be approached only by way of the marsh. No frontal attack could be made on him unless Sir William Stanley allowed it to pass through.

Regrettably we have no first-hand written account of the battle so that the numbers engaged and the tactics employed must necessarily be conjectural. A rough estimate is that the King had mustered 12,000 men, whereas Henry had but 7,000, though he had more horsemen than Richard. Sir William Stanley commanded 3,000 men from North Wales and the Dee Valley and his brother a further 5,000. If these joined Henry, the King would be outnumbered.

The key point was Ambien Hill. Whoever gained this would control the battlefield. It lay like a large plum on a green cloth, waiting to be picked up by whoever was quickest and strongest. That it had not already been occupied was probably because the armies needed rest after their long marches and were uncertain of each other's intentions. Each eyed the others warily, waiting for the false move, the rash attack, the tactical blunder that would provide opportunity.

The tradition is that the King after a disturbed night made the rounds of his camp, and finding a sentry asleep at his post, ran him through with his sword, saying he had left him as he found him, fast asleep. He then held a council of war, attended by the Lord Chamberlain, Lord Lovell, the Attorney General, Sir William Catesby, and Sir Richard Ratcliffe. He is said to have had terrible dreams that night, seeing dreadful devils which tugged and pushed him about without allowing him any real rest. Fear flooded his soul when he awoke, and he came out of his tent sombre, depressed, with a sense of foreboding. Nevertheless he dissembled his feelings to prevent his friends from losing confidence in the outcome of the battle. As dawn broke, he studied Henry's position, and ordered his army to draw up in order of battle. They presented an extremely wide front to the enemy, probably because so large a body needed as much space as possible for manoeuvre.

About 1,200 archers were posted in the forefront, aided by two hundred horsemen, led by John, Duke of Norfolk and Thomas, Earl of Surrey. Behind them and the accompanying footsoldiers sat the King himself, conspicuous on his white horse in the centre, at a spot today called Dickon's Nook which stretched towards the northern end of the field, 1,500 horsemen being on the wings. The rearguard was commanded by the Earl of Northumberland with 1,000 billmen and 2,000 pikemen and lay along the top of the ridge close to Dickon's Nook.

Holinshed has given a largely fictional version of Richard's address to his men, according to which he castigated Henry and his friends as 'a number of beggarly Britons and faynte harted Frenchmen, traitors, theeves and outlawes and renegades', called Henry a Welsh milksop of little martial experience and less courage, and pointed out that the Earl had been a captive of the Duke of Brittany for years. At dawn he marched from the direction of Sutton and occupied the summit of Ambien Hill. Sir William Stanley was now on his left, while directly to his right was Lord Stanley.

At 4 a.m. Henry, displaying his banners in his turn, ordered the trumpets to sound. He, too, addressed his troops, repeating his claim to the throne, and alleging that Richard was a usurper, homicide, murderer and commander of unwilling men. He promised rich rewards if victory were won, and that day should find him 'rather a dead carrion upon the cold ground than a free prisoner on a carpet in a ladies' chamber'.

The Earl of Oxford commanded the thin body of archers on the right of his line with Talbot and Savage. Their task was to observe the movements of Lord Stanley. Henry, with the main body, held the centre, accompanied by Jasper Tudor, Earl of Pembroke, as his lieutenant and counsellor, his horsemen being posted on the flanks. He had more cannon than the King, but neither had many, and those they had were small, probably hand-guns, so that the inhabitants of Hinckley, eagerly listening, heard little gunfire. The French and Breton contingents fought under Barnard.

Henry now advanced to capture Ambien Hill from the King, and seeing this, Richard sent Brackenbury to Thomas Stanley with an order to move up with his men and assist him in drawing up his battle order for the forthcoming fight. Stanley now showed his hand, returning the cold reply that Richard should draw it up himself, and he would come as soon as convenient. In a fury Richard threatened to cut off Lord Strange's head, which drew the immediate and brutal retort from Stanley that he had 'other living sons' to take Strange's place. Richard at once ordered Strange to be beheaded, and the block was actually made ready, but his Council dissuaded him on the grounds that the battle was more important than revenge, and the execution could safely be left till afterwards. So, at least, the story goes. Meantime, the young man was quietly taken from his tent and placed in the custody of Lord Ferrers of Chartley.

Another version is that Lord Stanley, leaving command of his own army to a deputy, rode into Richard's camp to lend the aid required, but this is extremely doubtful, and was probably an invention to make Stanley appear more treacherous than he was. Henry also is said to have sent Sir Reginald Bray to Stanley with an appeal to join him, whereupon Stanley, drawing Bray on one side, asked him to urge Henry to attack at once, possibly to save his son.

The King of England was no impressive figure despite his gleaming Italianate armour and his fine big white horse. He was of medium or short stature, estimated by some at 5 ft. 4 in., and according to such evidence as we have, one of his arms was withered and as a result one shoulder higher than the other. That he was a hunchback is improbable. Some writers have argued that because the four known portraits of him show no deformity, he was as whole as other men, but in those days what painter of royalty would have dared to show a king as he was, this one above all? The people named him 'Crookback' and for this there must have been some reason.

Nonetheless, he is said to have been 'comely', with red-gold hair, a smiling face, bright grey eyes, and an almost ascetic appearance. There has been no suggestion at any time that he lacked courage in war. He now wore the same polished armour of the finest steel and most beautiful design as he had worn in 1471 at the great battle of Tewkesbury. His helmet carried as ornament only a crown, which some say was merely a crest.

Henry, too, fully armoured and helmet in hand, rode among his horsemen and addressed them from the top of a small rise in the ground. The officers of both armies wore helmets, plate armour and mail, and used swords and spears. The horsemen also used spears, the footsoldiers bills for the most part, battleaxes for the rest.

Seeing that Richmond's tactics, to judge from the slow advance of his infantry, were to capture from him the key position of Ambien Hill, Richard waited immobile on his lofty ground to watch the progress of Henry's army over the swampy stretch, which could be crossed only at Sandeford. The weather remained fine, and he believed he now had the Tudor force at every possible disadvantage. They were bound to be bogged down in the mud, the sun was right in their eyes, they were heavily outnumbered and would have to come uphill. Soon they would be at his mercy.

The Tudor army continued to move cautiously in the direction of the hill, crossed the Tweed, still facing the sun, but suddenly, on reaching the marsh, turned sharp left. By the time they had executed this movement the vanguard had reached the point now occupied by the present Glebe Farm, and the sun was no longer in their eyes. The King's archers waited, flexing their bows, and his gunners fired a few shots from the hill-top, doing little damage, being mainly useful in signalling to the Stanleys that the battle had begun.

Sir William Stanley, having left his overnight camp, hovered over the approaching conflict like a carrion crow. The chronicler says: 'Lord! How hastily the soldiers buckled on their helms; how quickly the archers bent their bows and flushed the feathers of their arrows; how readily the billmen shook their bills and proved their staves, ready to approach and join, when the terrible trumpets should sound the blast of victory.' Henry is said to have called for a bowl of Burgundy wine, and addressing Rhys ap Thomas, said: 'Here, Vychan, I drink to thee, the finest Welshman I ever saw!' Emptying the bowl, he tossed it over his shoulder, giving the command to attack. 'A very terrible cry to them that should see them afar off... The trumpet blew, the soldiers shouted, the King's archers let fly their arrows, but Henry's bowmen stood not still, they paid them back again. Then the terrible shot once over, the armies came to hy strokes and the matter was dealt with blades.' So the chronicler writes.

As far as one can judge, the royal archers in the centre of the line

5—H VII

stepped forward a yard or so, let fly their arrows, then quickly withdrew. On each side of them were two bodies of men clad in steel from head to toe. As Henry's men began their climb of Ambien Hill, Richard's men under Norfolk swept over the brow of the hill to meet them in a bold and fierce attack. Where they met is now the present Shenton railway station, it is held. The battle was soon joined in earnest. Taken by surprise, Oxford saw his advancing ranks give way and his men in danger of being surrounded and destroyed. Shortening his line, he rallied his men to their standard in a compact central mass, urging them forward. Though still hampered by the marsh, which hindered reinforcement at speed, they fought fiercely, and it was soon obvious that the royal footsoldiers were uninspired, fighting to save their own lives rather than defeat the enemy. When Oxford counter-attacked they wavered.

Seeing this, Norfolk extended his own force on each wing in a thin enveloping line, hoping to encircle and roll up Oxford with his horsemen by attacking both their right flank and their rear. He is said by Holinshed to have been secretly warned to keep out of the battle, and on his gate the previous night someone wrote:

> Jacke of Norfolke be not too bolde
> For Dikkon they maister is bought and solde,

but Holinshed confirms that Norfolk rejected this advice.

For a time the issue was in doubt, the King's men greatly outnumbering Henry's at this stage. Had Northumberland and the rearguard on their ridge watching Lord Stanley joined in, there is good reason to believe that Richard would have won, but Northumberland refused to move, his excuse being that he had been told to report on Stanley's movements and was merely obeying his orders.

Rhys ap Thomas is said to have appealed at this critical moment to Sir William Stanley, who, seeing both Oxford's danger and his own opportunity, poured men into the gaps left when Oxford shortened his line. The Duke of Norfolk now found himself confronted by a new, fresh and numerous army, on whose neutrality he had relied. 'In array triangle' the struggle continued. Recognizing Oxford by his emblem, a star with rays, Norfolk, displaying his own sign, a silver lion, engaged him in hand-to-hand combat. They charged on horseback with spears couched, and met head on, their weapons being shattered by the impact. Flinging the useless butts to the ground they battled on with swords. Norfolk wounded Oxford in the left arm, but in return the 'beaver' or lower chin guard of his helmet was severed by Oxford, which left the enemy's jaws unprotected. Chivalrously refusing to take advantage of an ill-defended man, the Earl turned away to fight elsewhere, but at that precise moment an archer's arrow pierced the Duke of Norfolk's brain and he fell dead from his horse.

Similarly, his son, the Earl of Surrey, who had already done considerable execution, encountered Talbot, an experienced old warrior, who outfought him. His strength ebbing and men closing in upon him, Surrey determined to die fighting rather than surrender. Clarendon and Conyers tried to rescue him, but were themselves cut down by Savage's men. An unnamed soldier seeking to capture the flagging young man had his arm cut off for his pains, after which Surrey, exhausted, held out his sword to Talbot in token that he was prepared to die. Instead, Talbot had him seized and made prisoner.

[6]

The battle had begun at 4 a.m. and it was now 11. It seems to have been a somewhat shapeless affair in which fierce single combats took place among the leaders over a limited area, the main bodies tearing at one another in surging masses, most of the action centring on Ambien Hill. Jasper Tudor had wheeled his men round to face Norfolk's attack, but as far as can be judged there was little tactical movement once fighting began.

Richard now made one of those blunders that have cost so many monarchs their crowns. A spy reported to him that Henry, but weakly guarded, had stationed himself behind the hill, and at its foot. Never having set eyes on the Tudor, Richard, having quenched his thirst at the spring, asked to have him pointed out. Sight of his rival astride a horse seems to have inflamed his always passionate temper, for gritting, 'grinding and gnashing his teeth' and couching his lance, he cried: 'Let all true knights attend me, and I will soon end the quarrel. If none will follow me, I will try the cause alone.' So the legend runs.

Spurring his horse and galloping recklessly downhill, followed by his standard-bearer and his personal bodyguards, he made straight towards Richmond and Sir William Stanley, who were directing the movements of their men. The unexpected onslaught burst through the ranks of Henry's guards. His standard-bearer, Sir William Brandon, too stunned to move, saw the wavering silken green and white banner showing the red dragon of Wales torn from his grasp and flung contemptuously to the ground, and was then killed outright. Richard's impetuous charge sent Sir John Cheyney flying from his horse with a crash of protesting steel. Even Henry was at first too startled and surprised to defend himself, but recovering, fiercely resisted. The royal horsemen hard behind their King laid about them with such a will that their opponents were driven back and panicked, and the Earl of Richmond was in great peril.

At this moment, however, a surge of howling, baying men 'in their coats as red as blood' came pouring through the retreating Tudor bodyguards, arresting their flight by numbers and impetus. Attacking Richard's flank, they surrounded the advancing royalists. These men coming, fresh and eager, so timely to the rescue were Sir William Stanley's, led by their commander himself, who promptly made the King the target of his attack. Sir William Catesby, seeing Richard's danger, shouted to him to withdraw, and forthwith took his own advice, but the King, cursing him as a poltroon, swore to perish rather than give way. Seeing that the battle was going against them, followers brought him a fast light horse so that he might escape, but he refused it.

Meanwhile Sir Robert Brackenbury, Lieutenant of the Tower, was confronted by Hungerford, a Richmond man, in one of those conflicts on the sidelines, so to speak, of this curious mêlée. Brackenbury snarled 'Traitor!' to which Hungerford growled the reply that his answer should be more solid than words, aiming a blow at the grey head before him. Brackenbury parried with his shield, which was shattered by the blow. Henry, near at hand, swiftly passed him his own, saying it would be unchivalrous to take advantage of the mishap. The combat was resumed. Brackenbury lost his helmet and fell, wounded to the death, his life ebbing as he lay.

Curious episodes of this kind were a feature of the battle. Thus, two friends, Byron and Clifton, now on opposite sides, had earlier sworn that if either were killed, the other would beg the survivor not to alienate the dead man's possessions from his family. During the conflict Byron met Clifton in combat, and overcoming him, besought him to surrender, but Clifton insisted on fighting to the end, and died.

It is possible, as Lt. Col. Burne has suggested, that seeing the day lost, Richard decided to escape, but his horse became bogged down in the marsh, and dismounting, he cried vainly for another. This would account for the story told by Shakespeare. Unable to reach his enemy, he saw his own standard trampled in the mire, and was himself felled to the ground with terrible wounds. The standard, the Welsh declare, was snatched up by Rhys ap Meredydd of Nant Conway as a trophy, Richard Howell of Mostyn laid Richard low, and Rhys ap Thomas, wearing plate armour, gave him the final blow. His helmet twisted and torn where fierce blows had penetrated it, the King lay at the base of Ambien Hill. His blood with that of the fallen is said to have made the water of the rivulet that fed the marsh run red for some time afterwards, while elsewhere the spilled gore, quickly congealing in the hot sun, turned much of the field of battle black.

Lord Stanley had taken no part in the struggle, but now advanced at the head of his men and coolly surveyed the field and the dead monarch. The royalists fled as soon as they saw their King die, and rushed southwards leaving lifeless on the field the Duke of Norfolk, Lord Ferrers of Chartley, Sir Robert Brackenbury and Sir Richard Ratcliffe. The Earls of Surrey and Northumberland were taken prisoner. Some of the fugitives fled through Hinckley with their enemies in hot pursuit, many being overtaken and ruthlessly slain, even more, perhaps, than were killed in battle. The horsemen chased them for two miles and farther, but Lord Lovell and the Staffords, better mounted than the rest, escaped, and reaching Colchester, took sanctuary there.

Though the armies had begun to deploy at 4 a.m., the actual hand-to-hand conflict lasted but a couple of hours. It has been estimated that of Richard's army nine-hundred died, and of Henry's only one hundred, but of this there is no proof. Lord Strange was found safe in his tent and restored to his father. So ended the last great battle of the Houses of York and Lancaster.

[7]

When all was over Henry knelt and gave thanks to God for victory 'with devoute and godly orisons'. The whole army sang a Te Deum. Crown Hill, where the new King knelt, is known today as 'King Harry's'. He now spoke words of praise and thanks from this eminence, and ordered the wounded to be cared for and the dead buried. His men once more shouted 'King Harry! King Harry!' and gave him loud applause.

Sir Reginald Bray had picked up from a hawthorn bush either the true crown of England, 'of exceeding value', or the crown ornament worn by Richard on his helmet, there is no knowing which, though it seems unlikely that the King would have gone into battle wearing the precious crown and risking its damage or loss. Bray handed it to Lord Stanley, who with his own hand affixed it to the victor's helmet amid renewed shouts of 'King Henry!' This event is said to have taken place near Stoke Golding, and is the only occasion in English history when an English king was crowned on the battlefield. Richmond there and then knighted Gilbert Talbot, Rhys ap Thomas and nine other brave men.

From that day on Henry called Rhys ap Thomas 'Father Rhys'. This valiant Welshman had a distinguished career in his service, becoming Knight of the Garter, Privy Councillor, Constable and Chamberlain of Brecknock, Chancellor of Haverfordwest, etc. On Henry's death he retired to Wales, living to the age of seventy-six and being buried, according to one account, in St. Peter's Church, Carmarthen, where his effigy is to be seen side by side with his wife's, whose emblem, a dove, lies at her feet. Another account declares that he was buried in St. George's Chapel, Windsor.

Fox and Christopher Urswick were also present at Bosworth.

Henry now began the first stage in his journey to London, but there was no vulgar elation in his bearing. His mind was probably concentrated on the problems awaiting him in his new role of King of England. The sight of his predecessor's bloodstained, mangled body in its battered, jagged armour sufficed, perhaps, to show him the tenuous hold any man had upon the crown.

Covered in blood-caked dust, Richard was now taken up, stripped and flung naked by a horseman over the back of the big royal white horse, his head hanging down on one side, his legs on the other. In this shameful manner he was carried into Leicester. As he crossed the bridge over the river 'his head hung like a thrum mop' and struck the selfsame piece of wood as his foot had struck when he marched out. This, at least, is the tradition. The body was set down for public view in the Franciscans' church, and exposed for two days, being then buried at Grey Friars near the town centre and close to the market place.

In 1495 Richard was given by Henry an alabaster tomb to his memory—an unusually magnanimous act—but both tomb and church were destroyed during the following reign, Richard's bones being thrown into the river Soar from the old Bow Bridge over which he had ridden on his way to Bosworth. In the form of a few fragments the tomb was still to be seen in 1760.

So, at the age of twenty-nine, Henry Tudor was King Henry VII of England.

CHAPTER FOUR

The New King

[1]

ENGLAND NOW HAD a population of about 3,000,000 and a new King, but irrespective of Henry's merits, what sort of England had he won? She lay supine before him, but she was not pretty. Over decades the terrible rivalries of York and Lancaster had imbued her rural areas with hopelessness, much as after World War II the shadow of the atomic bomb and a future cataclysmic war hung over the young of Europe. Men could not bring themselves to believe in any peace of more than a few months' duration. Winter was in the offing, and there was a dearth of food. The grazing grounds were held in common, and in the November of every year cattle were slaughtered by the hundred and their meat salted down for storage or men would have nearly starved, since there was no other means of keeping it. A chosen few beasts only were retained for breeding and fed on the trimmings of trees and whatever else they could find, such as moss and ivy. In consequence stunted animals only were to be seen in the fields, and borough records have revealed that oxen, steers and cows, for example, were but a third of the size and weight of their modern counterparts. Indeed, the present-day sheep is believed to be larger and bulkier than many medieval bulls.

The crown was no longer a symbol of unity and nationhood. So many invaders had landed in England determined to win her that from one day to the next the common folk hardly knew whether King Log or King Stork was their master. The nobles had shown themselves not chivalrous, disinterested lovers of their native land, if indeed they had been born in it, but greedy tyrants, bursting with envy, hatred and ambition. The feudal customs had exposed themselves as merely convenient arrangements whereby the lords could call upon their servants and retainers at will for their own private wars. They were as likely to find themselves fighting men from the next county as the foreigner.

The towns were choked with the helpless, hopeless residues of the armies—the blind, the lame, the disabled, the sick, the diseased and the mendicants. Lepers were not uncommon. There was little or no money with which to repair damage or maintain collectively-owned edifices such as market halls. Pirates roamed the Channel and raided the southern ports. The Treasury was almost empty, and even the crown jewels had been pledged to pay for guns and munitions. Exports and imports had declined from the swelling torrents of Edward IV's latter days to thin trickles. The island was regarded in Europe as the home of warring barbarians, even its lords being often unable to read and write. As an ally she was considered negligible by all but a few minor princes in desperate straits, such as the Duke of Brittany.

As statesmen and administrators the clergy, both high and low, had little popular esteem. Such prestige as they still possessed attached mainly to their religious functions, for which, like witch doctors, they were considered indispensable. As defenders of the poor against oppression they had lost all their people's trust. They were more often than not oppressors themselves, though there were, of course, exceptions.

Parliament was called only when the king of the day needed money, or formal sanction for decisions already made and being acted upon. Its members were passive instruments of his will or that of the principal nobles, on whom he depended. Having ceased to expect anything of Lords or Commons, the people took little interest in their activities. As for Ireland, this was virtually self-governing, while Scotland was a separate, independent kingdom.

Among the common people some hysterical emotion could still be aroused by the actual presence and glittering display of a crowned head, but the identity of the man under the crown was relatively unimportant. He commanded little personal esteem or affection unless local ties allied to local popularity gave him a hold on a particular section. The crown had been bandied about too freely and frequently, won by means too obnoxious or cruel, for any great majesty or love to attach to its holder. It had come to be looked upon as the perquisite of a 'clever devil'. Like the successful gangster of our own time who has robbed a train and gained a fortune, he was envied by some and admired by others, but seldom reigned long enough to win love or affection. Edward IV had been the first king for many years to achieve for the crown a genuine popularity by means not always dignified, which popularity Richard had quickly lost and Henry had to regain.

Furthermore, life and property had once again lost their sanctity. The calm years of Edward IV's later reign, when men began to look up again, rebuild and hope, had been shattered by the violence and tyranny of Richard 'Crookback'. Once more extortion, theft, robbery and murder, especially by night, made the dark hours unsafe in towns and cities, and sometimes even in the rural districts. The right of sanctuary was, as earlier indicated, being grossly abused. Criminals fled into the nearest cathedrals and churches during the day to claim protection, then slid out after dark to kill and rob again.

Even the rich stole from each other—particularly land—and from the poor. They ran up debts and bilked without shame those poor tradesfolk who gave them credit. They hired assassins to remove whoever stood in their way.

The navy had been whittled down to a few ships, and there was no such thing as a national army. The people struggled for their beef and ale, eating and drinking to excess when they could because in the months to come they might starve. The new king had a difficult task before him.

Vagrancy was still a terrible problem. The less stringent measures of previous years against it had had some result, for a further relaxation of the law reduced the penalty for this offence to only a day and a night in the stocks. There was even talk of building refuges for the wretched wanderers in their native places or in the villages or towns where they had lived for at least three years. Strict rules were to govern these refuges, which were to be properly administered.

[2]

Henry did not hurry to London to marry the Princess Elizabeth of York and fulfil his vow. His first royal act before leaving Leicester, whose town hall, I am told, still carries slates he ordered to be supplied, was to make sure that she was lying safe in the remote castle of Sheriff Hutston. In the same castle, as a prisoner, was the young Edward, Earl of Warwick, the ten-year-old son of George, late Duke of Clarence. He had been put there by his uncle Richard, nominally his 'guardian'.

Elizabeth was summoned therefore by the new King's messenger, Sir Robert Willoughby, to collect her belongings and repair to her mother, the Queen Dowager, in London, who would be responsible for her. She set out at once, escorted by Willoughby and accompanied by a retinue of nobles, and by her women.

Willoughby had orders to take charge of the Earl of Warwick also. The boy had on one occasion been declared official heir to the throne, but since this endangered the claims of any son Richard himself might produce, he had speedily cancelled the declaration. Henry, too, was threatened by the continued existence of this Edward, whose claims might be considered by the Yorkist faction superior to his own. Willoughby was therefore ordered to bring him to London and have him placed securely in the Tower—a decision of personal policy rather than of national necessity, it seems, but though cruel not necessarily harmful to the state.

The day after Bosworth, Henry drew up a general order that none of the prisoners, of whom there were many, should be robbed or despoiled, but all could now go home with their horses and armour, undertaking to keep the King's peace. Otherwise they would be hanged. Any man threatened with robbery or spoliation could get a warrant from Richard Barrow, the King's 'serjeant', for his body and goods till the King had examined his case and made known his decision. He presented Richard ap Howell with the belt and sword he had worn the previous day and urged him to come to London as a member of his Court. Richard, the legend tells, replied: 'I dwell among mine own people.' At all events, the sword and belt are said to have been carefully preserved in the 'Mostyn House' till the late nineteenth century. The original window of the house still exists, I am told. Rhys ap Thomas was allotted part of the booty from Richard's tent, and a silver rose bowl was sent by Henry at a later date with an ewer of the same metal to the Lord of Mostyn.

From Leicester Henry moved by easy stages to St. Albans, where he spent a few days, his royal progress being marked by intense popular excitement. The roads along which he passed were lined with cheering spectators, and wherever he paused for refreshment tables were quickly brought out and burdened with poultry and meats roasted on spits before an open fire, while there were pies, pasties, bread and cakes, and sometimes, when available, herrings baked in pasties, spices, sauces, oatmeal cakes, almonds and rice. Goblets were filled to overflowing with mead, beer and cider. The beer must have been exceptionally good, for at that period any brewer who produced bad ale or gave short measure could be reported and fined—usually 2d. (Every manor had its taster of beer and bread.) This rejoicing indicates the relief felt at the passing of Richard.

The King carefully avoided martial pomp, wishing to present himself less as a successful warrior than as a humble man whose sole aim was to bring his people peace and teach them its arts and virtues. Only when entering London on the 3rd September, 1485, did he allow his trumpeters to crack the skies with their brazen notes and display to public gaze the treasures and booty he had wrested from the conquered, but he himself is said to have come in in a clumsy coach of the type used by women.

His welcome in the city of London was equally enthusiastic. It had already been decided to make him a gift of 1,000 marks. Richard, the feared and hated, had been overthrown, and the new and dreaded civil war was over almost as soon as it had begun, certainly before any had thought possible. The country 'gaped and rubbed its elbow' at the news of Henry's victory. Moreover, the recently fought battle had been decisive. Whatever the justice of the new King's claim, this man riding proudly through the streets had no rival of his own stature. All who might have challenged him were dead except Elizabeth of York, whom the King had vowed to marry. He stood, therefore, even with the common people, for a union of the two great houses and an end to civil conflict. Yet even so, it was not believed he would introduce a new and better way of life.

He was officially received by the Mayor—Hugh Brise, a goldsmith and Master of the Royal Mint—the aldermen and the sixty-six city companies, all in their gowns of scarlet velvet, to the number of 435. The reception took place at St. Magnus Church in the Bridge Ward at Shoreditch. As he came from Blackheath over London Bridge, he was accompanied by many nobles and gentry, his escorts riding two on a horse after the French fashion. People broke out of the crowd on each side of the street 'gladly to touch and kiss that victorious hand which had overcome so monstrous and cruel a tyrant'.

Cheapside was a colourful dance of banners and gaily coloured tapestries suspended from innumerable windows and flapping in the breeze. The water conduits thereabout were running with wine. In the streets the clothing of nobles, knights and armed men was variegated and attractive, though the dyes of their day gave harsher and more strident colours than the subtler ones of our own time. Everywhere the sparkle of gems, the rustle of silk, the soft sheen of flaming velvet, the vivid flashes of red from robes and cloaks, vied with the shimmer of sunlight on the tips of spears, the heads of battleaxes, the cuirasses and shields, the helmets and swords, of men. A continuous roar of voices made the narrow ways resound.

Bernard André, Henry's blind poet-laureate, sang in his praise verses he had himself composed. In the great Cathedral of St. Paul's the King offered up the standard of St. George, with whose figure it was emblazoned, and another showing the red dragon of Wales and Cadwallader 'beaten up white and green sarcenet', [sic] as well as a banner with a dun cow 'painted upon yellow tartern', all of which had been displayed at Bosworth. A Te Deum was sung and prayers recited.

Throughout the city 'plays, pastymes and pleasures were shewed' as well as processions and pageants. In the pageants the trading companies were represented by allegorical figures drawn on carts. For example, the Salters were shown as 'Salina', a maiden wearing azure robe and mantle and gown with white and yellow roses. In another, a mighty giant standing with drawn sword and figures of three 'empresses' representing 'Nature, Grace and Fortune' stood with seven maidens clad in white, symbolic of the seven orders of the host of angels. These delivered a poetical address to the new King. In the past, disputes had often broken out among the trading companies over their order of precedence, but the Goldsmiths' Company had finally established its right to be first. (In the following century the Mercers, Grocers, Drapers, and Fishmongers took precedence of the Goldsmiths.) Three sides of Leadenhall were largely reserved for the 'making and rewtyng' of these pageants.

Such entertainments were extremely expensive. A nobleman's dress could cost as much as £50, and all his retainers and servants had to be specially clothed for the occasion.

The King finally made his way to the lodging prepared for him at the Palace of the Bishop of London with its great hall, on the north-west side of old St. Paul's. Here he remained for a few days. On the eve of St. Simon and St. Jude he dined with Cardinal Thomas Bourchier, Archbishop of Canterbury, at his Palace at Lambeth, then, crossing London Bridge with a magnificent escort on the 27th October, he came to the Tower and there rewarded his uncle Jasper Tudor, whom he created Duke of Bedford, restoring him also to his Earldom of Pembroke with a yearly income of £40. Baron Stanley was made Earl of Derby and Sir William Stanley was also honoured, as were Rhys ap Thomas and other leading men. Later Thomas Stanley was made forester and keeper of the King's game in the northern lands beyond the Trent.

The Stanleys, an old English family, were a power to be reckoned with. Sir William, a man of enormous wealth, had fought for Edward IV. His brother, Thomas, Lord Stanley, had also inherited great estates and had been steward of Edward IV's household. He was the King's stepfather, but had tolerated Richard's usurpation of the throne and kept out of Buckingham's rebellion, becoming High Constable of England on the Duke's disgrace. During Richard's reign and with his permission, if not altogether to his liking, Stanley had retired to his home in Lancashire, and Henry had never been sure how he would react to his landing. At all costs he had to be placated.

[3]

The mind of a man about to command an entire nation is an enigma to most of us, whom the prospect would appal, but the mists of time have dissolved sufficiently to give at least an impression of the way this new King's brain was working during those first few days of his arrival in London.

What exercised him most at this juncture was his claim to the throne and its legitimization, next his coronation and finally his marriage. The first he allowed to rest for the time being. The third he also set aside as he did not yearn for it, and perhaps cherished a faint hope that he might even now wriggle out of it. The urgent thing was his coronation, fixed for the 30th October.

Unfortunately, his arrival coincided with the breaking out of a deadly disease which soon achieved the proportions of an epidemic. Some have suggested that it was introduced by the French or Breton forces he brought to the capital with him. At all events, it was so immediate and terrible in its effects that it made the coronation date doubtful, and has no modern parallel or name.

The disease, known as the 'sweating sickness', gave its victims a most offensive odour and killed them in less than two hours, though whoever could hold out for twenty-four hours survived. It was marked by a high fever, and in their agony men shed their garments, and craving for cold drinks, drained their pots dry. 'At the longest, to them that merrily dined, it gave a sorrowful supper' wrote one medical man of the time. It is said that most of those attacked succumbed, the Mayor being one, his successor following him five days later, as well as six aldermen. Men are said to have died on opening their windows, others while playing with their children in the streets or at their doors.

The epidemic quickly spread to all parts of the country, though it never reached Scotland and Ireland. The prescribed remedy was to go to bed fully clad, lie quiet for twenty-four hours, and increase perspiration gently and naturally by adding more and more clothes. No food was to be taken, and any drinks had to be warmed. Even to put one's arm out of bed was declared fatal. Nevertheless, those who followed this advice died as readily as the rest.

The sickness came to an end, however, before October was out, a violent wind being given the credit. The King had moved to Guildford to avoid infection, and a common saying was that 'he should reign in labour because his reign began with a sickness of sweat'. The sickness was to return several times, but never so violently.

Having had a few days in which to ponder, Henry called his Council together, with other important personages. After confirming the honours already awarded, he allotted to Katherine, widow of Henry, Duke of Buckingham, now the wife of Jasper Tudor, an annual 1,000 marks. To his own mother he restored her estates. Restitution was also made to Elizabeth Woodville, widow of Edward IV, the Queen Dowager. Rhys ap Thomas, Edgecombe, Conway, Urswick and the Earl of Oxford were given posts of honour, pensions and marks of goodwill, Oxford being appointed Lord High Admiral and also Constable of the Tower, in which capacity he had to keep the lions, lionesses and leopards there, for which he received a shilling a day, and half as much for the animals' food. Courtenay was created Earl of Devon, Morton, Bray and Fox were appointed to the Privy Council, and Sir Giles Daubeney was made custodian of Bristol Castle. Even the plain yeomen who had fought 'at the late victorious felde' were given reward and recognition. Richard's treasury was officially transferred to Henry himself. Lastly, the King made financial provision for the mother of Edward IV, Cicely Neville, now Dowager Duchess of York.

The matter of his marriage was raised almost at once. According to Lord Bacon he repeated his pledge to take Elizabeth as his Queen, but thought it better to postpone the wedding until after the coronation and his first Parliament. No objection seems to have been raised.

[4]

Although in the eyes of the nation and in fact Henry's claim to the crown rested primarily on his victory at Bosworth, he knew that for the world in general and Parliament in particular it would have to be based on a firmer foundation than military success alone. He therefore made its legitimization and establishment the second essential item in his programme. Various possibilities lay open to him. He could argue that since he had already vowed to marry the Princess Elizabeth, he as her husband would rightly wear the crown. He could claim it by right of the formal legitimization of his birth previously established in an earlier session of Parliament. As the surviving male representative of the royal House of Lancaster, he had a claim in his own right to the succession, or he could declare bluntly that he had won the throne by conquest and meant to keep it.

This cautious, intelligent and far-seeing man weighed each possibility with the greatest care, finally deciding to use his own right of succession as the primary argument and the second and third contentions merely as potential reinforcements in case of challenge. He had excellent reasons for his decision. If he used marriage with Elizabeth as primary support for his claim he would be 'a king by courtesy' only, and if his wife died, could be got rid of without scruple. Even if Parliament gave him a civil right to the crown, a rebellious and popular rival might easily set this aside. On the other hand, to rely exclusively on his victory at Bosworth, would make him feared rather than respected. He would be regarded as a potential tyrant, and suspected by the Yorkists of secretly preparing to favour the Lancastrians, restoring them at the first opportunity to their former pre-eminence. Then, if Elizabeth died childless, civil war might break out again, for there were still Yorkists with the blood royal in their veins, such as the boy, Edward of Warwick, and the Suffolk family of De la Pole.

By putting forward a *personal* right to the crown by virtue of his ancestry he would at a blow achieve an unchallengeable position, and his victory at Bosworth would seem then the needful removal of a usurper rather than a naked conquest.

Immediately after Bosworth, therefore, he declared himself King without any reference whatsoever to the Princess Elizabeth, ordering Parliament to assemble on the 7th November at Westminster Hall. His coronation was to take place at Westminster Abbey on the date originally appointed. His reign was said to have officially begun on the 21st August, though the battle took place on the 22nd. This was a legal device to enable Richard III to be formally attainted.

6—H VII

Meantime he took steps to strengthen his hold on the country. First, he instituted, after the manner of the French kings, a permanent personal bodyguard of fifty archers, picked out for their loyalty. These were given the now famous title of 'Yeomen of the Guard', but were not mere hirelings, being as their name implies of the yeoman class. They came into existence on the 16th September, those summoned to this service having been with Henry Tudor in Brittany and having sailed in his ships. A warrant in the Public Record Office reads 'to William Brown, Yeoman of the Guard', and refers to his good service 'as well beyonde the see as at our victorieux journeye'. Their full original title was 'Yeomen of the Guard of [the body of] the King'. They were paid 6d. a day and well supplied with bows and crossbows.

Their first collective appearance was at Westminster Abbey when Henry was crowned, and they accompanied him throughout each twenty-four hours, whether in his English palaces or overseas. They were sworn to safeguard him with their lives at all times, made his bed, and after 1605, searched the vaults of Parliament before each session. Many ultimately became guardians of royal castles or custodians of ports and filled other important offices. As a body they dined together and kept a good table, whence may have arisen the term 'Beefeaters'.

Henry had the advantage of having lived long abroad, so that he was less hidebound by tradition than some of his predecessors. He looked at England almost as a foreigner might, and saw that she had a great deal wrong with her. Before he could 'mould it nearer to the heart's desire', he had to make himself and his dynasty safe. Straightforward in action and unaffected by that part of medieval custom that seemed to him nonsensical, he brought to the government of Britain a Gallic realism combined with the toughness of his English blood and the subtlety of his Welsh. These he reinforced by a determination to keep his throne by fair means rather than foul, by wisdom rather than terror. He had fought what he hoped would be the last battle of the Roses, and meant to make it so if he could.

His first measures were all designed to strengthen the defences of the country. A commission appointed on the 16th October mustered men in the southern and eastern counties for movement at an hour's notice in emergency. Four days later the north was told to relax, for some raiding Scots had gone back over the Border, fearing the vengeance of the now all-powerful English King.

In choosing his Council the King gave greater weight to personal efficiency and devotion than to rank. He meant to govern, not be governed, and chose therefore men whose positions depended on himself rather than on hereditary title, men who would give advice only when asked, and who, once instructed, would do their work competently and without quibble. The Privy Council was to constitute a body of knowledge and experience on which he could draw, and to execute his personal policy thereafter without exceeding their instructions.

Inevitably this made them subservient to his will. The apparatus was that of an autocrat, but this was the inevitable consequence of the state of virtual anarchy existing in the land. In this instance the autocrat happened to be a reasonable and prescient being, whose firm hand was dedicated to ending civil conflict and restoring peace and order to the realm.

Every action of Henry's at this period was aimed at destroying the private armies and overweening arrogance of the nobles. To begin with he abolished the wearing of emblems by their retainers and by those of the keepers of castles, so that they could not be instantly recognized as the exclusive warriors of their masters. He then stopped the forcing of men to swear allegiance to their lords or bind themselves legally to give whatever service was demanded of them. He forbade both the unauthorized mustering and use of armed men and secret bribery to prevent justice from taking its true course. The sheltering of escaping lawbreakers in places that were not recognized sanctuaries was prohibited, and everything possible was done to render those charged with a royal commission, warrant or order from being obstructed in the performance of their duties.

In short he focused upon himself his countrymen's hopes of security and repose. Quietly he put down disorder, appointing men he could trust to the lieutenancy of his fortresses. Lastly he asked the City of London for a loan of £4,000, but they would advance only £2,000. However, he did obtain restitution of all the royal estates given away by Henry VI since the 2nd October, 1455.

[5]

His coronation was attended by Innocent VIII, Pope of Rome; Frederick III, Emperor of Germany and his son Maximilian; Charles VIII, King of France, with whom on the 12th October, 1485, he signed a truce for one year; and that impressive and capable couple, Ferdinand and Isabella, King of Aragon and Queen of Castile. Also present—a disturbing mark of interrogation in Henry's mind—was James III, King of the Scots, those traditional enemies of England. However, nothing occurred to disrupt the harmony. All was, outwardly at all events, friendship and warmth.

Everything had been done to give the King an impressive public appearance. He wore a doublet of cloth of gold and white and green satin, the Tudor colours. Over this was a 'long gowne of purpure velvet, furred with ermyne, laced with gold and with tasselles of Venys gold, with a rich sarpe' (collar or scarf) 'and garter'. Through the streets of London he rode on a fine horse caparisoned with cloth of gold. Four knights, two on each side, supported over his bare head an awning, also of cloth of gold. Following him came a troop of seven other men, mounted and bareheaded, and clad in crimson and gold, leading a spare horse for his use.

Now came the royal servants of every degree wearing their formal livery of Tudor white and green, and after them an array of heralds in magnificent attire. At this period the heralds were basically carriers of messages from potentates to each other. The Greeks and Romans had had them, but now their functions had become more diverse. They organized tournaments, looked after the royal arms, were skilled in everything pertaining to them, and had the gruesome task of counting the dead after battle. Richard III had enlarged their duties still further. They had become a close company known today as the College of Arms, and were deputed to grant or allot armorial bearings to subjects. In Henry's day, however, the arms assigned by a herald had no more authority than those a man had assumed for himself. 'Armys bi a mannys proper auctorite take, if an other man have not borne theym, be of strength enogh.'

After the heralds came trumpeters, equally emblazoned and displaying their gleaming instruments. Banners and streamers showed both the Lancaster red rose and the Tudor portcullis, emblems of great significance to those who saw them.

Arriving in Westminster from the city, the procession entered the Abbey. Here the sword of state was carried by the former Lord Stanley, now Earl of Derby. The crown was the responsibility of the King's uncle, Jasper Tudor, now Duke of Bedford, the King's spurs being borne by the Earl of Essex. The Bishops of Exeter and Ely walked in stately fashion, one on each side of the advancing party. Mantles and special caps of estate were worn to represent the former English provinces of Guienne and Normandy in France, lost during earlier reigns.

It is said that Henry's mother, Margaret, Countess of Richmond, 'wept marvellously', but whether from joy at her son's triumph or because she feared what might follow cannot be said.

Clothing the King and the rest for the coronation depleted the royal treasury by the total sum of £1,556 18s. 10¾d., colossal for those times. Great haste had been made to get the royal robes ready in time. From the careful accounts kept, one learns that twenty-one tailors and fifteen skinners worked by the light of lanterns and Paris candles day and night for three weeks, firmly bolted and barred in their workrooms to keep them at it, and to prevent pilferage or robbery of the expensive materials used.

[6]

Some indication of the havoc wrought among the nobility by the Wars of the Roses and the conflicts of the previous reigns will be gathered from the fact that only eighteen temporal lords were present at this opening Parliament of the reign.

The coronation was over at last. The King and Parliament could now settle down to business. This session was one of the most important of the reign, for under the guidance of the King the legislators laid the foundations of a new form of governance. Above all, civil disturbances had to be prevented, laws made and enforced by strong and capable administrators, order not only restored but maintained, anarchy prevented by whomsoever fostered, and the nation given a code of rule and behaviour that was both understood and accepted. Thus, by degrees, England should become a united kingdom.

This was exclusively the policy of the King. Whatever its merits and defects, they were his and his alone. Though Richard had stigmatized him as a rebel, this in his own view he had never been. No man who took up arms against a usurper could be called a rebel. Today he can be more justly described as one who gradually instituted a system of regal autocracy so unusual that it had in it the seeds of democracy.

It was arranged that Parliament should be opened by the Lord Chancellor, Thomas Alcock, Bishop of Worcester, its first task being to elect a Speaker, which took two days. Thomas Lovell, a member of the King's Council, was finally chosen, his election receiving royal approval.

The Speaker elected on the 9th was on the 12th appointed Chancellor of the Exchequer. The assembly now got down to work. Some immediate practical difficulties had to be got out of the way. For example, neglect had caused many rivers and waterways to be choked up, so that they were impossible to traverse or cross. In consequence a Bill was laid before Parliament concerning the Isle of Thanet in Kent, where, at Sarre, the river was so choked that there was 'no ferry or passage there, nor elsewhere adjoining and convenient by boat or otherwise except at high spring floods', to the impoverishment of 'owners, landholders, inhabitants of said island and country and great jeopardy in war' should an enemy land.

Powers were therefore sought to build a bridge at the ferry large enough to let 'boats and lighters . . . pass to and fro under it' whenever the water was sufficient.

On one thing the King was determined. His Court should not be a haven of wine-bibbers, gamblers, pimps and adulterers, as in Edward IV's day, but a place of dignity and splendour. Affairs should be conducted in seemly fashion, without slackness and informality. Rules should be rigidly observed, and the royal person revered and respected.

To this end he paid great attention to outward show. His palaces and residences became dignified, handsome reception halls, enriched by glowing cloth of gold and tapestry of arras, littered with carved chests and articles of costly woods. The massive dining tables glittered with gold plate. The Tudor rose was everywhere—on curtains, carpets and cushions. Hundreds sat down each day to dine on the delicacies a King alone could provide. One reads of swans, peacocks still displaying their gorgeous plumage, lampreys in galantine, 'crane with cretney', 'pike in Latimer sauce', 'shields of brawn in armour'.

This was the Court of neither a curmudgeon nor a Harpagon.

CHAPTER FIVE

The Simmering Pot

[1]

THIS PARLIAMENT LASTED for over two months. It granted the King tunnage and poundage customs duties on wine imported in tuns or casks and on every poundsworth of goods imported or exported, 'for the defence of the realm and especially the safeguarding and keeping of the sea'. This reveals that Henry had already observed the military and naval weakness of his kingdom, and was preparing to remedy it. It was laid down, however, that the grant was not to be taken 'in ensample to the kings in England in time to come'. 3s. a tun on wine and 12d. in the £1 on other merchandise was its amount.

Henry was given a loan of £14,000 to cover his personal needs and expenses, which were to be kept apart from the national expenditure. He undertook to set aside sums from customs and estate duties to meet this grant, which would be repaid in one lump sum, for it had been a sore point with Parliament that in previous reigns there had been 'constant appropriation of property and cattle for expenses of the royal household, for which the owners do not receive satisfactory and proper payment'. He also obtained a loan of £2,105 19s. on the same conditions to cover the cost of his wardrobe.

He was now formally and legally accepted as King in his own right, his reign having as earlier stated been officially considered to begin on the 21st August of that year. That he began with general goodwill can be gathered from Alcock's opening address, in which he referred to the King as 'a second Joshua, a strenuous and invincible fighter', from whom great things could be expected.

The crown was entailed to his issue, the inheritance to 'reste, remain and abide in the King and the heirs of his body'. Nevertheless, the omission of all reference in the Act to Elizabeth of York showed that Henry had not yet committed himself irrevocably to making her his Queen, a point that did not pass unheeded. It was, indeed, a clever means of avoiding any open support of Yorkist claims, designed to prevent Lancastrian resentment and hostility and make it plain that his title to the throne was not based on any matrimonial alliance, past or future.

Henry's own estates were restored to him by an Act of Resumption, the Act of Attainder against him, his mother and Jasper Tudor, being repealed as 'a notorious lie and a blot upon the statute book', and deleted instantly from the records. Nevertheless, it was decided that neither Jasper nor the Countess should resume their original rights until Parliament had finished its deliberations. Jasper was, however, appointed Lieutenant of Calais.

Many knights and burgesses entitled to attend the session had felt unable to do so because of Richard's Act of Attainder, as they could not legally take their seats until this Act had been repealed. This nice point had been submitted to the judges present, who had ruled to this effect. As for the King, who could himself have been excluded on the same grounds, they ruled that the crown 'takes away all defects and stops in blood, and that from the time the King did assume the crown, the fountain was cleared and all attainder and corruption of blood discharged'. (Circumstances can always be altered to meet royal cases!)

Sterner duties now devolved upon the Members. They declared that all who fought for Richard at Bosworth were traitors and their property forfeit to the crown, so Henry could now dispense with further special grants of money. Included in this sweeping denunciation and the Act that made it legal were the usurper himself, the Duke of Norfolk, the Earl of Surrey, Viscount Lovell, Lord Ferrers, Lord Zouch, Sir Richard Ratcliffe, Sir William Catesby, and about eighteen other knights and esquires. Some opposition came from the Members, 'but it would not be, for it was the King's pleasure'. The Act of Attainder was duly passed.

On the 19th November, the King being present, a most important event took place. The lords and ecclesiastics of the royal household, numbering only forty-eight, having been gravely addressed by the Chancellor, swore solemnly to give up various rights, such as to rebel or stir up disturbances against the King, to bind men to their service by oath or document, and to employ illegal liveries. Vowing on the Gospels, they submitted themselves to the law as laid down by their sovereign, refusing also to protect declared criminals.

At a blow this destroyed the overwhelming influence of the great lords and bishops, and with it their private armies, their oppression of the weak, their behaviour as if above the law, their refusal or distortion of justice, and their brutal violations of decency.

After this ceremony, the knights and esquires of the Lower House were called on the 19th November into the Parliament chamber, again in the King's presence, and there took the same oath. From that day on the power of the monarch and his law became supreme. That of the nobles and ecclesiastics waned. This result was not achieved without discontent. 'There is much runyng' (grumbling) 'amongst the lords, but no man wot what it is; it is said it is not well amongst them.' One suspects that the Chancellor's address had been so adroit and the Bill so carefully worded that many of these almost illiterate men had taken the oath without fully grasping its implications until it was too late.

Christopher Urswick, now the King's almoner and clerk, was formally appointed Master of King's College, Cambridge 'with all rights and profits and 8 marks for 2 robes out of the issue of Cambs and Hunts'. A Lancashire man, born in 1448, he was eventually made Dean of York, and in 1495 became Dean of Windsor. There he did a good deal of construction, one of the chapels of St. George's Chapel being still named after him. He was a friend of Sir Thomas More and outlived the King.

By now the omission of the Princess Elizabeth of York from all legislation thus far enacted was disturbing to both Houses. Consequently the Lower House petitioned the King on the 10th December to keep his promise and marry her. The Speaker himself presented this petition to the King while the lords stood up with lowered heads facing the throne, adding their voices to the request. Warned by this unanimity the King confirmed his intention of celebrating the marriage on the 18th January in the coming year.

Other business transacted by this, his first Parliament, was the suppression of 'purveyance', an iniquitous but ancient custom whereby the King, when travelling, was legally entitled to claim provisions and other needs for himself and his company at prices fixed by his own steward or 'purveyor', as well as the use of horses as required. This custom had been greatly abused in previous reigns because the King's retinue was often numerous and extravagant, the prices were fixed far too low, and payments either made only after great delay or not at all. This was one of the main complaints made in 1450 by the rebel, Jack Cade.

The attainder of the Bosworth combatants was mitigated by a pardon proclaimed for all who swore allegiance to the King, as long as they gave themselves up within forty days. This brought many fugitives out of sanctuary.

Some of the revenues from forfeited estates, etc., were devoted to meeting claims upon the King, the object being to cover the expenses of his household and to remove any need for royal extortion. Lord Chandos was made Earl of Bath, Sir Giles Daubeney became a lord, and Sir Robert Willoughby, now Steward of the royal household, who had brought Princess Elizabeth and the Earl of Warwick to London, was rewarded by being created Lord Willoughby de Broke. Edward Stafford, heir of the late second Duke of Buckingham, was reinstated in his father's estates as a recognition of his father's rebellion against Richard.

On the 11th December, Sir Reginald Bray, Chancellor of the Duchy of Lancaster, was appointed steward and surveyor of these estates at an annual salary of £40, until the heir should attain his majority. He eventually became High Steward of the University of Oxford, a Member of Parliament and a knight banneret.

The enduring misery of the country outside London is indicated by an exemption from dues and payments granted next day to the city of Shrewsbury by reason of the 'ruin, poverty and decay of their town'. Bishops were given greater power to punish clerks guilty of immorality. There was also dissatisfaction with the law regarding 'benefit of clergy'. (See p. 118.)

[2]

The system of government introduced during this session of Parliament was somewhat similar to that of the Nazis in Germany in 1939, in that it was a tyranny supported by the goodwill of the bulk of the population and upheld by a combination of unchallenged authority and a resentful, non-aristocratic mass, with bitter memories of war and hunger. These calamities were rightly attributed to the excessive power of the nobles and its misuse. A common practice was to send young men of gentle birth to serve great lords in their houses where they acquired knowledge, polish, and skill in the arts of politics and war. Every family with sons so employed felt obliged to take up their masters' cause in any disputes, so that the circle of civil war widened to embrace more and more normally decent, unaggressive folk who might otherwise have remained peaceful country squires or tenant farmers.

Henry sought to be both ruler and leader of the kingdom in his own person, and to represent to powers abroad, whether hostile or friendly, an England strong and united. After careful assessment of his financial and military position he saved much money by allowing useless castles to fall into disrepair, their garrisons being withdrawn. Those more important, such as Berwick and Calais, were strengthened so that neither Scot nor Frenchman should readily overcome them. The Governor of Scarborough Castle was ordered to admit no foreigner into its precincts. Armed troops were stationed at Portsmouth to hold the naval base there against attack by land or sea. Even hired soldiers from Flanders were brought over to reinforce the King's still inadequate army. He thus developed and increased his power, being the first medieval King of England to break the great barons by military and legal means combined, so buttressing the crown against them.

This task was easier than it would have been in previous reigns. The great houses had been seriously weakened by the bloodshed of the civil wars. Few heads of ancient families had wisdom, age, experience and ability. Younger sons, mere boys, or remote branches of families had found themselves suddenly ennobled by executions and by deaths in battle or from disease. The King gave them neither time nor opportunity to adopt the vices of their predecessors, while promoting few to their ranks except his own supporters.

[3]

On the 17th January, 1486, the truce with France was extended by two years. The wedding of Henry and Elizabeth on the 18th was an affair of great pageantry and public enthusiasm. By now the King had seen his prospective bride and found her more attractive than he had expected. Possibly she had inherited the wonderful beauty of her mother, which had won the heart of a gay young King. He had never doubted that politically the marriage was indispensable, and even had he found Elizabeth unattractive, would probably have accepted his mother's advice and married her.

Technically he should have awaited a papal bull giving him leave, but he made do with one obtained from James, Bishop of Imola, the papal legate in England. The Pope confirmed this in the following year, his bull of the 6th March reading: 'By the Counsell and consent of the College of Cardinalles approveth confirmeth and stablishyth the matrimonye and coniuncion made betwene our souryn lord king Henre the seventh of the house of Lancastre of that one party and the noble Princess Elyzabeth of the house of Yorke of that other [party] with all the issue laufully borne betwene the same.'

This bull is said to have been printed by William Caxton. It is also related that the marriage was even more splendid than the coronation. Certainly both King and Queen must have been splendidly arrayed, for no less than £53 4s. 8d. was spent on the velvet and collars that adorned the King's gown of cloth of gold, together with a few additional pieces of clothing, and £11 5s. 6d. on 'black silk of damask and crimson satin' for the Queen's use. The ceremony was performed by the Archbishop of Canterbury, Thomas Bourchier, who said: 'His hand held that fair posie wherein the white roses were first tied together.'

Nevertheless, Henry was still but the iron lid on a simmering pot. Away in the north, the fun of the coronation being over, the Scots were once more threatening invasion. Warned in time, he promptly put the border lands into a state of defence. This alarmed the Scots King, James III, who abandoned his intentions on the 30th January. A man of thirty-four, he had occupied the throne of Scotland for twenty-four years, and had had a chequered career, being constantly at variance with his brothers, his nobles and even his own son. Loving solitude and peace, he was forced to make war against his will. His hobbies were music and building.

Instead of sending troops over the border, he now sent ambassadors to the English Court. They were well received, being given presents of bows and arrows, and entertained by hunting parties at Eltham Palace—about two miles south-east of Greenwich. This palace had been greatly extended by Edward IV, who had loved it, a passion Henry shared. The ambassadors were also plentifully supplied with bread, wine and other provisions. Parliament had been prorogued on the 23rd January.

The first real danger had thus been averted. The critical few months had passed, and the King could look back with a degree of relief. No great rival had appeared. No foreign menace had loomed up. There had been no alarming decline in his popularity, and no resurgence of Yorkist discontent. His first Parliament had done a great amount of good work and sanctioned many measures he was convinced were for the good of the realm and conducive to the establishment of his kingdom. He had reason to feel satisfied; consequently this wise, young, but experienced man could now turn his attention to the future with some confidence that he would be there to see and direct it.

[4]

The Marquis of Dorset and Sir John Bourchier had necessarily been left in the King of France's hands as surety for the loans made to the King. Henry now repaid the loans and requested their release and return. The repayment had left him short of money, so he asked the city of London to lend him 6,000 marks, but had to be content with 3,000, which he repaid at the due date. At the same time as his envoys went to Paris, others went into Flanders to summon John Morton and Richard Fox to England as members of his Privy Council.

Fox, thirty-seven years old, born at Ropesley, near Grantham, was of obscure parentage. In fact, all his early life is a mystery.

He appears to have studied at Cambridge, and was living in Paris when summoned or invited to join Henry, but what he was doing there is uncertain. A learned man with much experience, he was quickly promoted. Although made a bishop and appointed to successive sees, he saw little if anything of the earlier ones, Exeter and Bath and Wells, being absorbed in his Court duties, but eventually settled in Durham. Morton was his superior till his death.

Both men obeyed Henry's order at once. Fox, made Lord Keeper of the Privy Seal, was frequently used as a confidential ambassador. Other men admitted to the Council were Sir Richard Guildford, Sir John Cheyney, Sir Richard Edgecombe, Sir Thomas Lovell and Sir Edward Poynings.

Up to the time of Henry VII the functions of the Council had been, firstly, to give the King expert opinion on all matters of law, secondly to do justice, and thirdly to perform such commands as their King laid upon them. As the affairs of the land broadened and became more intricate, additional functions devolved upon it, such as control of the royal exchequer and the drawing up of legislation. The members had to swear to give wise counsel, to safeguard the King's interests, to do justice honestly and to accept no bribes. Petitions from the Commons when finally approved were drafted by them into Statutes. Sometimes the Statutes had not been quite what the Commons intended, for the Council had often been corrupt, but by the time Henry came to the throne, petitions were being presented more formally as Parliamentary Bills, and when passed, were left unchanged when the eventual Statutes were recorded. It will be later seen that Henry gave a distinctly new twist to his Council, of whom the largest number attending at Court was never above forty, including seven or eight ecclesiastics.

During January, 1486, the Earl of Oxford sought to have the facts concerning his mother's 'imprisonment and coercion' by Richard III when Duke of Gloucester established by witnesses in a Court of Chancery. In February, another request came—that certain English freebooters who had attacked and plundered a Breton ship off the Normandy coast and taken it to the Isle of Wight should be arrested and compelled to return the cargo. This was sanctioned by the Council.

In the same month the King examined the matter of a Spanish ship carrying alum, property of the Holy See, from Piombino to Flanders. She had been attacked and brought into an English port. The sale of alum was a monopoly of the Pope, who at once declared that the cargo must be forfeited. Henry's legal advisers claimed, however, that the wares of a trader voyaging by the King's leave were protected, and that the Pope had no jurisdiction in the matter. Henry ordered the alum to be locked up till the dispute had been settled. Eventually he ruled that as he had known nothing of the ship's capture, and the entry of alum into his kingdom was prohibited by law, he would both punish these men and prosecute the Florentine merchant who had suborned his seamen into making this attack. Later, however, the Pope pleaded through the Archbishop of York and other Bishops for the guilty Florentine.

The frequency with which English ships were captured in the Channel by those of other countries, had long been a sore point with the merchants of the kingdom. One hesitates to call these affairs acts of piracy, for at that date no hard and fast distinction existed between pirate, privateer and royal naval craft. All carried out what were virtually acts of war, sometimes with the permission, secret or open, of their governments, and sometimes without it. Foreign and neutral vessels were regarded by these hard seafaring men as their legitimate prey.

Hitherto English merchants had suffered more than most, but as Henry's reign proceeded and the new ships he had built sailed from his ports, the boot passed to the other leg. It was the English now who robbed Spanish galleys of their cargoes and took them home, boarded and plundered the ships of the Genoese Republic, and in the Channel pounced upon the small barques of Brittany and Flanders.

Yet another instance of this occurred on the 1st March, when a ship called the 'Bréhat', coming from the small Breton island of that name with wheat, wine, salt, mercury, gold and silver, made towards Ireland. Attacked and captured by the 'Anne of Fowey', she was brought into Fowey harbour and her cargo distributed among the inhabitants and crew. The King ordered its restitution, but the wild Cornishmen refused, whereupon the Earl of Devon and his friends, Sir Henry Bodrigan and Richard Ford, as the King's representatives enforced his will.

These examples indicate clearly the extent to which lawlessness reigned in the English Channel and English coastal waters, and the difficulty of enforcing royal commands in distant areas.

On the 5th March, Henry granted to Elizabeth Woodville, widow of Edward IV and his mother-in-law, not only a large number of 'lordships and manors', but also annual payments from several towns and a monastery. In this way he both placated the Yorkist faction, gratified his wife, and, he hoped, assuaged the possible rancour of his mother-in-law. His mind was essentially that of a master chess player. He studied deeply each problem that arose and thought out well in advance his moves and their probable consequences. In this he was the direct opposite of both Edward IV and Richard III.

On the 30th March, Cardinal Thomas Bourchier, Archbishop of Canterbury, died, and the King was at last able to promote John Morton to his See, being greatly pleased with his work in the Privy Council and his service generally. Though Morton, being a man of integrity, vision and intelligence, on occasion openly disagreed with his sovereign, Henry showed no resentment, appearing even to honour him for it.

The King now determined on a royal progress through the counties. The Queen did not go with him, probably because she was pregnant and because of the uncertainties of travel, and not, as Bacon thought, because the King disliked her or they had quarrelled.

In rapid succession Henry passed through Waltham, Cambridge, Huntingdon and Stamford, pausing next at Lincoln, where he spent Easter and followed there the ancient custom of washing the feet of as many poor men as he had lived years. He passed on to Nottingham, but omitted Newark because an epidemic was raging there, then moved to Doncaster, Pontefract and ultimately York. Plague was more prevalent in England than for decades. The Wars of the Roses, devastating so many rural areas, had led to a great multiplication of flea-bitten rats and the spread of disease.

The Corporation of York had registered disappointment at his victory at Bosworth, and had opposed a nominee of his for their

Recordership with such vigour that at that time, still nervous of the Scots, he had withdrawn his nomination and allowed them to choose their own man. There had also been loyalist uprisings at Ripon and Middleham in Yorkshire, Richard's own castle, but when it was known that the King was coming north with many nobles and supporters, these quickly subsided, and though he knew the northern city might be hostile to him, he took the risk.

On the way, news was brought that the three dangerous refugees from Bosworth, Francis Lovell, Humphrey and Thomas Stafford, who had been sheltering in sanctuary in Colchester, had emerged and disappeared. By the time he reached York on the 22nd April, these men were reported to be in arms. Lovell had in fact planned to take York while the two Staffords moved south to besiege Worcester. There was also a plot to seize the King as he celebrated the feast of St. George in York, which only narrowly missed success, being discovered and thwarted by the Earl of Northumberland. Several of the conspirators responsible for this were hanged.

However, Henry was greatly heartened by the unexpected warmth of his reception by York. The Mayor and Aldermen rode five miles beyond the city walls to meet him and escort him in. The citizens thronging the streets shouted: 'King Henry! King Henry!' and 'Our Lord preserve that sweet and well-favoured face!' Pageants were presented, in one of which 'Solomon, the King' hailed him alliteratively as 'Most prudent prince of providential provision, sovereign in sapience'. Elsewhere was the representation of a cloud, whence emerged royal red and white roses crowned, together with other flowers 'louting low'.

Rich tapestries decorated the streets and from their dwellings the inhabitants flung down sugar plums and other sweetmeats 'as it had been hailstones'. The city also provided sumptuous repasts and provisions galore, stirred to this generosity by the restraint the King showed in not demanding from them a grant of money. Indeed, in appreciation of their welcome, perhaps, he exempted their city on the 18th June from part of the payments due from her, on the grounds of her 'ruin, poverty and decay'. The weavers, both in and outside York, were particularly hard-pressed and suffering, and the King was advised that unless some relief were granted, they would move to other towns, to the great detriment of the city. He freed them from their annual payment of £10 to the crown, while other concessions were made to these worthy citizens.

Nevertheless, despite this display of goodwill, Henry took no risks. The Lovell rebels were between him and his capital, and he dared not leave them at large. He had no armed force at hand with which to meet and overcome them. However, Jasper Tudor, Duke of Bedford, scratched up about 3,000 men from the King's own following and from local tenants and yeomen, who hastily made themselves ready and put on fine armour of leather, while the Pope, in a bull dated the 27th March, had threatened excommunication of all who rebelled against the King. Henry instructed his uncle that his heralds should proclaim a pardon for all who gave themselves up.

As anticipated, the unwillingly-impressed soldiers of the rebel force at once surrendered. 'The heralds were the great ordnance' of the encounter, and even the two Staffords could place no trust in the courage and loyalty of their men. Losing heart, Francis Lovell fled by night towards Lancashire, lay hidden for a time in the home of Sir Thomas Broughton, then made his way to the Isle of Ely to seek sanctuary or find a ship. From Lavenham on the 19th May the Countess of Oxford wrote to John Paston in Norfolk ordering him to watch all ports and creeks so that Lovell should not escape abroad. Nevertheless, the Viscount disappeared again for a time.

The Staffords galloped to Culham, near Abingdon, and tried to take sanctuary there, but high treason was not now covered by sanctuary law, so the church would not shelter them. The King was within his rights, therefore, in forcibly removing them from their refuge. They were thrown into the Tower, and eventually Humphrey Stafford was tried by a Court of the King's Bench. Although he protested cleverly that a former king of Mercia had authorized Culham as a sanctuary for *all* offenders, his judges rejected this plea. He was condemned to death and beheaded at Tyburn. Thomas was pardoned, on the grounds that he had been instigated by his elder brother.

[5]

Easier in mind, Henry, leaving York after a stay of some weeks, returned through Nottingham and the village of Birmingham to

Worcester, where Bishop Alcock on Whit Sunday delivered a sermon, then read out a second Papal bull confirming the King in his title and sanctioning his marriage. Alcock, from Beverley in Yorkshire, had been born in 1430. After reading at Cambridge he had become Dean of Westminster, Master of the Rolls, and Edward IV's representative at the Court of Castile. Appointed Bishop of Rochester in 1476 and of Ely in 1486 by Henry on Morton's promotion, he was a scholarly man, keenly interested in architecture, and largely responsible for building Jesus College, Cambridge.

Free from the fear of attack by rebels, Worcester welcomed the King with spectacles and pageants, at which he was likened to former heroes and honoured as a direct descendant of Cadwallader. He moved on to Hereford, Gloucester—which made little fuss of him—and Bristol, where an enthusiastic housewife flung down wheat from her window, shouting 'Welcome and good luck!' The city took advantage of this royal visit to draw the King's attention to the dilapidation and decline of their port and shipyards owing to the increasingly reduced shipments of cloth, and the sorry state of the navy.

The King was better pleased by these sensible complaints than by the fulsome compliments. He responded admirably, telling the city to go ahead and put new ships on the stocks, leaving the rest to him. Indeed, he was so concerned for English shipping that he has been called 'the father of the English navy', to which title he has, indeed, a better claim than his son Henry VIII.

Bristol was delighted by this encouragement and the royal demeanour. Indeed, their Mayor remarked that they 'had not this hundred years of no king so good a comfort'. The port was London's great rival, and the conviction he instilled into the people that they would no longer be overlooked heartened them.

After this Henry returned to London. On the 5th June he went by river from Sheen to Westminster, being joined at Putney by the Mayor of London and other dignitaries in numerous gaily beflagged barges, and proceeded to the Abbey for the singing of a Te Deum. About this time he spent over £16 on a gold holy water stopper garnished with 'rubies, pearls and a great sapphire', weighing '11 oz. 1 qr.', and other jewelled luxuries. He also bought materials for the Queen's lying-in, had the great bed of state repaired, hired a couple of beds for himself, had two swords fitted with cloth of gold, and arranged for stuffs to be carried from London to Winchester. In July he made a trade treaty with Brittany.

This man, so often portrayed as a lean, dry, austere person, was, on the contrary, a great lover of display, and when he could, delighted in organizing entertainments for his guests—the feast, the joust, the ceremony, the game, the hunt. He is known to have spent £14,000 a year on a liberal table, and to have shown himself on almost all occasions a generous and kindly host. He himself was temperate and his needs few, but he would indulge in no parsimony where his friends were concerned, regarding it as a royal duty to see that they were properly received and treated.

Returning to Sheen on the 12th August, he spent some time in the New Forest, hunting. Queen Elizabeth was near her time, and with her husband travelled to Winchester, where, about four weeks prematurely, she bore a son. As usual on these great royal occasions Te Deums were sung in the cathedral, on whose walls hung brilliant and beautiful tapestries. Glittering processions delighted the eyes of the populace, who made merry and rejoiced. Great bonfires roared and blazed in the streets.

Then came the christening on the Sunday, with all the majesty that could be given to the ceremony. The absence of the King on this occasion was probably so that he might watch over the Queen, who had picked up an infection and was herself not present.

The infant boy, heir to the throne, was carried under a crimson canopy to the waiting font of the cathedral by Lady Cecily, the Queen's younger sister. The child himself was clothed in a mantle of crimson cloth of gold, gilt-edged with ermine, the immensely long train being held up by Sir John Cheyney and the Marchioness of Dorset.

The boy was christened Arthur, after the traditional British hero, to suggest a symbolic link between his birth and the ancient kings, his father's reputed ancestors, while Winchester was chosen for the Queen's lying-in because of its association with Arthur and his knights and Alfred the Great. Here in this once splendid centre of learning and culture a son was born who united by blood, indissolubly, in his own person the rival Houses of York and Lancaster.

Henry's joy was overwhelming. The infant, despite his inevitable small size, was sturdy. When the Queen had recovered from her illness, the Court returned in September to Greenwich Palace.

[6]

The astute and prescient monarch had had insufficient time to gain general popularity. There had been too much bloodshed and bitterness over the previous decades for passions and hatreds to have completely died down. The Yorkists had gloomy memories, while the more fanatical Lancastrians, resenting the King's union with the Yorkist princess, studied his every action for over-fondness to the rival House. Nevertheless, the Yorkists were the more active in their dislike. Offended by the original delay in marrying Elizabeth, they angrily noted that she had not yet been crowned. Ugly rumours went flying round that the younger son of Edward IV, not having been assassinated by Richard after all, was actually still alive and hidden away in a cell in the Tower.

Another grievance was that the boy Earl of Warwick had been thrust into the Tower without justification or trial, and with no indication that he would ever be released. It was believed and whispered that one night this boy, too, would be secretly murdered in his prison, if he had not been murdered already. This was the more dangerous story of the two. Indeed, men were not lacking to mutter that he was already dead or soon would be.

Under no illusions as to his precarious position, the King went carefully and cautiously on his sagacious way, doing his best to meet just demands and calm inflamed passions. He still needed money, which, however, he raised by borrowing from individual lenders. In October he again aided Cicely Neville, mother of Edward IV, instructing the cities of Chichester and York to pay to her the arrears of their annual due payments. Defaulting Somerset and Devon authorities also received the same command.

Towards the end of the year Henry granted a soldier of his maimed at Bosworth £20 out of the fee-farm payment of Monmouth town. This payment was a perpetual fixed rent on lands let for farming, not in recompense of some service.

An ancient custom existed whereby herring fishermen when ashore could dry their nets on the King's land for a small charge. In November the King gave the monies from this source, together with the profits from a rabbit warren he owned and from some grazing rights, to Thomas Barowe, a clerk, and his brother, for seven years. These, too, may have been Bosworth men.

On the 11th December he leased a water mill at Merchington and a piece of land to Nicholas Agard. Agard undertook in return to keep the mill and weir in repair together with some adjoining houses. On his side the King had to supply timber and piles as required. If mill and weir were damaged by flood waters, the King was also legally bound to carry out the necessary repairs whenever the total cost exceeded five marks.

[7]

About this period Richard (some call him William) Simons, an ambitious and crafty young priest, twenty-eight years old, residing in Oxford, was entrusted by Thomas Simnel, an organ builder (not a baker) of that city with a new pupil, his son Lambert. The boy, about ten years of age, was unusually good-looking, with natural ease of movement and a courtly bearing. He was also mild in manners and intelligent. Simons had heard the current rumour that Richard, Duke of York, was still alive in the Tower, and saw a chance to win a bishopric for himself.

If young Simnel could be prevailed upon to impersonate the Duke and the people to accept him as their rightful king, preferment for himself would surely follow. Ecclesiastics who had served their sovereign well in adversity were being well rewarded. Even an eventual archbishopric might not be beyond attainment.

Then another rumour came to Simons's ears that Edward, the young Earl of Warwick, son of the Duke of Clarence and popular by reason of his misfortunes, had been murdered in the Tower. Seeing the advantage of this to his schemes, the priest changed his plan. Simnel should be coached 'in royal habits and good arts' to assume the person and character of the supposedly murdered Earl, who should be said to have escaped by some ingenious method.

It seems highly probable that Simons was instigated, aided and advised in all this by a more influential personage, John de la Pole, Earl of Lincoln. The Abbot of Abingdon and the still lurking Francis Lovell are also said to have encouraged him. Lincoln, a nephew of Edward IV, had secret aspirations arising from the royal blood in his veins. Meantime, the priest, having cajoled the boy into compliance, determined to remove him to Ireland, where there was less risk that he would be detected as an impostor, and where there was still great affection for the House of York. The Queen Dowager, Elizabeth Woodville, another high personage, was believed without much foundation to have helped promote this conspiracy.

Francis Bacon, a great statesman of later years, also believed this. A member of the Privy Council of his own day, he may have had access to documents that have since disappeared. In any event his knowledge of political motives and people makes his views worthy of consideration. Nevertheless, he wrote many decades after the events concerned and is not a dependable source of fact. He argued that Elizabeth Woodville was furious because her daughter had not been crowned, not even with a purely matrimonial crown. This she considered a humiliation. A rash and changeable woman, she disliked the subtle, powerful new King, hated the Lancastrians and wished to see a man of Yorkist blood in Henry's place. Lambert Simnel was to be a pawn in the effort to remove Henry, and discarded when his work was done, either the young Earl of Warwick or Lincoln himself taking the vacant throne. Elizabeth may also have been privately assisted and encouraged by Edward IV's mother, Cicely Neville, or so the theory goes.

Meantime, Henry was probably too preoccupied with learning to govern his country to worry about distant Ireland, which had been left to look after itself. His power there was strictly limited, being largely confined to 'The Pale', an area consisting of Dublin, Louth, Kildare and part of Meath, ruled for him by the Irish Earl Kildare. Beyond the Pale was a miscellany of 'free' cities, including Waterford, Drogheda, Dundalk, Cork, etc., and to these regions English law did not often extend.

The King's supporters in Ireland were the great Butler family, whom the Yorkists had deprived of their rights and exiled. These rights Henry restored, taking good care, however, not to offend the rival family of Fitzgerald, of which Kildare was a member. In consequence, much of the land was controlled by men hostile to him, being mainly the home of half-savage barbarians, tearing one another to pieces in furious clan warfare.

Thomas, Earl of Ormond, head of the Butlers, a courtier appointed Queen's Chamberlain, was a member of the Privy Council, and a royal ambassador to France and Burgundy. He was necessarily absent from Ireland by reason of his duties, and therefore of little service to that country. Consequently Henry made his uncle, the new Duke of Bedford, Lord Lieutenant. The title, which he retained till 1494, carried no great authority, and the post was virtually a sinecure. Thus, the Lord Deputy Lieutenant, Kildare, a Fitzgerald, remained the strong man of Ireland.

When Simons and Simnel landed, they made their way first to the Chancellor, Thomas Fitzgerald, who took them to his brother, the Earl of Kildare. The two Fitzgeralds were speedily convinced, or feigned to be, that Simnel was in truth Edward of Warwick. The Earl of Kildare confidentially disclosed to his party the startling news of Warwick's escape, and they were soon satisfied that the story was true. Before many days the delighted Irish were cheering Simnel with fervour. Only a few towns loyal to the Butlers, such as Waterford, remained sceptical and unmoved.

Simnel was conducted with pomp and ceremony to the capital, Dublin, where he received all the respect and reverence due to a king. The Chancellor took care that the boy preserved dignity and a regal carriage, doing and saying nothing that might lead onlookers to doubt his identity. In the city a few days later he was proclaimed without opposition, vocal or military, King Edward VI of England.

[8]

This news, reaching Henry at Sheen, alarmed him. It was something he had neither expected nor foreseen. Fearing, even perhaps knowing, that his wife's mother, Elizabeth Woodville, had been active in this business, he persuaded the Council to send her forthwith without trial or inquiry to the nunnery at Bermondsey, and deprived her of all her possessions, which he later transferred to her daughter, his wife. Bacon gives as his pretext that she had left sanctuary and entrusted her daughters to Richard III, after giving her word not to do so, but the true reason he did not reveal. She was allowed four hundred marks a year on which to live.

The King did not lose his head over the news from Ireland. At all times he preferred to defeat his enemies by guile rather than force. After a council at Sheen on the 2nd February, 1487, he brought Edward Plantagenet, Earl of Warwick, out of the Tower, and had him taken one Sunday through the main streets of London so that all could see him. In addition the boy was allowed to take part in the service and pray in St. Paul's, where he conversed with highly-placed courtiers, particularly the Earl of Lincoln, who the King suspected was among those hostile to himself.

Next, Henry alerted all the ports, ordering them to arrest Lovell or any others seeking passage to Ireland or Flanders without good reason. Urswick was sent into Lancashire to report on the ability of the ports there to accommodate big ships. He found them quite deep enough to take such ships as might come from Ireland, and his work done, returned. Meantime a treaty to last for a year had been made with Maximilian, King of the Romans.

[9]

In Ireland the parading of Warwick in London had not gone unnoticed, but the Irish ridiculed the credulity of the Londoners, declaring that Henry had merely taken some boy of good family, dressed him up as Edward, and presented him to the gullible crowds in that guise. Kildare and Simnel were communicating with known malcontents in England and Flanders, and indirectly as a result of this, John, Earl of Lincoln, now openly joined the conspiracy against the King. This Earl, a brave and knowledgeable man, had been nominated as a successor to Richard III should he die without issue. Not without cause, Henry had been suspecting him of treachery for some time, but the storm over the young Earl of Warwick's imprisonment had debarred him from taking prompt action. He could not afford to be accused of two scandalous imprisonments. Lincoln is said to have visited Ireland at this period.

The greatest encouragement the rebels received came, however, from Margaret, Dowager Duchess of Burgundy, Edward IV's eldest sister, who had induced Lincoln to support the Pretender. At that date Burgundy was a duchy, lying between the Jura Mountains and the river Saône. Its boundaries over the centuries had constantly changed. In the fourteenth century it also included Flanders, while in the fifteenth Brabant and Guelderland were added. The French, coveting the Burgundian territories, nibbled away at them by annexation, and the resulting wars were causing many European potentates, including Henry, to cogitate and plan.

Though Margaret had no belief whatsoever in Simnel's claim, she suggested to her advisers that a false claimant was better in the circumstances than a true king, since the false would in course of time 'fall away of himself', so opening the way for the Earl to assume the crown. She detested the Queen of England, her niece, 'as the means of the King's ascent and assurance therein'.

By this time the elusive Lovell, despite the vigilance of all the harbourmasters, or by the connivance of one, had escaped to Flanders in January, 1487, where, later, Lincoln joined him. The Earl had attended the Privy Council meetings at Sheen in February, and reported all their decisions to his colleague. Lovell took counsel with Margaret, who had 'the spirit of a man and the malice of a woman'. She had been left a wealthy woman by the death of her husband, Charles of Burgundy, and by careful management had increased her fortune. Having no children of her own she passionately desired to see her own House once more ruling her native country.

[10]

At the end of March Henry left Sheen, having learned by now that Lincoln, Lovell and the Dowager Duchess, who came to be known as 'Henry's Juno', were backing the young Pretender. He foresaw a double invasion, one on his north-western coast from Ireland and the other on his east coast from Flanders. Accordingly he ordered his subjects in each area to arm and assemble under the respective commands of the Earl of Oxford and the Duke of Bedford. Warning beacons were placed in readiness on hilltops or posts in Norfolk, Suffolk and Essex. He himself undertook the command of a third force designed to support whichever commander needed it the more. Leaving nothing to chance and more fearful of defeat by the men of Flanders than by the Irish, he moved slowly into the eastern counties to assure himself that their muster was proceeding satisfactorily.

Passing through Colchester and Ipswich he came to Bury St. Edmunds, where he was advised that the Marquis of Dorset, still living in France, was sailing home to avoid being thought guilty of treason, an allegation already made. The King, distrusting him, ordered Oxford to seize him as soon as he landed and lodge him decently in the Tower 'to try his truth and prove his patience'. No harm would be done to him there, but at the same time, he would be doing no harm to his sovereign.

CHAPTER SIX

The Pot Boils

[1]

IN ENGLAND, Sir Thomas Broughton, Lovell's protector in Lancashire, was serving as a postbox for the exchange of letters between the conspirators in Ireland and Flanders. It was finally agreed that Lincoln and Lovell should take about 2,000 seasoned soldiers, mostly Flemings, not to the well-watched and well-guarded eastern coast of England, but to Ireland, to reinforce the Fitzgeralds and their protégé. This would strengthen the eventual blow in the north-west, and also shorten the lines of communication. Moreover, the Irish and their supporters in England would be heartened by the union of the two forces.

Martin Swart, a brave and war-hardened captain, having been appointed leader of the Flemings, the army sailed, landing in Ireland on the 5th May, to the joy of the inhabitants. The Earl of Kildare promptly took possession of Dublin Castle, where on Whit Monday, the 24th May, 1487, Simnel was borne through Dublin and crowned by John Payne, Bishop of Meath, with the diadem from the Statue of the Virgin, in Christchurch, the principal church of the city. He was borne on great D'Arcy of Platten's shoulders, and took the title of Edward VI. The coronation was greeted with vociferous applause.

A general council was now held, before which two proposals were laid, the first, to invade England at once, the second to content themselves with occupying and controlling all Ireland so that eventually the King would be compelled to invade her, opening the way for an uprising by the Yorkists at home. Against this it was argued that Ireland, unable to support a large, idle army, could not pay regular wages to the Flemish troops, who would soon protest.

Moreover, since a static cause quickly runs to seed, the enthusiasm of the people ought to be used while at its height.

It was decided to invade. Command of the combined force was given to Gerald Fitzgerald, Earl of Kildare. The Irish Sea was crossed without incident, and the army landed on the 4th or 5th June at The Pile of Fouldrey, near Furness in Lancashire, close to the Fells. With Kildare were Lincoln, commanding the English, and Lovell, his lieutenant. Thomas Fitzgerald led the Irish, while Swart had charge of the Flemings. On landing they were promptly joined by Broughton with a small company of horsemen. The English troops and the Flemings were reasonably well armed, but the Irish were, after the manner of their countrymen, almost naked, having virtually no armour, and mostly short knives and spears, being, indeed, little more than wild tatterdemalions. This motley company had probably no high hopes of Lancashire support, for the Tudors were popular in the county. They were quite satisfied to have landed safely without loss or opposition. Their aim was to march into friendly Yorkshire, in the hope that lovers of the White Rose would flock to Kildare's standard and that of the new 'King'. They advanced, therefore, without delay towards York, taking particular care to avoid ravaging the country and to show restraint and courtesy to the people, so that all should perceive the kindly disposition of 'Edward VI'. Nevertheless, despite proclamations to this effect, rigid discipline and their own self-interest, many offended.

To the dismay of the leaders, the 'snowball did not gather as it went', for the countryside was bleak, wild and more than ever weary of strife. Some of its inhabitants had been charmed by Henry on his recent visit and by his just and firm measures, while as Yorkshiremen they resented the impertinence of 'Germans' and wild Irishmen in daring to march uninvited into their province. Lovell at least, they thought, should have known better, for his earlier failure had made him highly unpopular.

The invaders, and particularly Lincoln, were worried by this cold reception and the tacit disapproval that accompanied it, as well as by the failure of the Yorkshiremen to come marching in. It was therefore agreed to change the direction of the march and going south, seek out the King and defeat him in battle as he had defeated

Richard. With this intention they entered Sherwood Forest and made for Newark Castle in Nottinghamshire, hoping to occupy it. On learning that the King was advancing more quickly than expected, however, they diverged again, crossing the Trent at Fiskerton Ferry, marching towards the village of Stoke, near Newark, and pitching their tents on the summit of a hill overlooking the Fosse Way to Newark. With what confidence they could muster they awaited the battle that would almost certainly be fought next day. Both Simons and Simnel, neither familiar with war, were with them.

[2]

Henry spent Easter in Norwich, and on Easter Monday rode to the shrine of Our Lady at Walsingham, where he prayed and made vows. He invariably tendered thanks to God for successes gained, and throughout his reign presented himself at many sacred shrines, awarding to each the image of a knight in golden armour on his knees.

At the suggestion of Kildare, he had earlier invited an envoy, John Estrete, to confer with him in England regarding the government of Ireland. Kildare sought to be confirmed as Deputy Lieutenant over a long period of years. The King had reserved his decision, which possibly alarmed Kildare and quickened his acceptance of Simnel's claim, but it is not certain that Henry's reply had reached him when Simnel landed in Ireland.

From Walsingham the King travelled to Coventry, arriving in time to celebrate the Feast of St. George with particular solemnity. Morton entered the cathedral at the head of five other Bishops and heard the papal bulls approving of his appointment as Archbishop of Canterbury gravely declaimed, while a papal curse with 'bell, book and candle' was pronounced on all rebels. This was an ancient custom, of Druidical origin, and applied even to those who had not actually taken up arms against the King. Here Henry was brought news of Simnel's landing by an Irish royalist, Lord Howth. Urswick also sent a courier with the same tidings.

Henry had been busy dealing with a request that a Spanish ship, 'The Holy Ghost', be allowed to dock in London with a vessel she had captured. He had also been coping with the problems of the town of Leicester, which had been put to great expense in housing and feeding him and his staff after Bosworth and in caring for his wounded, and he had granted the Mayor and Burgesses an annual sum of £20 to cover this. He also found time to grant to his Queen the goods and monies of fugitives and felons, and their chattels. Now the King summoned all available members of his Council to a conference.

His advisers opined that he 'should be well enough able to scatter the Irish as a flight of birds, and rattle away this swarm of bees with their king', nevertheless the energetic and cautious King ordered a number of nobles to return to their counties and assemble their levies. Others were to accompany their sovereign, mustering their men meantime by messenger. His 'continual vigilancy did suck in sometimes causeless suspicions which few else knew', says the chronicle. Taking no chances, Henry meant to crush the invaders before they could seize any important stronghold as a focal point on which to concentrate.

However, he had no genuine cause for alarm, because men poured in. The Earl of Shrewsbury and Lord Strange arrived with seventy knights and about 6,000 men. A large body under the Earl of Devon followed. Old Jasper Tudor, Duke of Bedford, Earl Marshal, declared himself ready for battle, and the Earl of Oxford, begging for a command, was given the vanguard.

Until his preparations were complete, the King lodged in Kenilworth Castle, where the Queen and the Earl of Ormond joined him, the army being centred on Coventry. He then moved towards Nottingham to prevent Kildare and Lincoln from taking that town. His spies had percolated the enemy ranks, and scouts mounted on fleet horses were roaming the countryside to receive their reports and locate Kildare's main force. It was thus that the news came of their arrival in Stoke. It was said that 'Henry was in Lincoln's bosome and knewe every houre what the Earl did'.

[3]

We have little to go on regarding the battle of the 16th June, 1487. Camping in Banrys Wood, the King appears to have taken up a position on level ground at the foot of the hill known as

Rampire, on which the Irish and their leaders were already perched. An old Roman road, the Fosse Way, separated the two armies. Henry's men were divided into three groups, Oxford in the van, Jasper Tudor in the centre, Rhys ap Thomas in the thick of the combat, and the King himself commanding the rearguard. Lincoln made the common mistake of rash medieval generals. Instead of cannily waiting for the King's men to start climbing the hill, when they would be at a disadvantage, he no sooner espied the royal army below than, sounding the charge, he led his men in a frantic rush down the slope.

As weapons the Irish had only the lance, the dart, the dagger, and knotted cords with which to strangle their enemies. They wore the kilt, their legs being bare. Their sole defence was their hide-covered, round shields of yew.

The struggle lasted three whole hours. Everyone, even the ill-protected Irish, fought manfully, but the bows and arrows of the English were too much for the Irish darts and knives and for the pikes of the Flemings. The attackers were massacred 'like dull and brute beastes', their leaders dying with their troops. Some, though not observed to fall, were never seen or heard of again. Lincoln, Plunket, Swart, all fought bravely, but left their bodies on the battlefield. Kildare was taken prisoner.

The only commanders of whose fate little is known were Sir Thomas Broughton and Francis, Viscount Lovell. According to tradition Lovell, that cat with nine lives, escaped once more un-hurt, and abandoning the struggle early, plunged into the Trent on the back of his horse, but having tried vainly to climb the opposite bank, found it too steep, being then swept away by the river and drowned, neither man nor horse reappearing.

However, an alternative, less credible legend states that he fled northwards, lived for a time as a peasant, then took refuge in a secret vault at his mansion at Minster Lovel, where he lived for many years hidden from sight. This unlikely story is based on a discovery made two centuries later by labourers working at the house. In an unknown subterranean chamber they found the skeleton of a man sitting in his chair with paper and pen before him, wearing a cap greatly mouldered and decayed, his head resting on a table. He had died of hunger or old age.

8—H VII

Not unnaturally Lovell's name was attached to this grisly find.

The King took no part in this battle, the brunt of which was borne by Oxford's troops. It is claimed that of Lincoln's army 4,000 died against 2,000 of Oxford's, while on both sides many were wounded. These figures seem to me exaggerated. Few commanders on the King's side lost their lives. Henry wished to take Lincoln alive, but when their chance came to kill him, his men were ruthless, believing that the death of the enemy commander would dismay and depress the rest of the rebels.

The greatest triumph was the capture, uninjured, of the non-combatants, Simons and Lambert Simnel.

Henry was much encouraged by his victory, believing that the enthusiasm of his soldiers and their leaders proved that he was accepted. The Irish had lost more than men. They had lost the captured Kildare, a powerful leader.

When Simnel was brought to him, the King stared at the youth with interest and some compassion. Here, he thought, was a nice, good-looking, well-mannered, impressionable lad, too early chosen as the tool of ambitious men. Nothing need be feared from him. Even had his own good nature not induced him to spare the boy's life, his intelligence would have done so, for he knew the danger of transforming men into martyrs by over-hasty execution. Instead, he told his head cook to find the boy a job in his kitchen. Simnel was set to turn a spit by the fire, but later in life became a falconer in the King's service. One writer suggests that he ended up in the service of Sir Thomas Lovell.

It is also said that Henry often allowed visitors to see him, and when they engaged him in conversation, Simnel revealed a humble and likeable disposition. He lived till 1534. Simons, though not executed, probably because of his cloth, was thrown into a dungeon and history is silent as to his fate thereafter. The Bishop of Meath cringed to Henry after the battle of Stoke and was pardoned.

Henry's enemies had spread a rumour in London that he had been defeated, and the city shook in its shoes. So much so, indeed, that the Lieutenant of the Tower handed the keys of the fortress to the Earl of Surrey, one of his wards, who wisely and honourably refused to leave unless the King sanctioned his release. Even the Middle Ages had its 'English gentlemen'.

The King now moved to Lincoln city, in whose fine cathedral he offered thanks for his victory. The banner used in the battle was presented to the shrine at Walsingham. From Lincoln he advanced into Yorkshire, pausing in York, then on to Newcastle for a few days, from which city he despatched Fox, Bishop of Exeter, and Sir Richard Edgecombe in July as envoys to James III of Scotland, to discuss the transformation of the existing three years' truce into a permanent peace treaty. Edgecombe, a Member of Parliament, came of a Cornish family and was one of the King's principal envoys, as on this occasion.

All that was obtained, however, was a two months' extension of the truce, James's hold on his crown being far too uncertain for him to offer a more lasting treaty. Among marriage proposals put before the Scottish king was that he should take Elizabeth Woodville, the Queen Dowager, to wife, a scheme of Henry's to get her out of his way without damage to his reputation, but this came to nothing.

Throughout his royal progress the King ordered a thorough investigation so that those guilty of assisting the rebels or speaking publicly in their favour should be brought to trial. He was particularly anxious to discover who in London had given out false reports of his defeat, for grave disturbances had taken place in the capital when these were published. Men emerging from sanctuary had run riot, doing dreadful deeds.

Arising out of this, Henry urged the Pope to make sanctuary more violable, promising in return to place himself and his army at his disposal if ever required. He referred incidentally to an offender who, mocking the Pope's authority, died on the instant, whereupon 'his face and his whole body became blacker than soot'. The Pope's reply was a bull cancelling the right to sanctuary of any man who, having secretly left it, then went back. Debtors also, though they could still claim sanctuary, could not thus prevent their creditors from taking over their possessions. Traitors could now have guards set to watch over them while in sanctuary in readiness to apprehend them when they emerged.

Minor offenders got off with fines, but a few were put to death. The King's crown still depended to a great extent on his reputation for probity, and therefore in July he repaid his creditors another £2,000 instalment of his debt of £6,000, leaving a balance of only £2,000. This greatly increased his prestige in the financial circles of London. It was obvious his wealth was increasing, for he was constantly buying precious stones, partly so that at some future date he could obtain further loans by offering these as pledges. This practice, indeed, he continued throughout his reign, but even so, his credit was always good since he never failed to meet his obligations.

On the 3rd November, Henry came back to Leicester, where he received ambassadors from Charles VIII of France, who, wishing to excuse his onslaught on Brittany and to obtain the King's neutrality, declared his action a purely defensive one. In reality Brittany had long been coveted by the French king.

[4]

His reception on his return to London on the 4th July was secretly witnessed by the Queen and her ladies from a window in a house in Bishopsgate, after which they all went back to the royal palace at Greenwich. The affair resembled a Roman triumph, and after it Henry repeated in St. Paul's his words of gratitude to God for victory. The following day, after listening to a sermon at St. Paul's Cross, he set the Marquis of Dorset free as well as the honourable Earl of Surrey, and made Morton Lord Chancellor. Morton, a statesman, though he never lost sight of his duty to the Church, also carried out his duties to the King and the state conscientiously and well. His bishopric of Ely had been given to Alcock as a placebo to compensate for his demotion in Morton's favour.

The Pope had asked the King to tax his people for a crusade against the Turks, but the wary monarch responded that if there was any money to spare, he needed it for himself. Increasingly sensitive to public opinion, he now deemed the time had come to have the Queen crowned. On the 9th he called Parliament together, John Mordaunt acting as Speaker, to discuss this and other 'great business'. At this session the rebel leaders were accused of treason and an Act of Attainder passed against them. This Act, however, made no mention of Lord Lovell, whom the Government evidently considered dead. Stern punishments were ordered, and it is significant that the Act appointed a special court to try them, consisting of the Chancellor, the Lord Treasurer, the Keeper of the Privy Seal, or any two of these, with a bishop, a temporal lord, and the Chief Justices of the King's Bench and the Court of Common Pleas, or two other judges in replacement of any unable to attend. This court was empowered to try cases of unlawful maintenance of rebels, the giving of licences, signs and tokens, great riots, unlawful assemblies, and whatever offence was too grave to be tried by the normal tribunals.

At the time of its foundation this new court was useful and even indispensable, for it struck directly at the power of the great nobles and those wealthy influential men whom the ordinary law courts could not reach. It proved to be the precursor, if not the basis, of the infamous Star Chamber, so called from the room in which it met, but the uses to which it was later put were not in any way foreseen when it was first introduced into the legislature.

Henry liked to sit in this court, which was later regarded as 'the great instrument of his extort doynge'. A saying common in his day was that there 'the King took matters in his own hands' and that if he used the phrase 'My attorney must speak to you' a severe financial penalty would invariably follow. Nevertheless, during his reign the Court was consistently well-intentioned, dealing as it did with a hitherto privileged class of offenders, too powerful to be affected by the normal processes of law. The common man had now virtually his own court of appeal against verdicts obtained elsewhere by bribery or coercion. Hitherto in far too many instances court trials had been duels between rival perjurers, while many jurymen acted as agents for those they favoured or by whom they had been paid.

The men who sat in the new Court were uninfluenced by self-interest, judging and sentencing even the high and mighty. They could be deterred by neither threats nor cajolery, did not clutter up their trials with complicated procedures, and were respected and approved by the common people, though the squirearchy of the House of Commons did not like the Star Chamber because of the powers it gave to the law. Not till many years had passed did the Court of the Star Chamber acquire and deserve an evil reputation.

Its founders intended it to codify the personal wishes of Henry and his advisers. Legal right was given to the Court to call before it any witness they wished to question, and take evidence on oath. Nevertheless, it was not so much a revolutionary advance in judicial procedure as a tidying up and extension of previous Acts on similar lines, giving them precision, order and firm authority.

[5]

Parliament voted to the King a money grant of two tenths and fifteenths, some of which was to be obtained by taxing native artisans and foreign merchants. Renewed sympathy for the Dukedom of Brittany was felt and expressed, for she had been invaded by France, and her Duke was penned up in Nantes. If he were to appeal for aid, England might be called upon to fight for him.

Despite this, the King decided that nothing must hinder the Queen's coronation, now fixed for the 25th November, 1487, for he was anxious to show the Yorkists that despite the recent risings, he had no prejudice against them.

It was a great occasion. That morning the Queen was brought up river from Greenwich, escorted by the Mayor of London and the liveried men in their own ornate and vividly pennanted barges, one of which, known as the 'Bachelor's Barge', breathed fire over the surface of the river from the mouth of a large red Welsh dragon. Elizabeth went ashore at the Tower, being welcomed by the King with courtesy and every sign of pleasure. In her litter beneath a canopy of cloth of gold, resting on pillows also cased in cloth of gold and silk, she was carried towards Westminster.

The denizens of the stinking, narrow, slop-dribbling city streets saw her floating past them like a gorgeous water lily. Her gown of white and gold, ornamented with ermine, was secured by a 'great lace curiously wrought and of gold and silke and rich knoppes' (tufts) 'of gold at the end tasselles'. Partly enclosed in a close-fitting net decorated with piping, her golden hair was allowed to cascade down her back. On her head a golden circlet sparkled with rich gems. On this dull November day she was, to the humble folk who watched her pass, like a dream that has suddenly become reality.

Drawing near Westminster Abbey, the Queen was met by children dressed as angels and virgins. After the ceremony had been performed, the company repaired to the Great Hall of Westminster, richly provided with tapestries. It had been rebuilt nearly a hundred years before by Richard II, and was used for state banquets, especially those accompanying coronations. Such a banquet was now held, the nobles, including Jasper Tudor in a leading place, all wearing their most handsome robes, so that the scene was an eye-dazzling riot of shimmering gold and brilliant colours. It is recorded that two of her Majesty's ladies in waiting 'went under the table' (literally, not metaphorically) 'where they satt on either side the Queene's fete al the diner time'.

The King was not present, but with his mother watched the proceedings from a platform erected outside one window. It was a common practice on royal state occasions for those not entitled to be present to watch unseen from above. In the Kremlin in Moscow an aperture through which the ladies of the Tsar's court could watch their men at the dining table in the great hall below, from which they were excluded, is still shown to visitors.

The banquet over, the Queen left the Hall with 'Godd's blessing and to the rejoysing of many a true Englishe mannes hart'. Two more days of processions and feasting followed, after which the watchful, hard-working King settled down once more to the problems of sovereignty.

[6]

Three matters now demanded the King's attention. One was the eternal question of money. He had honourably repaid the whole of the loan of £6,000 received from the city of London, but this time the problem was different. A common difficulty in most medieval kingdoms was the lack of hard currency to finance their transactions. Consequently, every ruler did his best to build up a private reserve of gold, jewels and other valuables, kept securely guarded in his treasury. Time and again, however, the need of gold and silver hampered governments. This was particularly true of England. The King's steady accumulation of these precious metals in his strongboxes may even have enhanced the shortage with which he was now faced. Every possible step was taken to obtain supplies of this lifeblood of the kingdom. It had been laid down in previous reigns that every trader must bring home a quantity of gold and silver as part of his cargo, but this plan had never worked. Instead, therefore, more exports were declared imperative, and permission for bullion to leave the country was refused.

The result had been that while the English traders could not pay cash for their imports, the foreigner had to pay for his from England with the money obtained from selling English cloth, wool, tin and other commodities. The present state of his finances compelled the King to enforce this law and include in it the merchants of Ireland and the Channel Islands.

His great desire was to build up the cloth industry, which was based on the unsurpassed quality of English wool. He had done everything possible to promote its manufacture at home and ensure the greatest possible output, and had made the shipping of raw wool overseas expensive by clapping stiff taxes upon it. He had prevented the Hanse and other foreign traders from shipping worsted out of England, as well as cloth not cleansed and thickened in English fulling mills. Now he insisted that all cloth must be 'carded' and sheared at home before it could be sent abroad.

The Hanse merchants raged. English shearing ruined the cloth, they declared, making it excessively dear. Moreover, cloths were sheared which were not suitable for shearing. To all these protests the King presented a bland indifference. On the other hand he was all courtesy to the Venetians, some of whose people off a galley had been set upon and killed during this year in England. He at once punished those responsible and compensated the sufferers. The Venetian skipper concerned was invited to dinner and told that the King's own artificers and stores were ready at any time to repair any injuries suffered by the vessel he commanded.

The second problem was the war between France and Brittany, which Henry called a Council to consider. Other urgent matters were the administration of Ireland, and England herself. He was inclined to deal with these in the order given. As regards Brittany, he was determined not to be pushed by either the French or Parliament into a foreign war. The French ambassador had carefully concealed from the English their King's intention to annex

Brittany. Consequently the Council 'bare aloof from it as from a rock'.

At that time English foreign policy was governed not by the collective brilliance or wisdom of democratic statesmen, but by the individuality, royal connections and family of the man on the throne. There had been no such thing as a purely territorial nationalism since Henry V, and although different nations often detested one another, although the centuries had filled many of them with bitter recollections of foreign savagery and death and the hatreds resulting, none of this necessarily influenced the monarchs to whom they owed allegiance. These coveted each other's possessions not only for personal prestige, to revenge insult or to achieve power and wealth for their immediate dependants, but also to protect their dynasties and ensure, as they thought, their personal popularity by conquest.

The French assault on Brittany—they had captured Vannes—had alarmed both the English and Maximilian, King of the Romans, while the Burgundians and Spaniards were equally agitated. All Europe stirred uneasily, and the astute Henry saw that by a rash act he might unleash a general war, which he did not want, for his own crown might disappear from his head in the misery it would bring to his people. At the same time he had no wish to see the French closer to his shores than they already were. They might decide, if victorious, to overrun Calais, his own remaining foothold in Europe.

The French King had greatly aided him in winning his crown, but so had the Duke of Brittany. The charge of being ungrateful to either was one he did not seek. Nonetheless, there was great popular indignation in England against her powerful neighbour, and before long this became manifest in action. In the spring of 1488 Sir Edward Woodville, now Lord Scales and Governor of the Isle of Wight, an Admiral of the Fleet, often termed 'Lord Woodville', came to Henry with a scheme to take a volunteer force to Brittany and fight the French.

The King would have none of this—he 'woulde in nowise geve the brydle to hys hote, hasty and wilde desire'. However, according to William Paston, writing on the 13th May, 1488, that 'valiant captain and bold champion', Woodville, boarded a ship that had arrived in Southampton with a cargo of salt. He and the two hundred men he had raised compelled the skipper to carry them to Brittany. On the way there they were challenged and themselves boarded by a French vessel. The English soldiers had meantime hidden away below hatches, and at the opportune moment rushed out, overpowered the boarding party, seized the French ship, and took both her and their own to a Breton harbour, St. Malo. Woodville immediately offered himself, his prizes, their cargoes and his men to the Duke.

This venturesome action threw Henry's plans into complete disarray. Charles VIII and his advisers would naturally assume he had winked at this expedition, even if he had not formally sanctioned it. In consequence he might be dragged into war despite himself. Reluctant to arm his people lest some of them use the arms against him, he had therefore to weigh this risk against the possible loss of trade and prestige for the kingdom if the French succeeded in annexing Brittany. He was prepared to fight if he had to, but he inclined to believe that with Maximilian's aid Brittany could throw the French back without him.

[7]

The border town of Berwick had long been a cause of dispute between England and the Scots, who claimed it as their own. In January, 1488, they had revived their claim even more pertinaciously, insisting that if the English would not restore it to them, they should at least pull down the fortifications.

Henry was saved from a tedious and dangerous dispute by James's overthrow. The Scottish King was deposed, and his young son occupied his throne as James IV. The King of England was neutral during these events, but in June, 1488, James III died at Sauchieburn, near Bannockburn. It is related that while escaping, he was killed by a rebel soldier in priestly disguise, in a shepherd's hut, but many in Scotland believed his own son was responsible.

In October the Scots, seeking a bride for James IV, studiously avoided England.

In June, Edgecombe was ordered by Henry to repair to Mounts Bay in Cornwall, en route for Ireland. On the 23rd June, 1488, he left that harbour with four ships and five hundred men, the Bishop of Meath accompanying him. Pirate ships were known to be in the Severn estuary and off the Isles of Scilly, and Edgecombe was eager and ready to fight, but he encountered none, landing safely at Kinsale four days later, and being welcomed by Lord Courcy with the keys of the town.

Edgecombe, a loyal and vigorous Devonian and a supporter of the late rebellious Duke of Buckingham, had once escaped death by throwing himself into the water and pretending to drown. He now accepted the declaration of allegiance to the King made by Lord Thomas of Barry, and went by ship to Waterford, which as a Butler stronghold had been loyal to Henry Tudor throughout the Simnel period. The Mayor was afraid that Kildare, still his enemy, would take revenge on the city for her obstinacy. Edgecombe assured him that his master was determined to prevent this, and after looking over the city, took ship for Dublin. Compelled by heavy seas to anchor off Lambay Island, he perforce came ashore at Malahide, and was escorted into Dublin by the Bishop of Meath, now acting as go-between with the Irish leaders.

For some days the loyalty of Kildare was suspect. He compelled Edgecombe to wait eight days at Maynooth before receiving him, and would not bow on coming into the royal envoy's presence. However, after both the Papal Bull of Excommunication for traitors and the King's offer of free pardon to all who submitted, brought by Edgecombe, had been read by the Bishop in the cathedral, Kildare swore over the Host at St. Thomas's on the 21st July to be faithful. The collar of the royal livery was then placed once more round his neck and publicly worn by him in the city.

At Windsor on the 14th July, 1488, Henry had agreed to extend the existing treaty with France, due to expire in January 1489, for another year. Jasper Tudor was appointed a Conservator of this. All reference to Brittany was carefully omitted, for the King's shrewd eye had observed his own lack of the military and economic power to intervene decisively in Europe. He also made a provisional treaty with Spain. In the belief that the negotiations so successfully concluded had eliminated the prospect of war, the King now turned his attention to the next serious matter—Ireland.

Edgecombe now visited other Irish towns, including Drogheda, and going back to Dublin refused to pardon the Prior, one of Simnel's greatest advocates, giving a loyal man the office of Constable of Dublin Castle, which the Prior had refused during the previous two years to surrender to him. Kildare received his formal pardon, after which Edgecombe felt safe in sailing for home from Dalkey on the 30th July.

[8]

He found the Court in a state of consternation over the news from France. The Bretons had put over a thousand of their own soldiers into sleeveless jackets with the red cross of St. George and mingled these with Woodville's men. La Trémouille, a young but able commander of an exceptionally large French army (15,000 men, of whom 7,000 were Swiss), well provided with guns and horsemen, had overwhelmed the Bretons at St. Aubin on the 2nd July, 1488. Sir Edward Woodville (Lord Scales) and virtually every man of his company had been killed, having fought well, and the French, who had lost only 1,200 men and a general, Jacques Galéot, were at the gates of the well-fortified city of Nantes, on the Loire, which they were besieging. Louis, Duke of Orleans, had been captured and imprisoned, and it was said that at least 6,000 Breton soldiers had been killed, while Dinan and St. Malo, small fishing ports on the Breton coast, had been seized.

As a result of this defeat the Duke of Brittany signed at Vierger on the 21st August a treaty of peace with his conquerors, the last clause of which was that his daughters should take no husbands unless Charles approved. His capital, Rennes, was, however, still holding out against the enemy, but the Duke was in no state to go on fighting, and died on the 9th September, some say of grief at his humiliation. The Dukedom descended to his eldest daughter, Anne of Brittany, a child of eleven, whose hand in marriage had already been sought by several suitors. De Rieux, his chief minister, was appointed her guardian.

Henry was caught in a dangerous trap, and now regretted the treaty with the French, which he had just agreed to extend for another year. It tied his hands precisely when they should have been free. The French still suspected him of having secretly encouraged Woodville's escapade, while his own people were enraged by the loss of so many brave countrymen and by the ruthless ambition of the King of France. They felt much as the British in 1940 when the Germans seized the Low Countries.

Anne of Brittany, now Duchess, appealed to the King for help, but although sympathetic, he could do nothing except to summon a Grand Council at Westminster. In November, according to one writer, both Houses of Parliament put to him through Morton, Archbishop of Canterbury and Chancellor, the point-blank question whether he would or would not wage 'auxiliary and defensive war' on Brittany's behalf.

The Chancellor pointed out that if France annexed Brittany, England would be 'girt about with the coast countries of two mighty monarchs'. Though the French claimed to be fighting in self-defence, he urged the King to go swiftly to the aid of the Bretons, for which Parliament would grant him a subsidy.

The King in reply admitted that he owed gratitude to the Duke of Brittany for enabling him to avoid capture by Edward IV and Richard III of England, but declared himself reluctant to risk his people's safety and welfare in a war such as this would be, for they would inevitably suffer great hardship. He would fight rather than be dishonoured, but if he did, it would be 'without passion or ambition'.

Nevertheless, to prevent censure, Henry got together a small force of about six hundred men and archers, designed to garrison Anne's fortress and release men for her army, but not to make war themselves on the French. They were under Sir John Cheyney.

Meantime, encouraging replies came in from the powers opposed to France, and the King consequently set to work to build up a system of alliances, not wishing to be left alone to face a powerful foe, while continuing his military preparations. For example, John Baker, a master mason, sent to the Tower five tons of hard stone from Maidstone quarries, 'rough hewn for bombard shot'.

[9]

Henry hastened to despatch Ainsworth and Edgecombe to Anne of Brittany on December 11th, 1488, as his ambassadors, and

Urswick to France charged with the repudiation of any royal responsibility for Woodville's rash action, while Savage and Nanfan went to Spain and Portugal, taking the King of Portugal the insignia of the Garter, and other envoys went to Maximilian and Philip of Burgundy, his son. The French had already shown great annoyance, and on the arrival of Urswick and his attendants, raging young men threatened for a time to infringe the ambassadorial immunity of these Englishmen. However, the mob were dispersed in time. Henry offered to mediate between France and Brittany, and to win time for their generals to develop their campaign against the Duke, the French accepted the English apology and the offer to mediate.

Thus encouraged, Urswick left France and arrived in Brittany, where he narrowly avoided being imprisoned, but he and Edgecombe made the same proposal to the Duke, who, however, was old and once more in no fit state to govern. His acting deputy, Louis, Duke of Orleans, was by no means enthusiastic, reminding the Englishmen of the debt Henry owed to the Duke and of the risk to England and Calais if France won the Breton coast, and soliciting help. This Louis was the third Duke of Orleans, the old French province known as Orléanais, covering the territory around the city of Orléans. At this period he was about twenty-six years old.

Returning to Paris alone, Urswick reported that the Bretons were lukewarm, but the French assured him they were still willing to accept Henry's mediation, so the ambassador sailed for England.

One of the King's schemes was to marry the young Anne of Brittany, the Duke's daughter, to the Duke of Buckingham, whose father had been executed by Richard III. His ambassador in Spain was instructed to suggest to Ferdinand, equally alarmed by the French threat, that his support in this would be valued, but the Spaniard's response was not encouraging. Maximilian, Ferdinand said, was now free again, trying to re-establish himself in Flanders, and proposing to marry Anne himself. There were other influential suitors for her hand, and Henry's proposal would, he hinted, increase the hostility of the French to Brittany. Accordingly the King dropped the idea.

This correspondence, if it did nothing else, revealed to the

King the strong feeling in Europe against the French. He foresaw that he might one day create a 'balance of power' on the Continent by allying himself with Ferdinand and Maximilian, both of whom had turned against that nation, but this was merely something to bear in mind for the future. He now made a formal treaty of peace with the French for three years, which was ratified; and as he was determined not to break it, he would use the respite to maintain his hold on Britain. However, he took care to strengthen the defences of Calais, which in October he reinforced with 1,500 men, artillery and stores.

Indeed, being appalled to discover how few ships he possessed and the lack of reserve stores for the fleet, he constructed perhaps the first truly naval warships. These new craft came off the slip-ways in 1488 and 1489. Much more had still to be done, however, before he had a navy of consequence.

The moving finger of Time was writing, but none as yet per-ceived the message it wrote. In 1488 an unknown Genoese living in Spain, Christopher Columbus, sent his brother, Bartholomew, to England with a request for money and support in his forthcoming attempt to sail by way of the Atlantic Ocean to Asia. Bartholomew is said to have been captured by pirates on his way over and com-pelled to work as a slave. Escaping, however, he reached London and lived as a poor man in a state of ill health, earning his living by making maps and drawing globes. He gave the King a map of the world and received a promise of aid for his brother, but the promise was worthless. Henry would have nothing to do with what he considered a wildcat scheme. His shrewd, practical mind had been plagued sufficiently in the past by adventurers and cranks, and for once he lacked vision. But for this the wealth of the Indies might have come to Britain instead of Spain.

A new Parliament was now called for the 13th January, 1489.

CHAPTER SEVEN

Treaties Galore

[1]

A NEW PARLIAMENT in January, 1489, was faced at once with a request from the King for a grant of £100,000 as pay for 10,000 archers for possible war. This was not relished, and the assembly debated the matter hotly for forty-one days, until in February the figure quoted was accepted, but it was decided that at that time they could spare only £75,000. A supplementary amount would, however, be allotted for each of the two succeeding years, should the war last that long. One tenth would be raised by a levy on the people, a further sum by a property tax, and the rest perforce made up by the clergy. The northern counties were, however, let off this sharp and worrying hook.

The widower King of the Romans, Maximilian, had now formally allied himself with Anne of Brittany, and was still anxious to marry her. Maximilian has been described as 'pious and not very intelligent, and was always poor . . .'. He continually wanted to conduct wars and yet had not the money. At times, when he intended to ride to battle, his servants were so short of cash that they (and the Emperor) could not pay their way out of the inns. In fact, the merchant-councillors of the city of Augsburg would not allow him to buy a house and live there, not wishing so indigent an Emperor to be forever on their doorstep.

He was an eccentric, who once firmly entertained the notion of becoming Pope of Rome, but lacked the money, and those shrewd bankers, the Fuggers, would not lend it to him. Nevertheless, though needy and inefficient, he had dash and charm. He loved to strut around in armour, even when it was becoming old-fashioned, and the wealthy men of Augsburg proudly paid for the steel plate he wore. The King of France, sneering, christened him 'The Burgomaster of Augsburg'. He would run dances for the municipality and compel young girls to dance before him.

Head of the great Hapsburg family, he was a strange blend of good and bad qualities. Though handsome, physically strong, simple in his way of life, friendly in manner, of broad outlook and courageous in war, he was also vain, untrustworthy, rash, unpractical and over-optimistic, all of which adds up to an inferior military commander. Politically he lived in a dream world, like a medieval Walter Mitty, seeing himself romantically as a 'great king' and starting one hare only to follow another. Restless, provocative, 'a gifted amateur in politics', he was forever flinging out novel ideas of varying merit, but mostly chimerical and dangerous. Too careless to think deeply before he moved or pledged himself, he buzzed about Europe like a bumble bee, yet was the earliest royal advocate of world government, and for his day a remarkably cultivated man, the exact opposite in temperament and action of Henry VII of England.

In 1488, as overlord of Flanders living in Bruges, he was heir to the 'Holy Roman Empire', a union of Central European states which had existed for six hundred years, and which was believed to have been divinely appointed to link Church and State in the person of the Emperor. It now consisted mainly of the German-speaking peoples. The elected Emperor was considered inheritor of the old Roman Empire. Maximilian, an unstable, capricious man, had been married to Mary of Burgundy, daughter of Isabella of Bourbon, which marriage had embroiled him with France, for Mary deeply resented the French annexation of Burgundy. She had died in March, 1482, after a fall from her horse, and had she lived, he, as her husband, would have possessed great power and authority in Europe.

Inheriting her possessions, he fought to keep the Low Countries out of French hands. The populace rose, seized arms, and on the 5th February, 1489, attacked his residence, slaughtering most of his staff. He himself was held prisoner, and not released till his father, the Emperor, had marched a large army into Flanders to rescue him. On his release, he promptly declared war on the Flemings.

His leading officer, Philip of Cleves, Lord Ravenstein, had

placed himself at the head of the rebels, who, under John Pic-
quanel of Bruges, took Ypres and Sluys, important strongholds,
and on the 13th June, laid siege to Dixmüde. As a result of their
successes, they appealed to Lord Cordes, the Anglicized version of
the name of Philip de Crève-coeur, Sieur d'Esquierdes, for military
aid. Cordes, Governor of French Picardy, was probably expecting
this call, for at extremely short notice he despatched a considerable
army which linked up with the Flemish rebels and joined them in
the siege.

Maximilian's commander sent riders to Lord Daubeney, now
Captain of Calais, with an appeal for help. Desiring Maximilian as
a future ally against the French, and pretending to fear an attack on
Calais, Henry agreed that Lord Morley should take 1,000 archers
to drive the besiegers from Dixmüde, in which they were successful.
In addition, with the King's sanction, Daubeney and Sir James
Tyrell mustered 1,000 pikemen and 2,000 'valiant' archers from
Calais and Guines with sixteen guns. One night they slipped out
and marched to Nieuport, their advance being covered from the
sea by seven or eight ships.

The French had not kept a sufficient watch, and the six hundred
German pikemen garrisoning Nieuport came over. With them as
allies, Daubeney infiltrated the besiegers' lines and won over some
of the Swiss mercenaries on the French side with eloquence so
moving that they enthusiastically prepared to do battle against
their original employers.

The attack was launched on the main gate, but the English were
at first repulsed with heavy loss. The Germans, reinforcing them,
fought bravely and overcame the enemy, despite losing all their
officers. The accounts vary, however. One gives credit to the
Germans for the victory, whereas the other holds that the English
bowmen slew the French gunners, put their guns out of action, and
so ensured their defeat. Next day a rebel from Ghent under sentence of death led the English to a weak point in the French defences in exchange for his life. Daubeney attacked again, and the
enemy, thoroughly beaten, lost 2,000 men, much treasure and fifty
guns. Many of the dead were afterwards found to be prisoners
murdered by either the people of the town or the mercenaries.

The English casualties were smaller than expected, not more than one hundred being killed, it is said, but their commander, Lord Morley, was slain by gunfire as, refusing to dismount, he rode by the walls of the town to observe the state of the French defences. Considerable booty was gained and carried back to Nieuport. Later, a chronicler wrote: 'They that went forth in clothe came home in sylke, and they that went out on foote came home on great horses'. The Calais men went back, leaving behind only their wounded and a few volunteers to garrison Nieuport.

This defeat stung the French and especially Cordes, whose men were determined to redeem the prestige of their arms. Daubeney had gone back with his men to Calais, and taking advantage of this Cordes attacked Ypres. He took the main fort and tower, and for a short time the French banner floated over the citadel, but the wounded went on fighting heroically from the town walls. Suddenly a ship from Calais with eighty archers on board and some small companies of footsoldiers came sailing in. To them the women of the town cried 'with lamentable and loud voices: "Helpe, Englishmen!" ' The archers poured arrows into the enemy, while the redoubtable women, sallying from their doorways, cut the throats of those stricken by the English.

Cordes, who once declared that 'he could be content to lie in hell seven years, so he might win Calais from the English', was compelled to retreat to Hesdin. To prevent further assaults, Daubeney reinforced the garrisons of Dixmüde, Furnes and Ostend.

[2]

In England, the King was seeking to have laws passed against usury, which he hated and was determined to suppress. He wished also to prohibit illegal exchanges and to have special attention paid to commerce, industry, the arts and handicrafts, as well as measures taken to prevent unemployment. Some restriction of imports from abroad should be imposed, he suggested, the money saved being spent 'on commodities of this land', so that coin should not flow overseas without a return demand for British exports. He requested also that his income from customs duties should be continued, together with other 'loving aids', since he was 'a good husband and a steward of the public', and ought not to be left with an empty purse.

Other matters dealt with were the Court of the Star Chamber, to use its later name, whose foundation was confirmed. Morton pushed through a measure rendering any servant of the King below the rank of lord who conspired to kill a councillor liable to execution. It was also made a capital offence to abduct any woman, unless she were a bondwoman. In all this the aim of the King was to procure through Parliament the suppression of violence, the tranquillity of the state and the elimination of injury and death for his subjects.

There crept into the law of the land one regrettable measure. Judges, sheriffs and magistrates were authorized to try in their own courts offenders accused by private informers. The only stipulation was that the informer must live in the particular county concerned, and if he did not prove his case, meet both his own and the accused man's costs. Such chastisement might then be inflicted on the guilty as their offences warranted. The power thus given to the courts did not, however, apply to treason, murder or other grievous crimes.

This new ruling marked a radical change in English legal practice, since it dispensed to some extent with the jury, and made the judge responsible for both prosecution and verdict. It has been said that Henry himself was behind this new measure, having imported the idea from France. What prevented immediate abuse of the Act was his lack of prejudice and the wisdom of his councillors.

Incidentally, this Parliament drove one of the first nails into the rights of certain clerical and other criminals to claim 'benefit of clergy', exemption from trial by a secular court. These men were continually breaking the law, and it was therefore laid down that in future any man not of the ecclesiastical profession, even if he came within the provisions of the earlier Act, could claim this right once only. Even then, he would be branded with a letter indicating his crime, e.g. 'M' for murder, 'T' for theft, etc. A member of the clergy would have to prove it by a statement from the Head of his Order.

It remained true, even so, despite the passing of this Act, that after committing one crime any literate man might go scot-free by claiming benefit of clergy.

Parliament at this session also prevented debtors taking sanctuary from assigning their property beforehand to a third person, to prevent their estates from being impounded, while drawing from them the income to live on. The prorogation was now commanded. Parliament was not to meet again till the 14th October.

[3]

Trouble now came upon Henry from a new quarter. The subsidy granted to him by Parliament was proving unpopular. As was customary, commissioners of the Crown came in February, 1489, into the various districts to collect the amounts due, but on arriving in Yorkshire and Durham encountered great hostility. Men refused to pay, saying they had endured misery enough. The memory of Richard III was 'so strong that it lay like lees in the bottom of men's hearts', while as always political agitators fished strenuously in these troubled waters.

Meantime, the French, far from ceasing their attacks in Brittany, had penetrated still further, and were besieging Guingamp, capturing it on the 18th January, 1489. While Parliament was still in session, Henry sent Edgecombe and Ainsworth as envoys to propose and draw up a treaty whereby, in return for aid, Anne of Brittany would agree to obtain his approval before taking a husband. Her council were to swear that they would ensure she did not break her oath. Moreover, Anne was not to ally herself with any potentate other than Maximilian or Ferdinand of Spain unless Henry agreed and was included in any such treaty.

This harsh and grudging proposal amounted virtually to blackmail, but in effect the King was insuring himself against Breton treachery. He had no faith in the honesty of European potentates and particularly their statesmen, for little true morality prompted international politics. He had already had one taste of their instability.

The advisers of the little Duchess persuaded her to sign this treaty at Redon on the 10th February, and it was ratified on the 1st April. All things considered, this was, perhaps, an appropriate date. That the treaty was fairer than it appears at first sight was proved when, on the 6th July, Maximilian broke his own pact with Henry, signed on the 14th February.

In the final form of the treaty with Brittany, England undertook to send 6,000 men for defensive purposes only, to be retained till the next Feast of All Saints, but no longer. In return, the Duchess would aid Henry to recover Guienne and Normandy, former English provinces of France, if called upon to do so. Five hundred Englishmen were to garrison a couple of Breton towns and their castles at once, and hold them against any attack and as pledges until the cost of maintaining the English army had been refunded. The Duchess would also ship them home, sending the cash for this at her own risk. Thus, if Henry did not get his money back, he would at least have the valuable Breton towns, Morlaix and Concarneau, to hold as pledges until he did.

Committed now to incurring French displeasure, Henry regarded an undertaking with Maximilian and Ferdinand of Spain as essential. He spent Whitsuntide at Nottingham, then returned to Windsor for more hunting in the near-by forest. The Bretons, he knew, could not withstand the full power of France unless they had an ally bound by strong ties to support them. The solution of this problem lay in the child Duchess herself, who must be given a husband capable of propping up her weak régime and mastering her quarrelsome advisers. His thoughts alighted upon a new suitor, the lord D'Albret, a dissolute, ill-favoured, crippled, middle-aged Gascon, son of the King of Navarre, but possessing great wealth and power. D'Albret was, however, bluntly rejected by Anne, who, when De Rieux suggested him to her, said she would sooner go into a nunnery. De Rieux at once lost favour with her, and she turned instead to Francophile advisers, such as Louis of Orleans.

De Rieux, accusing her of being in league with Louis, refused to let her make a ducal entry into Nantes. In consequence the Duchess took herself off in a huff to Rennes, and did all she could to decry her guardian to Henry and other supporters.

Thinking it better to play fair with the French, the King advised Charles that he was in honour bound to assist Anne. In March, therefore, Charles secretly sent the Archbishop of Sens to England to reproach and dissuade him. Henry was far too clever to lay himself open at home to a charge of underhand dealing, and for this reason insisted that the Archbishop should present himself publicly. When he did so, he was told plainly that his master had no right to invade Brittany. The French King received this curt message in his castle of Chinon in western France.

In April, the 6,000 men promised under the treaty were shipped off to Brittany under Robert, Lord Willoughby de Broke, steward of the royal household, and Sir John Cheyney, Master of the King's Horse. They were splendidly equipped and had been carefully chosen. The crossing was good and needed fewer hours. On landing, the army moved at once to relieve Guingamp. Far from their base and suffering all the difficulties of supply in rugged, hostile country, the French besiegers were in no state to fight a pitched battle against fresh troops. Consequently, they dug themselves in, but the English archers did great execution among them, and at intervals mounted men raided their lines in surprise attacks. Afflicted and depressed, the French in September abandoned Guingamp after setting fire to it and badly maltreating the inhabitants, on whom they imposed a tribute, taking hostages to ensure payment.

De Rieux was blockading the large French-held port of Brest by land and water, but the French reinforced the garrison, and in October he was compelled to raise the siege and retreat, abandoning all his artillery.

Winter was approaching, and instead of being united by war, the members of the Breton government went on bickering among themselves. De Rieux again offered to help England regain Guienne if Henry agreed to make Anne marry D'Albret, but Henry, warned by her expressed detestation of this match, would not commit himself. Anne for her part wished him to wrest Nantes from her guardian, against whom she again levelled serious accusations, and though the King tried in vain to bring the two of them together, he was forced to give up the attempt.

[4]

Throughout this period the King was steadily pursuing his courtship of the great Ferdinand of Spain. Born in Spain in 1452, Ferdinand, King of Aragon and ruler of Spain, was Henry's great rival and political sparring partner in Europe. He had married his cousin, Isabella, Queen of Castile, and at this time was busily engaged in ridding Spain of the Moors. Astute, unscrupulous at times, dedicated to the preservation of his royal authority and power, he was probably the one man of the age equal to the King of England in political stature. The moves and countermoves of these two great men make a remarkable study of medieval haggling and bargaining, sometimes fascinating, sometimes merely sordid.

A tricky and experienced statesman with a strong-minded, but somewhat pious and narrow wife, he was splendidly built and had a rosy complexion. A missing front tooth caused him to lisp slightly, however, while he had the suspicion of a squint in his left eye. He could smile to deceive, and almost every treaty he made contained a snare, being usually so worded that it could be interpreted in various ways, from among which he chose the one most favourable to himself. He kept his great wealth securely in a formidable stronghold.

Not unnaturally his attention was divided between southern Spain, where the last Moorish armies lay, and his European rivals and neighbours, especially the lumbering Maximilian. He kept also a particularly sharp and watchful eye on the French King, whose intentions he distrusted. This, in fact, was the lever Henry used to move him. On the 11th December the English mission to Spain, consisting of Dr. Thomas Savage and Sir Richard Nanfan, set sail in two Spanish ships to convey the King's proposals to Ferdinand. Their sea voyage was extremely rough, taking nearly a month, and they did not arrive in Medina del Campo, south of Valladolid, until the 14th March following. Fortunately we have the Richmond herald's own story of their remarkable adventures.

The coarse and ill-tempered landlady of one hostelry at which they put up nearly forced them to surrender their beds and go. They rested a couple of days at Medina, then sought an audience of the King. Ferdinand's strong-willed, upright, intelligent Queen Isabella passed frequently before their eyes in shimmering gold apparel, one of her dresses alone being worth 200,000 gold crowns. The Bishop of Ciudad Rodrigo welcomed them on the King's behalf, responding to the greetings of men he regarded as 'boors from England'. His speech was marred by inaudibility, for he was a decrepit old man with no teeth, 'so that only withe great trouble could we understand what he said'.

Ferdinand was not yet ready to talk business, and until he was, the envoys were entertained by dances, tournaments, feasts, bull-fights and whatever else the Court could devise to please them. At last, however, on the 23rd March, 1489, they were summoned to his presence and discussions began, concluded two days later by the signing of the Treaty of Medina del Campo, the terms of which, briefly summarized, were:

1. The two countries would defend one another against hostile attack.

2. Intercourse between them would be unfettered.

3. Neither King would aid rebels against the other.

4. Both would make war on France, and England would not militarily ally herself with that country.

5. No separate peace would be signed, and either kingdom would make war at the other's side if called upon to do so.

6. Henry would begin the war when his truce with France officially ended. Ferdinand would join in after he had expelled the Moors, and at latest in 1490.

7. The war would end for England only if Guienne and Normandy were returned to her, and for Spain only when the territories of Roussillon and Cerdagne she claimed had been ceded.

8. A treaty of marriage between Prince Arthur of England, then about one year old, and the Infanta Catharine of Spain, a child nearly four, would be concluded as soon as they were old enough. The Infanta's dowry would be 200,000 crowns, one half handed over on her arrival in England, the other half following two years later. As the daughter of Ferdinand and Isabella, she would inherit the crowns of both Castile and Aragon on their death, and her rights in this respect were not to be forfeited by the marriage.

This treaty was Henry's first of its kind, and to him immensely important. Alliance with an upthrusting new power strengthened his position at home, gave his sovereignty European recognition, and promised him invaluable support against France. He is said to have been overjoyed when he learned that the match with Catharine had been negotiated.

Nevertheless, every treaty with Ferdinand had a catch in it.

This one bound the King of England to attack the French before Spain had put a single soldier in the field. In truth, neither monarch was anxious to start a war. Both were playing for time, but whereas Ferdinand could back out as soon as he had regained his two minor territories, which the French might relinquish without great loss of prestige, Guienne and Normandy, claimed by Henry, were huge tracts of territory which the French would certainly defend to the last gasp. The English ambassadors were quick to see the danger and declined to surrender their King's interests. The Spaniard's demands were, they declared, 'against right, against God, and their conscience'.

[5]

The French, thwarted in their attempt to recapture Calais, were alarmed by the hostility of the English and weary of war. They probably knew of the pacts Henry had made with Spain, Maximilian and Brittany, and consequently their cunning statesmen set to work to disrupt this triple alliance, whose peril to themselves they foresaw. Of the three allies Maximilian was the weakest and the most impressionable in character. They made him the target of their diplomatic offensive, sent a secret mission and agreed a truce for six months.

To alarm the French even more, Ferdinand made a token attack with a small force on Roussillon, and sent 1,000 men to Brittany, where they laid siege to Redon. The Diet of the Empire was meeting on the 6th July at Frankfort to discuss help for the King of the Romans. The French sent envoys to negotiate with him, and by dangling before him the tempting bait of an end to his troubles with the Flemings, aroused first his interest, then his enthusiasm. A treaty, whereby it was agreed the English should be sent home and the fate of those Breton towns occupied by the French settled by arbitration, the English-occupied being handed back if Brittany undertook not to appeal again to England, was negotiated on the 22nd July, 1489.

This treaty, known as the Treaty of Frankfort, showed how little concern Maximilian had for the English. It was both dishonourable and selfish, especially since no time was lost in forcing it on the child Duchess of Brittany. Henry, to whom De Rieux, her guardian, remained a good friend, encouraged Anne to resist the pressure put upon her, but failed and in consequence refused to recall his troops. Indeed, in September, 1489, they blockaded and finally captured the Breton fishing port and strong fortress of Concarneau, but Anne accepted the treaty in November, and by February, 1490, the bulk of the army was forced to withdraw to Guingamp, leaving garrisons only in Morlaix and Concarneau as pledges covered by the treaty with Anne. By this time, however, the English soldiers were restive, their pay being irregular and inadequate, so that their discipline inevitably became lax, for with the breaking up of feudal loyalties and attachments they had lost much of their original spirit and order.

Henry reinforced his army. The Earl of Oxford ordered Paston at the royal cost to muster his armed men to do the King's service. Although in theory Brittany was no longer at war, the King refused to abandon the struggle. He renewed in August an ancient alliance with Portugal. De Rieux also maintained hostilities, aided by that rejected but still hopeful suitor, D'Albret. Ferdinand instructed his officers in Brittany to work better with the English than they had been doing. They had hitherto refused to work with them at all.

Charles, the French King, having cut off two branches of the alliance against him, noted the marked slackening of discipline in the English soldiery. Believing Henry could be persuaded to make peace and accept the Treaty of Frankfort as a *fait accompli*, he sent over in August an imposing mission to England, knowing his treaty with Maximilian worthless as long as Spain and England maintained armies in Brittany. He also wished Henry to join with him in an attempt to have Maximilian's marriage annulled.

Henry was now as tired of the war as Charles. Indeed, he had never embarked upon it with enthusiasm. It was said in London that 'though their subjects' swords clashed, it is nothing into the public peace of the crowns', and this was certainly true of the struggle with France. The King still hoped to get some advantage out of the war-weariness of the French, but he dared not go over the head of Parliament. On the 18th October, therefore, he recalled them and laid the French proposals before them, as the existing truce was on the verge of expiry.

Both Houses concurred with the King in coldly rejecting the French terms. Parliament was prorogued on the 4th December till the 25th January, 1490, by which time it was expected that the French ambassadors would return from Paris with a new offer. They did indeed return at Christmas, all three of them—Francis, Lord of Luxembourg, Lord Wallerand of Maignu, and Robert Gaguine, General of the Friars of the Trinity in France. Henry gave them an official banquet on the 27th December, but still found the proposals they brought unacceptable, though a message of support from the Pope accompanied them.

He had never forgotten that Edward IV had once won a magnificent annuity by claiming the throne of France, invading her with a great army, yet never fighting a single battle. If he hung on long enough, he believed he might himself win just such a rich prize. Accordingly he revived the old claim to the throne of France, and was quite prepared, if need be, to ravage Brittany and kill Frenchmen, though he preferred not to do so if it could be avoided. What he wished to avoid was the recall of his army and the confession to Parliament that all their money had been wasted. When the House met again he asked for more money to continue the war. He was not altogether secure in his monarchal position, but with the tenacity and patience that invariably marked his behaviour, waited and worked, trusting in luck and his knowledge of the men over whom he ruled.

Once again Parliament moaned and murmured at this new demand, but after seven weeks of argument, it was agreed to grant £82,000 less a deduction of £6,000 for the relief of towns in great need, such as Lincoln, Yarmouth and New Shoreham. In return for this somewhat grudging allowance the King agreed to cancel any portion of the previous grant not yet collected. The small grant made on this occasion was considered sufficient to maintain the English garrisons in those fortresses of Brittany held as pledges.

The King now played a waiting game. He had no intention of pulling European chestnuts out of the fire for Ferdinand. His spies had already brought him unpleasant rumours of secret peace negotiations between France and Spain. Indeed, during the summer of 1489 the French had been trying to thwart Henry by allying with Ferdinand themselves. Their Regent, Anne of Beaujeu, had even offered to meet Isabella of Spain to discuss the future of Roussillon.

The 'dame de Beaujeu' as she was called, eldest daughter of the late Louis XI, had been entrusted by her father with the care of his young son Charles. She and her husband, Pierre de Beaujeu, were virtually rulers of France until 1491, when Charles himself took up the reins. Nothing had come of this attempt at an alliance, nor of the rumour, current among the suspicious Bretons of the Orléans party, that Henry and De Rieux were themselves plotting a separate peace with the French. This rumour, nevertheless, caused dissension between the Bretons and the English. The King could have saved his country money and himself much worry by pulling his troops out of Brittany, but this would have been at the expense of his cherished alliance with Spain and his popularity at home. In January he signed a treaty of alliance with Denmark.

Innocent VIII, Pope of Rome, now took a hand in this tortuous game. A Genoese of about fifty-eight, who had held his sacred and powerful office since 1484, born Giovanni Battista Cibo, he was ferocious against heretics. Nepotist, popular, but too readily dominated by his more powerful cardinals, he abused his office by having several children.

In the February of 1490 at the request of France he sent Bishop Lionel Chieregato of Concordia, his nuncio or ambassador, to Boulogne to reconcile Charles and Henry, so that both might unite with him against the all-conquering Turks. The Bishop met both Henry and his Chancellor, but had no better success than Charles himself. Nevertheless, Henry sent Fox, Bishop of Exeter, Thomas Goldstone of the Order of St. Benedict, and Thomas, Earl of Ormond, as his envoys to a peace conference in Boulogne arising out of this, attended by representatives of France, England, Brittany, Maximilian and the Emperor Frederick, his father. Henry insisted on compensation for what he had spent in putting his army into Brittany, but after much argument, the conference was suspended.

Meantime, he received in May a secret message from Maximilian seeking to persuade him to join in an attack the King of the Romans was planning on France.

In June the conference met again at Calais, but once more failed to agree. Henry maintained inflexibly that the cost of bringing his men home again must also be met, half by Anne, the Duchess, and half by France. Otherwise he would take them at once out of the Duchy. However, he said that he would not object if the French paid for Anne's reoccupation of the fortresses at that time in his hands as pledges.

On the 23rd September, after a long delay, he ratified the Medina treaty, having previously made a treaty with the Duke of Milan on the 27th July providing for joint defence against the French King. He also made it clear that Spain, if she wished, could join in any secret arrangement he made with Maximilian, suggesting also that the Medina treaty be modified so that if Spain entered the war against France, the signatories to the various treaties would all be bound in the same way. However, when this was put to him, Ferdinand demurred, for it meant he might have to make war on France within three years if she should annex territory belonging to one or other of his allies, and to carry on the war with massive armies for at least two years more unless victory had been won or his allies agreed to peace. Quietly, therefore, he removed his signature from his copy of the Treaty, so destroying its legality.

In October the peace conference was once more resumed.

[6]

Great rivalry existed between the chief traders of London and those of other cities. Bristol disputed the capital's supremacy as a port, and intense competition in internal trade took place between them. London tried to shut her rivals out of her markets, persuading Parliament to deny them the right to sell their wares outside her walls. This caused an uproar. The provincial towns wailed that their trade would be destroyed, since they would be unable to buy anywhere but in the capital, which would involve long and costly periodical journeys. The clamour was so great that the decree was rescinded.

The wealthy London traders were, nevertheless, helping England to become more prosperous, so that Polydore Vergil praised the King for fostering their commerce 'in order to improve this art, which is at once useful and excellent for all mortals'. Nevertheless, at times the Londoners caused the King great concern by cutting across, as they often did, his home and foreign policies.

The Merchant Adventurers, for example, having extended their activities, sought not only to cut out their rivals abroad in amplification of their existing trade, but also to open up new markets wherever they could be found.

The King wished consistently to sell more English cloth and less raw wool, so fostering the home weaving industry. He had probably perceived the value of native cloth manufacture during his early years in Europe, and is said to have 'secretly procured a great many foreigners who were perfectly skilled in manufacture to come over and instruct his own people here in their beginnings'. He forbade the export of wool and white ashes, to ensure adequate raw materials for the production and finishing of cloth at home.

He was, indeed, said to be 'a king that could not endure to have trade sick'. He also forbade his subjects to import silks, bows, and woollen cloths capable of being made in Britain, and introduced a system of specially chosen advisers to help English merchants abroad.

His spinners and weavers were given the right to buy unshorn wool, and even to buy in advance the next year's output for ten years, at the same time arresting, as indicated, the sale of shorn wool to foreign traders at least until his weavers had taken their pick of the market. Some concession on this point was, however, made to the Venetians.

Henry also brought in new laws designed to benefit particular centres of the cloth industry. At one time it had been decreed that only those apprenticed for seven years could become worsted shearmen, while in Norfolk, the principal area of worsted manufacture, only the children of substantial citizens could be apprenticed. For some time Norwich had been losing ground as the source of heavy woollen cloth, tapestry, etc., largely because she could not obtain sufficient labour. The King persuaded Parliament to cancel the decree for this town, and in effect the rigid exclusiveness of the worsted manufacturers was abolished.

Other ordinances controlled manufacture and trade. It was laid down that a coarse cloth known as 'fustian', containing a proportion of wool, was no longer to be singed. Butchers were forbidden to cut up and sell their meat anywhere except outside the town walls. Shopkeepers and those who made goods in their own workshops were protected against itinerant pedlars and salesmen, and a 'ceiling' was fixed for the price of headgear.

Silk had been banned as an import, but now the ban was moderated to include only those silken goods that could be made in England. Thus, it was legitimate to bring in stuffs in the piece, but not ribbons, laces, and the plain backs of women's caps, though the Act covered only those fabrics mentioned in earlier laws.

A great fire destroyed a considerable area of Norwich in 1508, and during the following month a second followed it. When all was over, little was left of the town and its cloth-weaving industry.

[7]

Ferdinand was annoyed by the discussions with the French, suspecting that the English were doing what he himself was secretly trying to do—get what he wanted and bring his troops home. He demanded that Innocent VIII should recall his nuncio from Calais, and once more proposed Charles of France as a husband for his own daughter, Joanna, in which event he was willing to offer him concessions.

Warned in time, no doubt, Henry dismissed the French envoys with his minimum conditions for withdrawal from Brittany. Broadly, he proposed a truce for three years with a separate conference to discuss the situation there. On their way home via Calais the French envoys crossed the path of the papal nuncio.

Now in July came Maximilian's renewal of his treaty with France, followed by the withdrawal of his forces from Brittany for a wild dash across Europe to do battle in Austria against the invading Hungarians. For over thirty years Hungary had been ruled by the great Matthias Hunyadi and his powerful, efficient army. Having turned his unruly, semi-barbaric country into a civilized and consolidated empire, he had driven the Turks back

Henry VII; a contemporary portrait by an unknown Anglo-Flemish artist, *c.*1500

Elizabeth of York, after a portrait by an unknown artist, $c.1500$

Lady Margaret Beaufort, mother of Henry, by an unknown artist, $c.1500$

into the Balkans. The sustained enmity of the Bohemians and Germans had, however, caused him to invade both countries, shatter them, and occupy Vienna, which he made his capital. When he died in April, 1490, his enemies sought to despoil his empire as he had despoiled theirs. Maximilian could not let this opportunity pass.

CHAPTER EIGHT

The Colossal Bribe

[1]

HENRY NOW SAW HIMSELF about to be left to carry on the war alone, but this was not his only worry. Things were going badly in England. Men were hungry, and in consequence there was an ever-present danger of sedition. To this, the narrow scope of England's agriculture at this period contributed. Little produce was exported, though 'were they to plough and sow all the land that was capable of cultivation they might sell a quantity of grain to the surrounding countries'. On the other hand cattle in great numbers roamed over the meadows 'especially as they have an extraordinary number of sheep, which yield them a quantity of the best wool'. This concentration on the rearing of sheep had made England's wool supreme in continental markets.

Sheep-rearing was favoured by landholders because they could obtain their rents more easily from a small number of tenants holding large areas than from a large number of tenants renting small areas, but the increasing enclosure of common land for sheep turned more and more labourers in the fields and small tenant farmers into unemployed wanderers and worse. Hence More's remark about 'the man-eating sheep'. Hedges sprouted around extensive tracts of land. Several farms would fall into the hands of a single man, who would turn them into grazing lands. A couple of shepherds replaced one hundred or more agricultural workers. Buildings, neglected or abandoned, collapsed and entire villages decayed and died. Population in these localities fell sharply, so that local churches were almost empty and their revenues disappeared.

Parliament consequently restricted the number of cattle kept, and placed a heavy customs duty on wool, which could not now be so easily bought. The King's aim was to bring down the wool-sellers' profits from selling abroad. Similarly, any owner of a house to which twenty or more acres were attached was prohibited from surrendering it, and many areas were assigned to the yeoman class. This benefited the State, which thus obtained a reserve of robust and contented men, lower than nobles or esquires, but ranking higher than villeins and serfs. They became the loyal, disciplined nucleus of the later, sound royal forces, and made splendid footsoldiers and horsemen to support their leaders. It has been said that in creating this intermediate class Henry 'sowed Hydra's teeth'.

Sheep were, however, much more profitable to rear than wheat to grow. Corn was cheap, owing to improved methods of cultivation, whereas wool fetched a high price, and once there was enough corn to meet home needs, the rest of the land could be safely abandoned to the cattle farmers. No duty was placed on exported corn, but little was sent abroad since most countries, at least those within reach of English ships, had enough of their own. Cattle, however, could not be shipped abroad, except for a few stallions, the breeders needing to retain their mares. Sometimes, however, a few oxen and sheep were exported by special permission.

The London merchants resented the ability of the foreigners to sell their wares 'retail' in the city. The King supported them, ruling that the Hanse and other foreign traders must pay him £4,000 for the right to sell there, and even so, their marketing must be done through the London merchants.

[2]

Although safely immured in the Tower, the Earl of Warwick was still a magnet, drawing towards him every ambitious ecclesiastic and malcontent. In December, while the King's mind was concentrated on Europe, the Abbot of Abingdon and a certain John Maine plotted to liberate the boy, but being detected, were beheaded at Tyburn.

In an endeavour to obtain relief from oppressive taxation the

Humber commissioners appealed to Henry through their overlord, the Earl of Northumberland, but the King sternly refused to ease the burden. Northumberland, therefore, with a small body of armed men at his back, tactlessly delivered the royal refusal exactly as conveyed to him, and made it even less palatable by imprisoning his own recalcitrant tenants. On the 28th April, 1491, however, he was attacked at Thirsk by hundreds of men under John a Chambre, 'a very boutefeu' (firebrand) 'who bore much sway among the vulgar and popular'. Northumberland was abandoned by his servants, and murdered. When John asked the King's pardon for this deed and his request was dismissed, he promptly persuaded Sir John Egremont and his followers to rise with him and his rabble.

At this moment Henry was entertaining foreign ambassadors in Hertford Castle (the ruins of which are still to be seen), hunting cheerfully, and enjoying himself. He was not particularly alarmed by Egremont's revolt, which was not that of a great and powerful lord, but of a mere knight, a 'simple fellow', and sent Thomas Howard, Earl of Surrey, to deal with it. Surrey's earldom dated from 1483 only, until which year he had been but a lord. His son was that Earl of Surrey later known for his admirable verse and his friendship with the two Thomas Wyatts, father and son.

When it was learned that the rebels were advancing on York, Henry took the matter more seriously and prepared to march against them himself. Gunners, smiths and carpenters were assembled, and the King's tents repaired.

Meantime the rebels mustered at Topcliffe, near Thirsk in North Yorkshire, and moved towards Ackworth, near Pontefract, where they were assailed by Surrey's trained and well-armed men and soundly beaten. Many were killed, and the rest fled: 'their hartes were in their heeles and their stomackes coulde as any stone'. Egremont fled too, leaving England in haste, and joined in Flanders the Court of Margaret, Dowager Duchess of Burgundy, but John a Chambre was captured. His body and those of some of his followers were soon dangling from gibbets in York, his higher than the rest. Those not executed sued for pardon, which was granted. This had been the first revolt occasioned directly by the King's financial measures.

The money for the King's archers was still slow in coming in, and by Whitsuntide only about £27,000 had reached the treasury. Those who had to pay the tax grumbled and growled, but no new rising occurred. Instead men paid up and looked unpleasant.

Henry never shirked meeting his dissident subjects and striving to win them over. Although the rising had failed, he travelled on into the north, doing what he could to appease the rebellious districts, but not once reducing his demands. Leaving Sir Richard Tunstall behind as Chief Commissioner to continue the collections, he returned to London, where a special Council was appointed to govern the north, Surrey being given his father's place on it as Chief.

The King had no alternative but to carry on the war with France. With his grant from Parliament he equipped a new army. Fortunately on the 27th July he had strengthened his position in Europe by signing a treaty of peace and trade with Ludovico Sforza, Regent of Milan, and this gave him a useful potential ally against the French. In Brittany, the hungry peasants of the Morlaix region, driven by despair, revolted with violence against their rulers, declaring that having suffered so much through the war, they would now choose their own Duke. The garrison of Morlaix put down this revolt for their own security's sake, killing some four hundred and capturing three hundred more. This did not make the English any more popular.

Anne now listened to her councillors. A courageous, strong-willed girl, she made her peace with De Rieux, obtained concessions from him, but successfully withstood all efforts to marry her to the unsightly D'Albret. For months, however, she had been urged to marry Maximilian instead, and giving in at last, agreed.

Meantime, Henry took advantage of the French rejection of his peace terms at a further conference in Calais to turn the coat of that impetuous, volatile potentate, the King of the Romans. The French, he pointed out, had flatly refused to leave Brittany, which was neither just nor reasonable. He himself, having tried to make a fair and honourable pact, would have no more truck with them. He had no faith in their promises, and would soon send a new army to hold Nantes as a safeguard against further attacks, though he was willing to surrender the city at any moment if this would ensure a good peace.

This new force was, indeed, despatched to Brittany, Lord Daubeney at its head, so that on the 26th July, Anne, encouraged, gave Henry 6,000 gold crowns as an equivalent to the revenues of Morlaix. The French did not, as feared, launch a new attack. Instead they strengthened their forces in those areas and strongholds already occupied, but sent the rest away, and on the 15th August granted the Breton government the long-sought armistice.

Meantime, influenced by Henry, Maximilian turned his back on the French and on the 11th September made a new treaty of joint defence and friendship with England, undertaking to resist any further advance by Charles in either Brittany or Burgundy. Henry, having lost the faithful services of Sir Richard Edgecombe, who had died a few days earlier at Morlaix, was secretly confirmed in his poor opinion of the fickle King of the Romans, but too sagacious to let his feelings override his needs, promptly offered to make him a Knight of the Garter, and made it clear that he would not oppose his marriage to Anne. The French made fresh efforts to make peace, but the discussions were broken off in October.

[3]

On the 29th of that month a new gold coinage was introduced in England 'according to the prynte and fourme of a pece of lead'. Made by 'Rede of London, goldsmith, masters and workers of the King's money within the Tower of London', this new coinage included the gold sovereign, now making its first appearance in English history, as well as the double sovereign and the half-sovereign. These gold coins showed the King wearing his robes and crown, seated on the throne against a background of fleurs de lys. Also introduced was the silver 'testoon', its name derived from the French *teste*, a head, because the King was portrayed on it in profile. In value it roughly corresponded to the modern shilling.

[4]

Maximilian, now affianced to Anne and encouraged by his ally, hastened to marry her, but being busily engaged elsewhere, could not or would not disentangle himself for the ceremony. Accordingly, in December they were united by proxy, Count Wolfgang von Pelham of Nassau, his ambassador, acting for the bridegroom. The ceremony, which took place at Rennes, was a curious affair. Before a concourse of Austrian and German nobles and spectators, both male and female, Anne entered the marriage bed naked. The Count 'stripped naked to the knee', placed his bare leg between the sheets, which was the legal equivalent of consummation and carnal knowledge. The proxy marriage was not revealed at the time and was in no way a true union, but 'an invention of the court'. It was remarked that 'it was a widower and a cold wooer that could consent himself to be a bridegroom by deputy, and that would not make a little journey to put all out of question'. However, Anne was but fourteen years old and Maximilian a man of forty-one, who had probably never seen her.

Flattered by Henry's offer of the Garter, Maximilian agreed to the investiture, and at Neustadt on the morning of Christmas Day, 1490, received the English ambassador, accompanied by Sir John Writh, Garter King of Arms. With the dignity consistent with his office, Sir John, Garter in hand, advanced between rows of Austrian and German nobles. In the Castle Chapel the seated Maximilian extended his knee, about which the Garter was gravely and carefully secured. Mass was then sung, and the treaty against France read out to the assembly. A Te Deum followed, trumpets blared, the royal heralds shouted 'Largesse! Largesse!' as they paraded the streets of the town, and the representatives of England were feasted to repletion. Before Maximilian could be accepted into the Order, however, he would have to be installed at Windsor.

It was all a great fuss about nothing, for little resulted. Charles took up negotiations with England again in February, 1491, and early in 1491, Anne, though she publicly declared herself Queen of the Romans, was in sore distress, being surrounded in Rennes by a garrison made up of riotous, ill-disciplined English, German and Spanish soldiers, all short of money, but stubbornly refusing to leave the city. The behaviour of the English abroad was hardly legitimate. For example Oxford protested to Paston at the way in which the fishermen of the east coast stole, robbed and extorted money from the inhabitants of the Danish islands, of which they had bitterly complained. In certain quarters it was no secret that Charles of France intended to annex Brittany at small cost by himself marrying Anne. To the young girl, however, her betrothal and proxy marriage to Maximilian were spiritually binding since they had been sanctified by the Church. She would not accept another spouse.

Despite this Charles was not discouraged. As the first step towards his objective he bought off the rejected D'Albret, who admitted the French into Nantes. On the 4th April, 1491, he received the surrender of both town and fortress, garrisoned them with French troops, and returned to Touraine to make ready for a final attack. He had liberated Louis of Orleans and ended the quarrel with his party.

Maximilian was still too busy with his Hungarian war to concern himself greatly with Brittany, expecting England and Spain to do whatever was necessary in this direction. Suddenly, with many apologies, Ferdinand took most of his army away to fight the Moors. There was little fighting for them to do in Brittany during the winter, he argued. Consequently, but a small force was left to assist in holding Redon, though their return in the spring was promised, while Ferdinand signed an armistice with the French to last six months. Meantime, he urged Henry to go on fighting till he himself had taken Granada from the Moors, when he would once more actively make war.

Poor Anne, deserted by two of her most powerful allies, could in May turn only to Henry, and sent Mort, her Chancellor, to speak for her. If England would come once more to her aid, he conveyed, his mistress would agree to take no husband of whom he disapproved.

Henry promised to help, being in the best possible mood, for on the 28th June, 1491, a second son, Henry, had been born to him at Greenwich Palace and baptized by Richard Fox, Bishop of Exeter. His dynasty was strengthened by two sons. Following the precedent set by Edward IV, he extracted money from the kingdom by means of 'voluntary' gifts from private persons—the Edwardian 'benevolences'. His commissioners ordered their victims to give what they could afford. This was the notorious 'Morton's Fork' or

'Crotch'. Those ostentatiously rich had to give because they could obviously afford it. The less perceptibly wealthy must have saved enough, they argued, to have something to spare for the King.

Sending a few more men to Brittany, Henry offered to bring Anne herself to England in one of the ships that had carried them, so that she could be conveyed to neutral territory whence she could join her husband. Anne had been compelled to raise money on her own jewels but would not abandon her homeland. Her government was now more stable, both factions having at last united in view of the overriding danger from the French. Nevertheless, before Henry could intervene on a massive scale (if this was ever his intention) Charles's great new offensive began. Henry, still struggling to bring Ferdinand back into the conflict, managed before the end of the year to get two new treaties signed which committed both Kings to the struggle, and also confirmed the betrothal of Prince Arthur to Catharine.

The French rolled back the opposing armies and in swift succession took Redon, Guingamp and Concarneau, though the English retained Morlaix. Finally they besieged Rennes, the capital, itself.

A curious medieval atmosphere surrounded this siege, which began with a 'joust' between 'champions' of France and Brittany, at the end of which the contestants drank spiced hippocras supplied by Anne.

The garrison of Rennes, made up largely of English and Flemings, still discontented because unpaid, refused to fight until they had received back pay to cover at least a month. When Charles guaranteed to provide this if they would abandon the city, they opened its gates. On the 15th November, therefore, the French King came in with pomp and splendour, and as a temporary measure suggested that the town should be held by the neutral Prince of Orange until a settlement had been reached. This having been agreed, he withdrew his army, leaving only a token force to hold the province. He now offered to make Anne his Queen.

The child—she was little more—was worn out and weary, and cannot be blamed for being tempted by this glittering prospect. Nevertheless, she still had religious scruples, but her Father Confessor assured her that by marrying Charles she would commit no mortal sin. The Pope had already given one formal sanction to cover their consanguinity. On the 15th, he provided another dispensation freeing Anne from her theoretical husband. All her objections overcome, she gave in, and on the 6th December, 1491, publicly rejecting the mock marriage with Maximilian, she became the Queen of Charles VIII, their formal wedding ceremony taking place in Langeais, a town of Touraine. Brittany as a separate state now ceased to exist. A rich prize had fallen to French arms and diplomacy.

Henry, wounded, railed bitterly against the French. They were always on the watch, he said, to increase their power by any villainy so that they might annihilate their neighbours to their own advantage. Maximilian too was enraged. He had not only been robbed of a wife, which did not greatly matter, perhaps, but he had also been humiliated. He appealed to both England and Spain to join him in full-scale war on Charles, sending Giaocomo Contebaldi, a statesman, to England as envoy.

Henry told Parliament that he would repay French insolence by leading an army against them himself, not merely to defend Brittany, but to oppose their rapacity, a danger to the whole Christian world. They had seized Brittany despite his efforts, aided the Flemish rebels against Maximilian, deluded, ignored and attacked his allies, refused due tribute, and deliberately made war rather than preserve the peace. He meant now to recover his country's original lands and old-established rights in France. If Parliament did not wish him to be humiliated in the field, they must see that the troops he led were well-fed, well-armed and well-paid.

Despite this hint of taxation to come, the war was popular, and this Parliament was called 'one of war'. The actions of the French were resented, and on the 14th October, Morton obtained for the King a grant of two fifteenths and tenths less £12,000 for the poor or battered cities of England. More was promised should the war last longer than eight months. Parliament was then prorogued till January 1492, the benefit of clergy having been revoked for any deserter from the royal forces, since this would injure King and country. Certain privileges were granted to those about to serve in the war. The Scots in England were ordered back to their own land as they were suspected of secretly favouring the French.

Chancellor Morton's minions once more used their notorious 'fork' to good purpose, the rich of London alone contributing 'benevolences' amounting to £9,000.

Parliament also took advantage of the session to remove one of the greatest obstacles to English trade—the extraordinary confusion in weights and measures. No set standards existed, and even those empirically arrived at and adopted in London and the larger towns were by no means general throughout the kingdom. Indeed, in the remoter towns and villages it is doubtful if they were known at all. Consequently the House of Commons implored the King to authorize and pay for standard metallic weights and measures which could be referred to as required. Replicas could then be forwarded to each important town. Confusion would be ended by making all conform to them. These new standards were approved and put in hand.

There was talk of making the port of Southampton a centre for the export of copper, tin and lead, but this came to nothing.

[5]

As allies in Europe Henry now had Spain and Maximilian, but the Spaniards would not agree to modify the Medina treaty as requested. In November he had the treaty split into two single documents, one covering the marriage of Catharine and Arthur, the other the alliance. He signed the alliance but continued his demand for modification of the marriage provisions. Although Maximilian promised 10,000 men, he became embroiled once more in Flanders, and did nothing. Spain, in the final stages of her grapple with the Moors, could not or would not commit herself to open war with France until she had taken Granada. Not even the Duke of Milan, to whom Henry also appealed, was willing to embark upon a struggle so dubious in its outcome. As in 1940, Britain stood alone.

Nevertheless, the King went quietly on, waiting for circumstances to change and bring him better fortune, meantime seizing every opportunity of creating trouble for his enemy. In January, 1491, some Bretons, ill-disposed to submit to French sovereignty, offered to hand over the port of Brest to his men, but the plot was betrayed and came to nothing.

Then, in the same month, Granada fell and the Moors were on their way out. Nevertheless not a Spanish man-of-war, not a Spanish pikeman, came back to Brittany.

[6]

Parliament reassembled in May, and the preparations for war intensified. Even had he wished, the King could not have extricated himself from it, for his people expected and wanted him to fight. Yet still he let the months drift by, hoping to avoid the wastage of wealth and the shedding of blood. A great tournament was held at Sheen so that his nobles and officers might practise the arts of combat. Here Sir James Parker quarrelled with Hugh Vaughan, a royal usher, and at their first course in a tourney had his tongue driven to the back of his mouth by his opponent's spear, and was instantly killed. For this a faulty helmet was blamed.

In June, mustering men at Portsmouth in large numbers and in many newly-made tents and pavilions, Henry also built three large breweries near-by so that they should not be denied their favourite beverage, and sent ordnance there in good time. When his ships sailed in this same month they raided coastal towns in Normandy and Brittany, carried off some plunder, and returned to port, having accomplished little of importance. In August, 1491, Kent and Sussex were warned to guard against already threatened French reprisal landings. Every man capable of bearing arms and armour was to be ready to take the field on the instant. Letters of the time reveal that much armour, many horses, knapsacks and carts, were being got together by the 'Gentlemen' who were to accompany the King. In August again a dozen English ships sailed up Channel under the flag of Sir Edward Poynings, with a force estimated at 2,500 men and many guns, to help retake Sluys, which had been seized by Philip of Cleves, the same Lord Ravenstein who had rebelled against Maximilian in 1489.

Now forty-three, Poynings had fled to the Continent to avoid trial for his part in the Kentish rising against Richard III, and had returned to England with Henry in 1485. He was connected through his mother with the Paston family.

Philip of Cleves, after commandeering all the vessels in Sluys harbour, had carried out piratical raids on shipping in the narrow seas, being privately aided by the French. Henry's expedition, which included Jasper Tudor, was sent not solely for Maximilian's benefit, but also because Philip's depredations were harming the English cloth industry overseas, whose representatives had strongly complained. The Duke of Saxony was suffering in the same manner, and had also been besieging the town since the 18th May.

Sluys was stubbornly and bravely defended, but the mixed body of English, Flemings, Germans and Netherlanders were equally brave. At low tide the English left their ships and attacked. Philip had built a bridge of boats between the two forts of the harbour to facilitate communication between them, but the English set fire to and destroyed this during the night. Not until the 13th October, however, were the forts captured, whereupon the defenders, having lost many men, surrendered to Poynings, probably because it was mainly he and his men who had forced the citadel, which had become virtually a pirates' lair. Arras was also occupied, but by the Germans.

Leaving Greenwich on the 9th September, Henry came to Sandwich, being entertained on his way through Kent by singers and a Spanish jester. With him he brought 25,000 footsoldiers and 1,600 horse in borrowed Venetian galleys. A large number of ships and cross-bowmen had, in fact, been hired as usual from overseas, the galleys mostly from Venice. Having entrusted the Regency to Prince Arthur on the 2nd October, he crossed the Channel in 'The Swan', spent his first night ashore at Sandyngfelde and the second at Margyson, where he was met by Oxford and his staff. After a further night in Wynelle, he arrived in Calais at 11 a.m. the following day, wearing a splendid suit of armour crowned by a pearl and gem-garnished helmet, as lustrous and beautiful as the merchants of Lombard Street could make it. Here he stayed for a fortnight.

The expected contingent from Maximilian had not arrived. He was 'sore sicke of a flux of the pursse', it was said. They were to have assisted him in taking Boulogne, but Henry was on the whole relieved not to have to deal with 'drunken Flemings' and 'crakyng Brabanters'. His heart had never been in this war. This new foray was intended as an impressive demonstration in force rather than a serious invasion. On the 18th October his guns battered away at the well-fortified walls of Boulogne, which was stocked with enough food for two years and had a garrison of nearly 2,000, but though the guns made a lot of noise, they did little damage. For a fortnight the army loitered outside Boulogne. Sir John Savage, riding under the town walls to observe the effects of the gunfire, was ambushed, fought back bravely, but was killed.

[7]

Throughout that summer and autumn messages had been passing secretly between France and England, each knowing that the other was not anxious to prolong the war. Lord Cordes, one of the bitterest and bravest opponents of the English, now privately conveyed his sovereign's overtures for peace, which the King is said to have received before boarding ship at Sandwich. He was all the more inclined to take them seriously because Cordes had a great reputation for sincerity and was a good soldier. He therefore sent Fox and Lord Daubeney to Etaples on the 27th to meet the French emissaries and discuss the matter.

The terms offered were most acceptable. The entire cost of his defence of Brittany, 745,000 crowns, would be met, Cordes said, in an annual subsidy of 50,000 francs, paid in half-yearly instalments. Charles would also agree not to aid rebels against the King, and would remove from his Court a young man with certain pretensions that were giving the King of England concern. Amity and freedom of commerce between the two kingdoms were to be encouraged.

Henry for his part was not to assist Maximilian if he continued hostilities. He had, in fact, already concluded that while Boulogne would certainly fall in the end, the winter might arrive first, and its capture would cost many lives. Accordingly, calling a council of his generals and officers on the 27th October he laid the French terms before them. Secrets are rarely kept for long, and a rumour ran round among the English that peace would soon be made.

These men, knowing quite well how the wind blew, begged their master to accept the terms, pointing out the little likelihood of adequate military aid from his allies, and the difficulties of a siege begun so late in the year, such as feeding the troops by sea in stormy weather, and the savage cold.

The King could now claim, if challenged, that peace had been urged upon him by his generals. On the 30th October the terms were formally agreed, and on the 3rd November, 1492, the treaty was signed at Etaples. The following day the English army was told that the war was over. The King left for Calais, arriving on the 11th and sailing for home on the 16th. No date had been set for the treaty, which would have to be ratified by Parliament. Charles, however, had already ratified it on the 6th, and many of the King's advisers had already received rich rewards from their royal adversary. In England men were not wanting to hint that these men had been bribed.

The tents of the English were now dismantled, the artillery, munitions and stores loaded into carts, and the soldiers despatched on their slow way to Calais, where ships awaited them. They were not, as one might think, overjoyed at the end of the war, for they had been looking forward to the sack of Boulogne. To them the news of peace was 'bitter, sore and dolorous'. One chronicler wrote: 'They were in great fumes, angry and evil content that the occasion of so glorious a victory to them manifestly . . . was refused.'

In London on the 16th the Mayor announced peace in the Guildhall, and Morton, the Chancellor, had a Te Deum sung in St. Paul's. On Saturday, the 22nd December, the King himself, returning via Dover to the capital, was met at Blackheath by all the civic dignitaries of London in their finery, who, as was the custom, rode with him from Blackheath to Westminster, whence he proceeded to Greenwich and rested.

[8]

For centuries men have disputed over this peace, which some still regard as shameful. The severest critics were those who had emptied their pockets to pay for the war. They remembered only too well Henry's declaration in the House at Westminster that 'after the war was once begun, he doubted not but to make it pay itself.' The discontented remarked with bitterness that he had now broken his promise, for 'the King cared not to plume the nobility and people to feather himself'.

Others, however, excused him, pointing to the failure of Maximilian and Ferdinand to support him in the field. Against this, it was argued, 4,000 of Maximilian's men would probably have joined the English, having already been assembled. Nevertheless, the reply was made, by the time they came winter might have set in and they would have been too late to be effectively used. In any event Henry could not be sure that his erratic ally would not go flying off in some other direction carrying his troops away with him. Perhaps he was weary also of fighting his allies' wars for them, having been twice bereft of sorely needed and long anticipated help, and left 'out on a limb'. Nevertheless, Parliament did not immediately accept the treaty, and the King of the Romans was greatly offended. He had not been consulted, he complained, but should have been, and it was a long time before he forgave Henry for this separate peace.

The truth, as far as one can judge, is that Henry had achieved all the objectives for which he had crossed the Channel. His nearest, most powerful and dangerous, continental neighbour had engaged himself to be his friend. England was safe from him at last. Secondly neither France nor Brittany could now be used as refuge or springboard by any English rebel, and by one in particular, a young man already mentioned claiming to be the Duke of York. Moreover, he had avoided draining away his monetary resources in a long and costly war.

In his cool, chess-master's assessment of the situation during those two weeks before Boulogne he had appreciated, perhaps, that a relatively small English army could no longer race spectacularly across France as in the days of Edward III, and engulf or re-engulf great slabs of her territory. No longer could massed and clumsy blundering knights in heavy vulnerable armour be shot down in dozens by arrows from bowmen concealed behind hedges and thickets. Warfare had changed. The French defences were strong now, their tactics and officers as good as his own, as he well knew.

Cardinal Wolsey, after an early sixteenth-century portrait by an unknown artist

Maximilian I; a woodcut after an original drawing by Dürer, *c.*1520

Henry VII, in the nineteenth year of his reign, presenting John Islip, Abbot of Westminster, with an illuminated manuscript. A fragment from the book

Though he might win local victories, he could never finally defeat the enemy. Strategically he had no chance unless great allied armies came to his aid, and these he did not for a moment believe would be forthcoming. To go on would be to ruin himself and his country, to encourage the Yorkists at home to rise against him, and to destroy England's trade, slowly recovering and expanding after a few years of peace. His people were being taught by experience that foreign war, like civil, was an expensive hobby, but the lesson must not be too drastic or they would make him their scapegoat. Nevertheless, much time was to pass before Parliament confirmed the treaty. Henry never again made war outside his own island.

There were other reasons, too. It was rumoured that Spain herself was secretly coming to terms with their joint enemy. Indeed, these rumours were eventually proved true, for in Barcelona on the 19th January, 1493, Ferdinand and Isabella signed a treaty of peace with France by which they regained the two territories of Roussillon and Perpignan, which Ferdinand's father, John II, King of Aragon, had pawned with the French for 300,000 crowns. The only promise extracted from Spain in return was that she would aid France if Henry and Maximilian made war on her, and would not allow the royal children of Spain to marry either of these princes or their offspring.

Maximilian was now as Henry had been—alone against a great power—but for all this he did not give up the struggle, fighting on till the 23rd May, 1493, when at Senlis he himself signed a treaty of peace again.

Disturbing events had helped to convince Henry that peace was essential. Hints of a new threat to his sovereignty were coming in, and to be away from England for any length of time would be unwise. Bacon declares that at this period he was haunted by the ghost of Richard, Duke of York, one of the two murdered princes, who 'walked', vexing him.

He had, after all, done what he had planned to do, wrested from the French King a sum of money, with more to come, that was all he could have expected, and this without fighting for it, without cost and with precious little bloodshed.

He was not the first English king deliberately to abandon territorial ambition in return for money. Edward IV had preceded him in this. Better even than Edward, Henry knew the changes that had come about in Europe, where he had lived for so long. What is more, he was the first English king to take an almost modern view of his world. Though no great innovator, he kept a realistic eye on events, worked out in his mind their possible consequences, and took what reason convinced him was the wisest course to follow.

[9]

English commerce, steadily increasing, was mainly in wool, cloth, hides, lead and tin. No foreigner in England was allowed to sell English wool abroad. It was carried from the grazing lands in sacks on the backs of packhorses or mules, over rough roads and 'packhorse bridges' to the nearest of the Cinque Ports, then taken by sea to Antwerp or Calais en route for the markets of Flanders. This trade was mainly monopolized by 'The Staple', an ancient trading company made up of those towns whose merchants by royal consent bought the primary products of the kingdom and shipped them overseas. The mayor and constables of each Staple town controlled its trade. They had numerous privileges and considerable freedom, being mostly elected by the merchants themselves, though on occasion the King himself was their nominator. Their statutory rights, privileges and activities were governed by a whole body of law.

The income of the Staple enabled Calais to be held and defended from the French. In 1487, for instance, the total duty on wool and skins received by the Staple merchants, amounting to £10,000, was allowed to that city and the strongholds on its borders.

Wool duties gave the King nearly two fifths of his income, for the Staple paid almost a third of the value of their merchandise in customs duties. Outsiders paid as much as seventy per cent. This trade in wool was consequently essential for the national exchequer. The wars with France and in Brittany had restricted the Staple's trade, many of whose members suffered heavy losses and even ruin. They at least had every reason to support the peace.

The State had on occasion to restore the prosperity of declining industries, as when Henry gave the Metal Staple of Southampton authority to carry on mining operations, and encouraged them by the concession of special rights and privileges.

At Henry's accession, English overseas trade was still clinging to the nearer northern shores of Europe, but the mercantile outlook was slowly changing, and the need for greater and more distant markets beginning to be felt. Every country believed its most important objective to be the acquisition of money, not in parchment deeds or written promises to pay, but in solid metal, such as gold and silver, which could be used as currency. In consequence, all sought to sell as much and buy as little as possible abroad. A nation was accounted rich only if it received more cash than it paid out. Whenever it experienced a serious dearth of coinage in its treasury, its ministers hastened to shut out foreign goods or charge heavy tariffs on them, while simultaneously subsidizing their own exports, and making every effort to prevent gold and silver from leaving the country.

Much of England's foreign trade was carried on by a body of foreign merchants known as the 'Hanseatic League', who for decades had imported her wool at a low price, then sold it back to her at a high price as woven cloth. This League included such North European cities as Lübeck, Bremen, Hamburg, Cologne, and many others—nearly ninety in all. They had a virtual stranglehold on all trade in raw materials carried on with western, northern and eastern Europe, and would when necessary fight to preserve this monopoly. In England their headquarters was the 'Steelyard' or 'Styleyard' in London, situated where Cannon Street Station now stands. Here all their goods for sale in England were stored.

Their rivalry with an ancient English exporting body, later to be known as 'The Merchant Adventurers', was steadily growing, but in addition to the 'Hanse', as London was the first to call it, the English merchants' guild was adversely affected by the traders of Venice, whose 'tall ships', oared and awkward, but powerful and well-armed, were emerging under the pressure of Turkish competition from the landlocked waters of the Mediterranean, and driving northwards to Antwerp and Southampton in an endeavour to capture new markets.

The English merchants had all the insular characteristics of their race. Indeed, a foreigner was to say of them: 'They have great affect for themselves and for all that they have. They fancy there are no other men but themselves, and no other world but England. Their highest praise for a stranger is that he looks like an Englishman. They have a dislike to foreigners, who they imagine only came into the country to take possession of it, and to appropriate their goods.' (Have we changed so much? Who has not heard similar sentiments expressed even within the past decade?)

Henry, though fully appreciating his countrymen's competitive difficulties, had to tread warily before trying conclusions with the autocratic and immensely powerful Hanse. Nevertheless, quietly and without braggadocio, he set to work to break the hold of the League on the foreign trade of his realm. First, he insisted that all laws affecting export should be strictly observed. No longer was a blind eye turned to breaches of the regulations if they favoured the Hanse. His ships even seized a Hanse vessel from Danzig and brought it into Calais harbour, while the King turned his head away when other English craft bared their teeth to the League's ships so that they dared not enter ports such as Kingston on Hull. Those Londoners in the city who in moments of fury attacked these foreign traders often went unpunished, and once, when the Hanse addressed Henry in terms he resented, he told them he would send them all packing if they did not mend their ways.

Finally, he had allied himself in 1489 with the Danes, also at loggerheads with the League, and in gratitude the Danes had given England remarkable trading privileges in both Denmark and Iceland, their colony, so that at least one market had been snatched from the greedy Hanse jaws. Henry had also reached agreement with the merchants of Riga, and nibbled through them at the trade of Prussia, but they backed out later, making their peace with the League and frustrating the English effort to capture more of the Baltic trade.

This struggle lasted for two years, at first underhand, then open, but the League, well aware by now that they had an able, subtle and powerful opponent, slowly realized that friendship with England would be better for them than open enmity. They sought peace, sending plenipotentiaries to Antwerp to meet their English counterparts. They came in vain. The English were not there, being unprepared to negotiate with such inflexible men, and did not arrive till a month later.

However, after arbitration had been rejected, the Hanse were told they would be wise to trust in the good faith and intentions of the King, who was fully aware of what the English towns had to put up with, 'which they would fain have written with a pen of iron on a hard stone that they might never more forget it'.

Only then, having shown their spirit and independence, did the English come to Antwerp. On the 28th June, 1491, after much discussion, they signed an agreement whereby the Hanse were confirmed in their former rights for eight years, Henry being granted in return concessions extending English trade in northern waters. Nevertheless, disagreements continued, and the discussions were eventually broken off.

So matters stood when the cloud 'no bigger than a man's hand' which had appeared on Henry's horizon blew up into a dark, sky-invading canopy.

CHAPTER NINE

The Boatman's Son

[1]

THE YORKISTS in both England and Ireland, deliberately stirred up by Edward IV's sister, Margaret of Burgundy, from her Flanders home in Tournai, a city of Hainault, on the River Scheldt, were never idle. Despite the strict and cautious impartiality with which the King had restored order, they continued to regard him as a Lancastrian, and were ever on the lookout for means of overthrowing him. They had hitherto relied on the French and Burgundians for aid, but were also in touch with the Scots who, though their King, James IV, had in 1488 signed a truce with Henry to last for three years, were a threatening presence on the northern border and on the seas around their own native land. For the moment, however, concerted and dangerous action on their part was unlikely by reason of their internal struggles, but the possibility could never be ignored.

Two Scottish parties existed, of which one, the pro-English party, had been in secret communication with the English Court since April, 1491, being headed by Lord Bothwell. Bothwell, a member of the Hepburn clan, was Lord High Admiral of Scotland and the third Lord Hailes. The more notorious later Bothwell, husband of Mary, Queen of Scots, was his grandson. Through them Henry sought, it is said, to have the Scottish King and the Earl of Ross kidnapped and sent to England by Earl Buchan and Thomas Todd, an exile in England, as hostages against invasion. King-kidnapping was by no means unknown among the Scots themselves.

James IV, born in 1473, was highly popular with his people, and despite plots of the nobles against him at the beginning of his reign, proved immovable. He is reputed to have had courage, liberality, sagacity and knowledge, but was at times rapacious and foolhardy. He agreed to a treaty of peace with England in December 1491, but did not confirm it, despite its having been accepted by the English King.

In 1489, a merchant of Exeter, John Taylor, an official of the Court and a supervisory customs officer in various harbours during the reigns of Edward IV and Richard III, had been found guilty of disaffection, was pardoned by the King in the June of that year, but had to leave the country. He went to Rouen in France, and unable to rest in peace there, embarked upon machinations that when rumours of them reached him made Henry uneasy. Taylor is known to have written on the 15th September, 1490, to a certain John Hayes, originally employed by the late Duke of Clarence, but now occupying an important post in Devonshire, and plotted with him to free the Earl of Warwick from imprisonment in the Tower, proclaim him the rightful king, and obtain help and support 'in three parties out of the Royalme', i.e. from three different foreign sources: the King of France, Margaret of Burgundy and the Yorkist sympathizers in Ireland.

Hayes's assigned task was to win over his friends to this scheme and proclaim Clarence's son the Earl, and therefore his feudal lord, as king by right of birth and blood. If this proved impracticable, they would find some youth willing and able to impersonate the young Earl, who should raise his standard in Ireland.

As if the gods had decreed that just such a tool should be placed in their dissident hands, a youth with precisely the qualifications required presented himself.

[2]

Tournai in Flanders was famous even in those days for its carpets. In that city lived a Jew, John Osbeck or 'Warbeck', who, it is said, had abandoned his religion and become a Christian, possibly to marry Catherine de Faro, a Catholic girl. Osbeck is believed to have been at one time a boatman on the Scheldt, but later became a customs officer. To this couple a son, christened Peter, was born in 1474 or 1475.

According to Lord Bacon, the Warbecks lived for a time in London during the reign of Edward IV, and were not unfamiliar with the Court. (Is it fanciful to suppose that John Warbeck may have supplied carpets for the palaces of the luxury-loving Yorkist King?) Indeed, Bacon asserts that Edward became the infant's god-father, and it was not at all uncommon for the genial King to act in this capacity for his servants. Catherine Warbeck was said to have become one of that King's numerous mistresses, and the boy to be a by-blow of Edward himself, though this has not been established.

It is known that the child was somewhat diminutive and girlish, so that he was nicknamed 'Perkin', short for 'Peterkin'. The nick-name stuck. He seems to have been looked after for a time by John Stenbeck, a relative in Antwerp, perhaps because he was an embarrassment to his parents.

He shuttled to and fro between that city, Tournai, Middelburg and other Flemish towns. Here he mixed with English folk, picking up a smattering of the language and serving various masters, until at the age of fourteen or fifteen he entered the service of Sir Edward Brampton's wife in Portugal. Brampton, a Yorkist, said to have been of Jewish blood and the first of his race to receive the accolade, presently recommended his wife's young servant, of whom he may have been a little jealous, to Pregent Meno, a merchant of Brittany trading regularly with Ireland. Warbeck, now seventeen, made himself conspicuous by parading the streets in rich silk garments when in 1491 his master landed in Cork. In fact he is said to have acted as a male 'model' for Meno, showing off in public the clothing and other wares he had brought for sale.

By his undoubted elegance and dignified carriage he attracted much popular attention, and many were the speculations as to his identity. The Irish in Cork, strongly Yorkist, remembered the Duke of Clarence, once Lord Lieutenant of Ireland, and fancied they saw in this youth a resemblance to that prince. Indeed, it soon began to be whispered that he was in truth the Duke's own son, Edward, Earl of Warwick, or if not he, then Richard of York, son of Edward IV, alive and not murdered in the Tower with his brother, as was supposed.

The Yorkists of the town saw their opportunity. The astute among them did not for a moment believe he was other than Meno's paid servant, but he was so much handsomer and better-spoken than Lambert Simnel, so well formed, self-possessed, attractive in appearance, dignified in bearing and demeanour, that they saw in him great possibilities. Taking him aside, they proposed that he should pass himself off as the young Warwick. Warbeck, affrighted, shrank from taking this step, declaring long afterwards that he even swore on oath to the Mayor, John Lewelyn, that he was neither Warwick nor any other member of Clarence's family. Because of his refusal, emphatic and unshakable, the Yorkists abandoned the scheme.

Presently, however, John Taylor, away in Rouen learned, probably through Hayes, of Warbeck's existence and qualities. He intrigued with others to prevail upon Perkin to change his mind. First John Walter, a respected citizen of Cork and formerly her Mayor, together with Stephen Poynton, an English Yorkist, put before the young man an alternative suggestion. Would he pretend to be the illegitimate son of Richard III?

Warbeck would do no such thing. However, the pressure upon him increased. He was advised that the great Earl of Kildare, Deputy Lieutenant of Ireland, together with Lord Desmond, would back his pretensions. Desmond ruled like a king over the eastern part of Kerry and the western part of Cork, possessing great power and virtual independence. Like Kildare, he was a hereditary enemy of the Butlers, who coveted his lands.

At last Warbeck, after much hesitation, gave way. Possibly he had shied away from temptation because none who approached him had adequate status, but the support of two great Irish lords was another matter. He undertook at last to assume the character of Prince Richard of York.

The conspirators could now set to work. Their motives appear to have been various—ambition, discontent, the eternal desire for change, disbelief in Henry's claim to the crown and plain credulity. The discontented blamed the King for the annexation of Brittany by France, his shameful coming to terms with his conquerors, his severe taxation and his suppression of the baronial power. Others claimed that he had put the Queen in an invidious position by making it appear that she held her title by her husband's consent alone rather than in her own right. They elected John Taylor, who had come over from France, Hubert de Burgh and John Walter as organizers of the plot. 'And so,' Warbeck later confessed, 'against my will, they made me to learne English, and taught me what I should do and saye.' Despite this statement, however, they had probably little need to teach him English, of which he seems to have known a great deal already, and if he had been genuinely reluctant, no one could have compelled him to achieve so laborious a task as learning a foreign language.

He was soon but a puppet in their hands. They made him write letters outlining his claim to Kildare and Desmond, and also to Yorkists in England. All of these he signed with his own hand, using as his code name 'The Merchant of the Ruby'. Other letters went off to the Kings of Scotland and France, possibly carried by merchant ships of the Hanseatic League, the Scots receiving theirs in March 1492. Desmond had already accepted Warbeck's claim, but Kildare, more cautious, left himself a loophole that would enable him to disown the young man if the plot failed.

The war with France was still in being, and eager to take advantage of whatever would weaken Henry, Charles invited Warbeck through his envoy, Stephen Frion, once a French correspondent in his service, but no longer so employed, to come to Paris. He was given a princely reception there and a guard of honour under Lord Congressal. As residence he was allotted a suitable mansion, and became known everywhere as 'the Duke of York'. As many as one hundred Yorkists hostile to Henry, 'mostly bankrupts and cheats', left England and came over to him, including Sir George Neal and John Taylor. It was planned to launch with French aid and simultaneously both an invasion of England and an internal insurrection there.

All these harebrained schemes were, however, frustrated when Charles and Henry made peace outside Boulogne. Warbeck may have been used by Charles as an additional argument in favour of the treaty. The young man was forced to leave France, but one court still open to him where he would be well received was that of Margaret, Dowager Duchess of Burgundy. He and his partners departed therefore for Tournai, while Henry, learning for the first time of the negotiations between Taylor and Hayes, took immediate steps to render them fruitless.

Margaret welcomed the Pretender, accepting him as her late brother's son, and with this powerful lady behind him the young man was able to proclaim himself boldly and freely as Prince Richard. So ended the first chapter of his remarkable career. Incidentally, the Milanese ambassador to Flanders did not scruple to assert on Maximilian's unsupported word that Warbeck was Margaret's own illegitimate son by the Bishop of Cambrai. Margaret gave her protégé thirty halberdiers, elegant in murrey and blue livery, as his bodyguard.

[3]

English commerce continued to occupy Henry's attention during 1492. A serious problem had arisen. Piracy was still rife, and despite their peaceful declarations, the French, with or without the connivance of their King, were forever seizing foreign ships on the high seas, taking them into their own ports, and keeping their cargoes. Among the sufferers were the Venetians, who depended on the prompt and regular arrival of English wool for the prosperity of their profitable cloth-weaving industry. Cargoes of wool had been intercepted on their way from England, so that weavers in Venice were being thrown out of work. These indigent men had clamoured for redress, forcing their rulers to solve the problem for the time being by a system of wool licences to traders to ensure fair shares.

The King's attention had already been drawn to the fact that his shipping, both naval and mercantile, so greatly strengthened by Edward IV, had declined in ten years to such an extent that it was playing little effective part in the commerce of the country. Malmsey wine from Greece and Crete was coming to England exclusively in Venetian and Netherlands bottoms. It seemed to Henry that to encourage his shipbuilders he must make the building of English ships more profitable and their charges for freight fully competitive with those of other lands. He was careful, however, to achieve this slowly. His first tentative step was to send ships to Greece, Crete and other near-eastern ports to load up with wine at a much lower rate of freight than the Venetians were charging. This proved so successful that the merchants of Venice retaliated by imposing a customs duty on every cask of wine from these territories of theirs carried in foreign holds, the duty exceeding the saving in freight rates made by shipping under the English flag, and so cutting off the English trade in wine.

The King was not alarmed. With his acute perceptions he had forecast some such action. Coolly, quietly, fully aware of the need for a strong fleet for his kingdom, his powerful will and lean dry hand stretched across the chessboard of Europe towards a new piece with which to check his opponent's hostile move. That piece was the Italian city state of Florence. On the 15th April, 1490, he signed a treaty with that flourishing collection of tall towers and rich bankers whereby the Florentines alone would sell the English wool needed by the entire Italian peninsula. Venice was to be rationed to a mere six hundred sacks of wool for each voyage, and the treaty was to run for six years. As long as Florence received all the wool she needed, she had no objection to its being carried *in English ships* to her principal port, Pisa.

This was indeed to call 'Check!' to Venice, which had to have wool. She had no greater commercial rival than Florence. The Venetians blustered, threatened, but finally pleaded for mercy. When their pleas were rejected and their threats ignored, they ordered their galleys to deliver no wine to Florence, and gave their own shippers a handsome bonus on every shipment made to northern ports, so that England could buy her wine from Venice only in exchange for wool loaded into Venetian galleys.

Once again the calm English monarch and his Council had their answer ready. Parliament, meeting in 1492, clapped so heavy an additional tariff on imported wine (18s. a cask) carried in alien holds that Venice could no longer sell her wine to the English market, which meant she could not buy English wool.

The English could buy other wines, so they went on selling their wool to Florence, whose bankers regularly gave the King good commercial and financial advice. The ships of the Netherlands were too busy transporting men and munitions to the war in France and Brittany to worry about carrying Venetian cargoes, so that at long last the merchants of Venice had to come to heel, allowing English ships once more to enter their ports and load up. Henry, calling 'Checkmate!', had won his game.

English supremacy at sea had emerged from the womb. Not only had the Venetians been discomfited and another nail driven into the coffin of their mercantile power, but also the Hanseatic League had been given cause to ponder and feel alarm.

[4]

In 1492, Elizabeth Woodville, Edward IV's Queen, died in Bermondsey Abbey, to which she had been sent by the King and his Council five years before. She had emerged from this refuge and appeared at Court on special occasions only, seeing few people throughout Henry's reign, most of them being afraid to visit her lest the King should be displeased. She was buried beside her husband at Windsor.

Henry was considered by many to have treated her cruelly, though, in fact, he had increased her pension from four hundred marks to £400. She had never been reconciled to him as her husband's successor, and as stated, may have meddled in the early conspiracies.

Like a chess champion playing simultaneous games against opponents of varying skill, the King kept a keen eye on the movements of that advancing, irritant pawn in Flanders, Perkin Warbeck. He knew he had no more bitter and relentless enemy than Margaret of Burgundy. Consequently, the men of his secret service infested her Court like blackfly on a bean row. To ensure military readiness he had caused Parliament to introduce severe penalties for desertion from the armed forces, which he meant should be trustworthy and essentially national. For this reason he now reintroduced the old system of local militiamen. Each town was required to supply to him, on demand, the greatest possible number of armed men they could muster.

His primary aim was to kill the privately-maintained, uniformed baronial armies, and substitute for them a royal army imbued with passionate devotion to their sovereign. Meantime, he set men to watch Warbeck himself, others to investigate his antecedents, and others again to feign support so that they might discover and report his intentions and sap the loyalty of his friends. Margaret of Burgundy was also spied upon, as were the movements, activities, and new accessions from England to the ranks of the Yorkists in Flanders. Their councils were permeated and their household staffs wherever possible suborned.

Maximilian, too, had welcomed an opportunity of revenging himself on Henry for the peace of Etaples. He gave as warm a welcome to Warbeck as Margaret. No more than she had he any fondness or cared a fig for the young man himself, their pawn, to be moved as suited them. The King of the Romans did not know it, but he was himself being subjected by Henry to the same secret observation as the rest.

As 1493 streamed past the banks of the year Henry knew all he needed or was likely to know about Warbeck's parentage and early career. In February of that year the so-called Prince was already communicating with partisans in Westminster, merchants of the Hanse acting as his 'postmen'. Henry had no fear of this intruding pawn, but to arrest his progress despatched in the summer two emissaries—Sir Edward Poynings and Dr. Warham, a doctor of canon law who ultimately in 1503 became Archbishop of Canterbury on Henry's recommendation and was the last English Archbishop to accept Roman supremacy—to the Court of Philip, Duke of Burgundy, Maximilian's son.

Henry's emissaries gave the Duke full details of Warbeck's humble origin and career, appealing to him either to send him to England or expel him from Flanders. Born in 1478, Philip had acquired Burgundy from his mother, Mary, his father having acted as his guardian until he was old enough to rule for himself.

Unfortunately, Warham seems to have offended the Dowager Duchess Margaret in Flanders, so that she prevailed upon the Duke and his council to reject Henry's appeal on the grounds that Tournai belonged to *her*, and they had no jurisdiction over her or her guests. In conveying this decision, the Burgundian council insisted, nevertheless, that they sought to remain on friendly terms with England.

For once the King was irritated by this rebuff, especially when he learned that the Duke was secretly aiding Warbeck, and he retaliated in a powerful and vigorous manner. Since both bishop and knight had failed to remove the offending pawn, he brought up another piece. In other words, he expelled the Flemings from England, confiscating their merchandise, calling his own merchants home from Antwerp on the 21st September, and setting up the wool staple for the Low Countries in his own port of Calais instead. This was in effect a declaration of trade war.

It was a double-edged weapon, however, because it inconvenienced his own people as well as the Flemings, giving the Hanse a wonderful opportunity, which they were quick to seize, to steal English trade in Flanders. It was one of the few false moves Henry made.

On the 15th October, the apprentices of London, many of them in the wool trade, seeing these foreigners robbing them of custom, took up weapons, rose in anger, and raided the great Hanse storehouses of the Steelyard, which they pillaged. Recovering from surprise and confusion, the tough, determined 'Easterlings', as they were called, fought back. The Steelyard had been provided with massive gates as a precaution against just such attacks. Despite resistance, they were closed by main force, and the walls circumscribing the area manned. The mob continued to attack, but a clever stratagem prevented them from breaking down the gates. A messenger, sent speeding across the Thames, brought back with him by water blacksmiths and woodworkers, who plied the tools of their trade so effectively that ingress was denied, the gates being strengthened wherever they threatened to give way.

By now the commotion had disturbed the civic authorities, and in the midst of it the Mayor arrived at the head of the civil guards, who charged the rabble with cudgels and sent them scurrying back, heads bleeding, into the alleys and hovels from which they had come. Eighty were apprehended, tried at the Guildhall, found guilty, and the ringleaders sent to the Tower. They were a mixture of wild young apprentices and covetous menials, headed by two servants of a mercer, John Pycton.

Yet another chessboard now demanded the King's attention, that at which the King of Scotland sat. A treaty of peace between the two nations had, as earlier stated, been drawn up in 1491 by the English, so that when the pact came up for renewal in 1492 for a period of seven years, Henry had had to pay the Scots £1,000 in compensation for the border offences of his subjects. Now, however, reports suggested that the Scottish King was in correspondence with Warbeck, and taking his claims seriously. He would have to be watched.

[5]

The state of England in that year was still bad. Churches were falling into decay. The Church of Stretton Baskerville in Warwickshire, for example, 'grew to such ruine that it was of no other use than for the shelter of cattle, being with the churchyard wretchedly prophaned'. Crime prevailed in many areas, even the wealthy, equally evil, in many instances, robbing the poor where they could. Sir Thomas More wrote later that the rights of sanctuary were still being shamefully abused, robbers fleeing into the nearest cathedrals and abbeys with their booty to claim sanctuary and still using their ill-gotten gains to pay for their keep. Each night they slid out into the reeking jennels to thieve and murder again, returning to their refuges as dawn approached.

The wealthy, he said, borrowed money, rushed with it into their chosen ecclesiastical place of safety, and laughed at the lenders outside, barred by law from entering to recover the sums on which their debtors were comfortably living. 'Benefit of clergy', the privilege of exemption from trial by secular court, lasted in English law till 1827, and applied not only to all clergy, but also to those *laymen* who could read and write, and were therefore held capable of taking holy orders. In consequence these offenders went free, while ordinary folk were arrested every day by the dozen 'like birds in a covey', especially in London, where some effort at least was being made to suppress crime and punish the criminals. More wrote: 'that strayte and rigorous justice, which at that tyme was there executed upon fellons, who . . . were for the moste part hanged together upon one gallowes'. More was in advance of his era in considering that hanging for theft was an excessive and 'horrible' punishment.

Warbeck seems to have visited Austria for the funeral of Maximilian's father, the Emperor, Frederick III, in November 1493. Here Albert of Saxony introduced him to Maximilian. The dead

Emperor, born in 1415, was described as 'a useless emperor, and the nation during his long reign forgot she had a King'. A handsome man, with many endearing qualities, he was indifferent to politics, allowing Maximilian, his son, to exercise power in his name.

Albert III, then fifty, was sometimes known as 'Animosus' or 'The Courageous'. He had helped the Emperor to release Maximilian from captivity in Bruges, and when the King of the Romans went off to Germany, Albert remained behind to carry on the fight against the rebels on his behalf. Thanks to him Holland eventually recognized Maximilian as her ruler.

After the funeral Warbeck made his way to Antwerp in the train of the new Emperor. He now had his own retinue of two dozen archers, whose surcoats bore the white rose of the House of York. In Antwerp he occupied a mansion which, by Maximilian's permission, was ornamented with the royal coat of arms of England, carrying the motto: 'The arms of Richard, Prince of Wales and Duke of York'. Some Englishmen passing through the city were so infuriated by this that, making a noisy demonstration, they tore down the device, hurled it into the mire, and fled before they could be arrested.

The Emperor, annoyed by the assault on the trade of the Netherlands, ignored Henry's evidence that the Pretender was an impostor, believing that if Warbeck dethroned Henry, the foreign policy of England would perforce be reorientated against France. In vain Ludovico Sforza, Duke of Milan, advised him that this plan would fail. Ludovico, 'el Moro', the Moor, as he was called, had usurped his Duchy from his nephew, whose guardian he was. He was at this period forty-two. By both him and Ferdinand of Spain it was believed that peace between England and France was now in all their interests.

The attitude of France to Warbeck is best revealed by Charles, the King, who called him a mere 'garçon', son of a boatman of Tournai.

[6]

At this stage in his career Henry was slowly surrendering to one of his greatest faults, an excessive allegiance to the letter rather than the spirit of his creed. He had always been devout and a loyal supporter of the Church, but became fanatical where heresy was concerned. Many accused of this were tied to the stake and burned in Smithfield, others, less seriously tainted, being put in the pillory. One shocking incident of this kind occurred in the April of 1494, when the King allowed an old crone of eighty to be burned. Though surrounded by leaping flames, the victim refused to recant and died unrepentant. Even the Jews were not safe, for the King gave his word to Spain that he would treat Jewish refugees from that country with the utmost harshness. Meantime he was angered by the embargo Maximilian and his son placed on English wool and iron in May.

CHAPTER TEN

The Holy League

[1]

THE KING WAS PRESENTLY forced by events to pay close attention once more to Ireland. The Earl of Kildare, head of the Fitzgerald clan, had fought at Towton for Edward IV against the Lancastrians, and as Deputy Lieutenant, ruled Ireland like a King. Nominally he was subordinate to Jasper Tudor, Duke of Bedford, who, though Lord Lieutenant, was rarely called upon to visit the island that was his responsibility, the work of government being done by his Deputy.

Reports came filtering through that all was not well in Erin. Fighting in the streets of Dublin had taken place between the Butlers and the Fitzgeralds. There were rumours that Kildare was tacitly supporting 'the French lad'—Warbeck—complaints being made against him by the Bishop of Meath, his former friend, but now his opponent, and by others in Ireland. Taking the hint, the King relieved Kildare of his office, temporarily appointing the Archbishop of Dublin in his stead, and dismissed all his underlings, giving their posts to members of the Butler family. Jasper Tudor being ill, Henry made his own son, Prince Henry, Lord Lieutenant, and sent Sir Edward Poynings to take over the position of Deputy from the Archbishop. Poynings sailed into Howth on the 13th October, 1494, backed up by 1,000 trained men-at-arms and a body of experienced officials. Their brief was to subdue the recalcitrant Irish, take over the government, and ensure that the revenues due to England were regularly collected and remitted to the royal Exchequer. This Kildare had never achieved.

In November, Henry strengthened his country's defences. He named Henry, his second son, Duke of York, the title the Pretender had appropriated, and made him a Knight of the Bath. The little Prince, a mere four-year-old, came riding into Westminster astride a horse, which occasioned great admiration. For the ceremony he was carried in the arms of the Earl of Shrewsbury. Preceding Henry and his Queen, wearing their crowns, were ten bishops in mitres and many titled men. The affair took place in Westminster Hall. The royal, public and private tables became gastronomic jousting grounds, at one of which the prize, a ruby ring, was given by the winner to Princess Margaret.

The festivities, the splashes of colour they created, the fanfares, noise and laughter, the ring of steel on steel, the clatter of hooves, the cries of street vendors and the capers of acrobats and jugglers, 'gave great gladness to all the common people'.

There had been at the Court of Burgundy for some time an enigmatic figure, Sir Robert Clifford, who, with William Barley, was among the first group of Yorkists to go over to Flanders, ostensibly to report to the King on Warbeck's pretensions. Many have believed that this man was one of the King's principal secret agents 'working by countermine', who, claiming to hold the Pretender's claim justified, and penetrating into the inner councils of the intriguing Dowager Duchess and her advisers, was present when Warbeck undertook to return to her all the property she had lost in England when Henry became King. Returning to England in the winter, Clifford disclosed to his sovereign all he had learned.

Another and more likely version, however, is that he was bribed to do this by the promise of a free pardon. It is significant that Henry never thereafter showed him any great respect or favour.

All unsuspecting, the principal Yorkists in England, busily engaged in preparing for Perkin Warbeck's landing in England, were suddenly arrested in December, 1494, taken to London and tried at the King's Bench in Westminster Hall. They included Lord Fitzwalter, Sir Simon Mountford, Sir Thomas Thwaites, William Daubigny, John and Robert Ratcliffe, Thomas Cressenor, Thomas Astwood, and William Worseley, Dean of St. Paul's, this last, though interrogated in November and January, 1495, not being subjected to trial. A leader of the Dominican friars, as well as one of his assistants and a couple of priests, were also arraigned. The churchmen were pardoned by reason of their function, but the rest were found guilty of high treason in accepting Warbeck's claims and undertaking to help him. Fitzwalter and John Ratcliffe were sent to Calais and imprisoned, but in November, 1496, having bribed a warder to let them escape, went free for a short time, but were soon recaptured and beheaded. On the 29th and 30th January, Mountford, Robert Ratcliffe and Daubigny were also beheaded, the other conspirators being hanged at Tyburn on the 27th January, 1495. Cressenor and Astwood, though taken to Tyburn, were reprieved at the last moment 'which gladded moche people, for they were both yong men', remarks the chronicler.

A considerable number of English Yorkists, including Barley, voluntarily surrendered themselves to justice and were allowed to go free, but unquestionably a wave of terror passed over the land, and for the first time since the reign of Richard III, perhaps, men went in daily fear of the hidden enemy and the secret informer.

Presently the King went to Greenwich Palace for Christmas, but ate his Christmas dinner at Westminster. 'On the twelfth day' he gave a magnificent banquet to Ralph Austry, Mayor of London, and his colleagues, knighted the Mayor, and took him to see the preparations for a feast in the great hall. After it, the guests joined in fun and games, which included dressing up. They ate dinner that evening at a stone table, sixty knights and esquires waiting on the King and his guests and a similar number on the Queen and hers. An identical number of dishes was set before Henry and Elizabeth, but none of these included meat or fish. The Mayor and his party were allowed, however, only twenty-four dishes, but were given an ample supply of different wines. At the end of the repast the royal pair were conducted 'with great lights' into the palace, the Mayor and his friends then taking barges up river. As dawn broke they entered once more their rich and prosperous city.

[2]

Behind all this gaiety, however, sombre men were moving. There was evidence that the edicts against trade with Flanders were being secretly evaded, and stern measures were taken to prevent this. For two years there had been next to no trade between the two states.

The King now returned to London, and took up residence in the Tower. That great fortress was ideal for secret conversations and also for the ease with which great personages of the Court could be quietly seized and thrust into the cells. Every member of the royal Court had to be within call of his sovereign in case he was needed. Consequently he had to lodge within the Tower walls, so that his arrest could be effected at any time unknown to the public.

Early in January Clifford received his Iscariotic 'thirty pieces of silver'—the sum of £500. He now awaited his King with further mortifying revelations, so grave that he had deferred making them, he said, till he could do so to the monarch himself. Henry listened, then went away to brood and meditate. A couple of days went by, after which, all preparations made, the King summoned his Council. Clifford, brought in to face them, knelt and was formally pardoned. It was a bitter story he had now to tell. The chief conspirator on Warbeck's behalf, he announced, was none other than Sir William Stanley, the wealthiest aristocrat in England and Lord Chamberlain, that Stanley whose army at Bosworth had by its timely intervention changed the course of the battle and set the crown of England on the Earl of Richmond's head.

The truth concerning this accusation may never be known. Such proof as exists would hardly warrant a conviction today. According to Polydore Vergil, Henry showed complete surprise, finding it difficult to believe that a man so greatly trusted, whose brother was the King's own father-in-law, and who had been in no personal danger or difficulty, should have betrayed him.

Clifford insisted that he had met Sir William in March 1493, before he went overseas, and that his accusation was true. Finally Sir William was arrested, confined to a room in the Tower, and examined next day by the lords of the Council. He said little in self-defence, relying on his past service to the King. Again according to Clifford, he believed that Warbeck, if what he claimed were true, had a title more legitimate than the King's to the throne, and therefore it was his duty to help him with men and money. Bacon, however, suggests that Sir William had grown too big for his boots and was dissatisfied with the rewards he had received. An ambitious man, he had coveted the Earldom of Chester, for which he had pleaded, but this Henry regarded as an impertinence, since by tradition it belonged to a son of the monarch. He refused the request.

On the other hand, though Sir William may not have believed in Warbeck, he may have secretly promised him support to cover himself in the event of his success. The Stanleys were great 'sitters on the fence'.

Prolonged gratitude is the rarest of human virtues. Henry decided that this man had to be broken, and broken he was. A chronicler attributes the decision to the King's 'convenient diligence for inveigling', declaring that Sir William's intended treason had been known to the King for some years, so that he had 'covertly watched him, keeping it secret and always gathered upon him more and more'. Henry is said by his detractors to have envied him his large fortune, Sir William being one of the richest landowners of England, and his power so great that even the King feared it.

His brother, Lord Stanley, now Earl of Derby, had married the King's mother, which gave the Stanleys even greater power, so that there was some excuse for Henry's distrust. He may even have suspected that the Earl of Derby himself was planning treachery.

Six weeks went by, but finally on the 30th and 31st January, 1495, the conspirator was arraigned before the King's Bench on a charge of high treason, condemned, and on the 16th February, beheaded on Tower Hill. His body was interred at the King's cost, his estates and wealth being transferred to the sovereign. In the following month Dr. Hussey, Archdeacon of London, and others were named by Bernard de Vignolles under interrogation as undetected and unpunished members of the plot. These men, he asserted, sought to kill the King, his family and his principal advisers. The method proposed was certainly unusual. From an astrologer in Rome they had obtained a box of deadly ointment. If the first conspirators failed to kill the King with it, another would spread the ointment across some doorway or passage through which he would walk, so bringing about his death.

As is customary when conspiracies are exposed, even minor figures were touched by the bony fingers of suspicion, while the Archbishop of York himself was called in February before the

Court of Justice in the Star Chamber, and freed only after being guaranteed by his ecclesiastical superior.

There is an interesting postscript to these unhappy events. The story goes that at a later date the King was being entertained by the Earl of Derby (Stanley) at Latham House, and climbed with his host and others on to the leads to see the magnificent view. Derby drew close to the parapet with Henry directly behind him. The jester of the household, who was present, uttered the sharp warning to his master: 'Tom, remember Will!' Taking the hint, Henry at once drew back. The allusion was to Sir William, whom he had condemned to death.

Giles, Lord Daubeney, became Lord Chamberlain in Sir William Stanley's stead, having the reputation of being competent, brave, kindly and reasonable. That the King felt strong enough to break one of the most powerful men in his kingdom reveals the security of his position.

[3]

Poynings had failed to subdue the fierce Ulstermen, but had succeeded in bringing the control of all laws and statutes into the hands of the King and his Council. He discovered in the course of his work that Kildare was in touch with the King's enemies, and calling a Parliament at Drogheda, arraigned him. The Irish Parliament at first pardoned the Earl, but afterwards changed their minds and attainted him, no doubt because Poynings insisted on having his way. Kildare was arrested on the 27th February, 1495, and sent to England together with the Irish lords who supported him, with the sole exception of the Earl of Desmond.

Henry gave him a cordial welcome, but he was compelled to stand trial. At Westminster he confronted his accusers with spirit, saying that as Counsel he would have none other to plead for him than the King himself. The Bishop of Meath exclaimed in dudgeon: 'See! All Ireland cannot hold him!', to which Henry made answer drily: 'Then he is mete' (fit) 'to rule all Ireland.'

At dinner, he and the Irish lords were told the King would send them wine to drink. It was brought by none other than Lambert Simnel, but they refused to accept it from his hand, and 'bade the great devil of hell to take him before they even saw him'. However, Lord Howth, who was no party to the plot and was a merry fellow, said to the youth: 'Bring me the cup, the wine is good, and I shall drink it off for the wine's sake and mine own sake also, and for thee, as thou art so, I leave thee, a poor innocent.'

Henry is said to have told the Irish lords: 'My masters, you will crown apes some day.' Disinclined to restore Kildare to his original authority, he sent him to the Tower where he could no longer trouble unhappy and combative Ireland.

Poynings went on with his work there, and the body of Irish legislation enacted by him, known as 'Poyning's Laws', effectively deprived dissidents of the power to honour officially any aspirant to the throne of England, and prevented the two opposing clans from making the population victims of their rivalries and feuds, pretensions and greed. In the long run, however, these very laws robbed the Irish of independence and put them wholly in the power of the Kings of England.

The collapse of the Yorkist conspiracy in England came as a great shock to Warbeck's party. They perceived too late that their councils had been penetrated by spies and informers. Their preparations to invade England were dislocated, for instead of an organized body of supporters pledged to take up arms the moment they landed, they had now to go ahead unaided and hope for the best. Until they appeared off the coast of England, they would have no clue to their reception by the people. It is said that they were 'like sand without lime, ill bound together', and 'at a gaze ... not knowing who was faithful'.

However, they had gone too far to draw back. In April, 1495, Warbeck's former employer, Pregent Meno, who had settled in Ireland, was granted £300 and given custody of a castle. He became a citizen of the country. Steps were already being taken to ensure the co-operation of the Yorkist Irish in the young man's future plans.

In the same month Henry gained another victory when the French took off at his request a duty imposed, and returned the overcharges. In May a new agreement was made and the losses caused by the raids of pirates made good. His success in wresting advantages from the agreements entered into with him, which left the French always in a position of disadvantage, annoyed both the French and their vassals, the Bretons.

A chapter of English history closed when, on the 31st May, Cicely Neville, Dowager Duchess of York, mother of Edward IV, Richard III, George, Duke of Clarence, and grandmother of Elizabeth, the Queen, died at the age of seventy-two, and was buried at Fotheringay Castle.

Henry knew that a fleet including some Scottish craft was being assembled by Warbeck for an attack on his shores, and therefore equipped a few of his own ships in readiness. The King of France generously offered a fleet to help him withstand the attack, but the English King declined the offer, saying he had no fear that the boatman's son would succeed. Nevertheless, lest the Scots should break their truce, he had his northern counties put in a state of defence.

In June, the Scots made their first move, sending envoys to the Court of Maximilian, possibly to consult him regarding Warbeck. Convinced by the Emperor of the young man's genuineness and sincerity, they agreed to supply some of his needs in ships. Maximilian undertook the organization and supply of the expedition, though what advice he gave to the Scots is uncertain. Margaret proposed that she and James should pay Warbeck a pension, but it is doubtful if he ever received this.

Warbeck's departure for Antwerp led to rumours that Maximilian had dismissed him. Margaret of Burgundy quickly denied this in a letter to Pope Alexander VI, in which she invited his support for the 'Duke of York'. Alexander, a Spaniard, born in 1431, had succeeded Innocent VIII. A rich and powerful member of the notorious Borgia family, he was both ambitious and dissolute. Margaret pointed out that the Emperor himself was providing not only some thousands of men for the invasion, but also no fewer than fourteen vessels for their transport.

What Margaret did not say was that neither she nor Maximilian were doing all this for nothing. They had already made sure of a considerable financial share in the success of the invasion. Margaret, as stated, would have all her possessions in England returned to her, and in addition she had obtained Warbeck's written promise to repay all she had spent on Lovell's and Lincoln's rebellions, as well as 80,000 crowns she was now advancing towards his own expenses. The 'Prince' had also promised her the castle and town of Scarborough.

Maximilian and his son, Philip, were even greedier, forcing Warbeck to declare Maximilian his heir should he die without male issue. In return, the Emperor, at no cost to himself, surrendered a purely fictitious claim to the throne of England. Lastly, this head of the Holy Roman Empire compelled Perkin to promise that as soon as possible after victory he would join in a concerted attack upon the French.

There were no other European potentates to whom the Pretender could turn, and the power of the Holy Roman Empire could not be lightly discarded. Perkin had already spent more than two years in Flanders, and although he had invited Ferdinand and Isabella of Spain to accept his claim to royal descent and support him, the Spanish pair had returned 'a dusty answer', having far too much intelligence and far too little faith in his pretensions to indulge in so risky a venture.

In June, Warbeck sent some of his Yorkist advisers to Stirling to obtain a promise from the Scots that they would invade England as soon as he was safely ashore. Meantime, Maximilian had whipped up a motley band of thieves, robbers, vagabonds, bankrupts and sanctuary men to make up the invasion force, and would have sent Warbeck off on his adventures much earlier but for the slowness with which his essential supplies arrived at the port of embarkation. He camouflaged his intentions by keeping up a show of friendship with the English, convinced that their need of Flanders trade would prevent them from taking overt action against him.

[4]

Towards the end of June or early July, Warbeck sailed with his fourteen ships and between 1,400 and 1,500 men, appearing presently off the little Kentish fishing ports of Deal and Sandwich. Before he committed himself to a full-scale landing it was essential for him to discover the reception the English would give him. Accordingly his ships anchored outside Deal harbour, and boats containing a few hundred men were sent to the shore, which they reached in safety. Landing, they displayed Warbeck's standard, boasting of the numbers to follow.

The Sheriff of Kent, who when the alarm was given had promptly raised men to defend the coast, set a trap. The invaders were accosted by a single mounted man-at-arms, the rest being kept carefully out of sight. He asked their master's name, and when told, 'The Duke of York', replied that his fellows would 'live and die with him'. The soldiers could safely disembark, he asserted, and meantime he would bring his comrades to join them and beer to quench their thirst. He rode off, and reinforced by a second party from the ships, the invaders, relaxing and cheerful, made themselves comfortable. Suddenly they were violently attacked and surrounded by archers and swordsmen under the Sheriff. One hundred and fifty were slain and one hundred and fifty-nine made prisoners. Four of Warbeck's captains—Mont, Corbett, White and Beet—were among the captured, two others were killed and two drowned. The captives were yoked together 'like horses drawing in a cart' and conducted to London, the officers being sent to the Tower, the rest to Newgate jail.

As a warning to the 'Duke', no fewer than one hundred and fifty were hanged after trial in London, Wapping, Kent, Sussex, Essex and Norfolk 'by the seaside'. A Frenchman and a Spaniard among the commanders seized were also executed in London, their heads joining others on the spikes of London Bridge.

Warbeck's appearance off Deal had alarmed the people of Yarmouth, and afraid they would be attacked, they petitioned John Paston and the Mayor of Norwich to aid them in such a case.

The news of Warbeck's defeat was brought to Maximilian, but he refused to despair, arguing that the bulk of the invasion force was still in being, and Ireland was sure to give him a warm welcome. On Ferdinand the effect was the reverse. Addressing his ambassador in London in his usual forthright fashion, he wrote: 'We now tell you that as for the affair of him who calls himself duke, we hold it for a jest.'

Warbeck himself had not been so foolish as to land with his advance parties, and making no effort to rescue his men, sailed away. He had lost three of his ships. One had been captured and a second driven on to the Normandy coast. The fate of the third is not recorded. He saw now that his only course was to make for Ireland. Towards the end of the month the remaining eleven vessels reached the Irish coast and made their way up river to Waterford, a blunder for which he was to pay dearly.

When Warbeck came up by river to Waterford, the Earl of Desmond, at liberty in Munster, joined forces with him. Together they sat down to besiege the city, Desmond having about 1,500 men, though some place the number as high as 2,400. It was a Butler stronghold, which as before remained loyal to the King. Desmond enveloped it from the land side while Warbeck's ships blocked the harbour, hoping to starve the citizens into surrender.

Waterford was, however, no home of cravens. Her guns thundered at the ships while her messengers sped to warn Poynings of the siege. Poynings swiftly mustered a strong force and marched. Eleven days went by with no breach in either the defences or the determination of the city. On the 3rd August, 1495, therefore, Warbeck abandoned the siege, hoisted anchor and sailed away, knowing he could not withstand a relieving army, while without body armour Desmond's Irish would be helpless against trained and well-protected English soldiery. The Waterford men sent ships after him. He lost three more vessels, one, the 'Kekeoute', by capture.

We have scant evidence as to his movements after he left Waterford, but one manuscript declares that he sailed to Cork, being welcomed there by the Mayor, James Walter. According to this same account, he perceived that he would find little support in Poynings's new Ireland, and determined to try his fortune in a more profitable field, that of the Scots.

On the way northwards he ran into a violent storm, his ships, all control lost, being driven back by a howling wind and wrecked on the Irish coast. Warbeck himself, getting ashore unharmed, made his way in disguise over the mountains, arriving in a small fishing harbour, where he hired a ship, setting out once more for Scotland, disappointed, but by no means defeated.

[5]

In England, the King was again poised over the widely-separated European chessboards. In the August of 1494 the Sforzas of Milan had joined Charles of France in a war against the state of Naples, which at that period was not only a town, but a kingdom, technically that of 'Sicily', comprising Naples and that portion of the Italian mainland 'beyond the Pharos', i.e. beyond Messina. This war gave much concern to both the Pope, who appealed to Henry, and to Ferdinand of Spain, who also looked round for an ally. With many self-exculpations for past misbehaviour, he suggested a union of Henry, Maximilian, the Pope and himself, a 'Holy League' against the French, who had swiftly and easily captured Naples, so that Charles contemptuously remarked that his troops had come provided with chalk as well as swords in their hands with which to scrawl on the doors of the houses they chose as lodgings.

Ferdinand impudently gave as his excuse for having made peace with France that Henry had continually referred to England's treaty with Spain as 'the concluded treaties', but had sworn never to ratify it, or so he had been told.

The King deliberated long, telling none his decisions. In fact, as was his way, he waited to see where England's interests lay. Cordial gestures were made by him to the exiled King of Naples, who had fled from his kingdom, and amicable letters exchanged with the Duke of Milan, which led the Milanese ambassador to declare later: 'In many things I know this sovereign to be admirably well-informed'. All the same, Henry had no desire to relinquish without good cause the regular payments made to him by France, nor had he forgotten the naval assistance offered by Charles against Warbeck, or the news of Warbeck's movements sent to him from time to time by the same hand.

He continued, therefore, to show goodwill to the French King, which irritated Ferdinand, who declared that Charles was not to be trusted, as he himself well knew, pointing out in his own favour that the Dowager Duchess Margaret's request that Spain should aid Warbeck had been ignored. He had not forgotten, he added, that the Infanta Catharine was promised in marriage to Prince Arthur, and had no intention of going back on his word in this respect. The quarrel between Henry and Maximilian must, however, be ended. To bring this about he offered his own services.

Henry called a Parliament, which met at Westminster in October, 1495. The most important Act passed by 'the obedient Parliament', as it was called, was that thenceforward no man could be impeached or attainted for obeying his sovereign's commands. There was one important and specific exception. The Act did not cover any man who deserted or betrayed the King. This made it clear that the *reigning* king alone mattered and none other. Arguments concerning who was to be obeyed and to whom loyalty was due were thus automatically prevented. Irrespective of the justice or otherwise of his claim to the crown, the *de facto* occupier of the throne, whoever he might be, was legitimately entitled to the support of his subjects until he died naturally or in battle. This measure safeguarded even the Yorkists as long as they remained loyal.

Parliament also strengthened the laws against crime, enabled the poor to sue in the courts without payment of fees, gave them free legal aid, protected them against injustice, and inflicted heavy penalties on dishonest juries. These steps, designed for the good of the ordinary people, were warmly welcomed. The King emerged with enhanced prestige in both his own country and Europe. Not for many years had so firm and wise a hand ruled Albion.

The King's mind now directed itself for the first time towards the New World across the Atlantic. A Venetian, John Cabot, born in Genoa, had settled in Bristol in 1491 or 1492, imbued with the passionate desire to discover a northern route to Asia by way of the Atlantic. When Henry revisited Bristol in March, 1496, Cabot petitioned him for permission to fit out a fleet at his own expense to discover new 'islands'. The petition was granted, and the document itself can be seen today in the Public Record Office in London.

In the following year, Cabot returned from his successful voyage, and was granted the not too generous sum of £10 for having 'founde the new Isle'. This was followed up, however, with a pension of £20 a year, not regularly paid, but this was not the King's fault.

[6]

There was now little labour trouble, for daily bread and other needs were within the reach of any willing to toil for his home. Parliament gave a slight increase in wages to carpenters, masons and other craftsmen, who received 6d. a day. A manservant was to be clothed free and paid 19s. 8d. a year, a maidservant to receive 14s. and money for her clothes, a child below the age of fourteen to be paid 12s. 8d. When men received board and lodging at their place of employment, twopence a day could be subtracted from their wages. Nothing was paid for holidays, and if a man downed tools before a job was finished, he could be jailed for a month and fined £1. His working day was from 5 a.m. to 7 or 8 p.m. in spring, summer and autumn, and from dawn to dusk in winter. To ask for higher wages was to be fined, and the same punishment was inflicted on any employer who granted the request.

Trouble was being caused by fishermen, whose nets and contrivances obstructed harbours and estuaries. Permission to remove these was therefore granted to any person they impeded, and their installation was forbidden. Trouble of this kind had been experienced by the merchants of Southampton in particular.

On the 16th November, the King and Queen attended a great banquet given by nine 'serjeants', a superior class of barristers, at Ely Place, one of the most splendid of London's mansions, town house of the Bishop of Ely. The King's presence was an honour to the men of law. It was said of Henry that he 'governed his laws by his lawyers', while Bacon wrote that he was 'the best law giver since Edward I'. He, if anyone, should have known.

[7]

Charles of France now suffered a setback, for on his return to his own country a revolt broke out in conquered Naples and the Spaniards recaptured the greater part of that state. The French reverse convinced the King of England that he might after all be wise to unite with the European potentates in a defensive alliance, though he was still not prepared to wage a major war. Parliament granted him the estates of the executed English Yorkists and other financial benefits, while a specific amount was voted for strengthening the fortresses of Berwick and Carlisle against attack by Warbeck and the Scots.

He was still distressed by the lawlessness prevalent among his people. Peasants, turned off the soil by the enclosure of common lands in earlier reigns, were thronging the woods and roads as robbers, bullies and murderers. Since they were all armed or could easily acquire arms, it was a great temptation to the hungry or violent among them to use force and intimidation to gain their ends. For example, simple men who objected to excessive rents or charges were often attacked with swords, bucklers and spears by ruffians in the pay of landlords, and were lucky to escape with their lives. Others were turned out of their homes by gangs with bows, arrows and swords. At times, as earlier indicated, foreigners in London parishes were set upon and beaten. The brutes who committed these offences were often the servants of abbots.

The measures taken by the King were aimed not so much at punishing the guilty as at eradicating the causes of these evils. Instead of being clapped into jail at public expense, rioters and vagabonds were exposed in the stocks for three successive days, then thrown out of the locality for good. Those who begged on the roads or in the towns were shipped back to the parishes from which they originally came, which did not want them and made them suffer for it. Gambling and gaming were prohibited to whoever might attempt to recoup their losses by crime. Drinking, a common cause of violence, was carefully controlled, magistrates being given power to stop the sale of beer in town alehouses if they considered it desirable.

Until these measures had been put into effect the King did not feel free to contemplate war, but his hand was forced, as he had foreseen it might be, by an alliance between the King of Scotland and Perkin Warbeck. By this time, however, he had constructed at Portsmouth the first dry dock capable of taking his new warships.

[8]

King James IV of Scotland, had, as previously stated, been convinced by his ambassadors that Warbeck was indeed the escaped

13—H VII

Duke of York. Consequently, when the young man landed in Scotland, he gave him the welcome customary for princes from overseas. They met on the 27th November, 1495, in the Chamber of Presence at Stirling Castle. James was immediately impressed by Perkin's charm and attractive appearance, while his courage, patience in face of disaster, and daring, particularly appealed to him. The Scottish King cherished all the ancient romantic traditions of his people.

The newcomer, bowing, embraced the King, retreated a pace or two, then narrated his adventures. He had lost everything in the wreck of his ships, but James took him in hand, had him reclothed magnificently at his own expense, and had tapestries brought specially from Edinburgh to hang on the walls of the castle chamber allotted to the young man.

At this period James was nearly twenty-three, a courageous, chivalrous, able and educated man, reading Latin, and parleying in Gaelic, Scots and English, as well as French. Tradition relates that he wore an iron belt under his shirt as penance for the part he had played in the death of his father. He had the reputation of being generous, audacious and honest, and of believing a king should never break his word. Some trained observers considered him, however, wanting in foresight as a commander in the field, and though a good and just ruler of his people, inexperienced and incompetent in foreign policy. He was temperate in habits, and had some knowledge of medicine.

His piety was extreme, so that he would not eat meat on Wednesdays or Fridays, never cut his hair or beard, and invariably walked to Mass on Sundays. He would attend two Masses before beginning his daily work, and follow these up with a cantata. He never omitted a prayer, and respected the counsel of his priests.

Having taken an instant liking to Warbeck, he went out of his way to entertain him with magnificent feasts, tournaments and royal processions from one Scottish town to another, granting him also the annual sum of £1,200. Peers and statesmen of the realm were presented to him, and if a church festival took place, Warbeck received in addition a proportion of the sums deposited in the offertory boxes.

Even this did not satisfy the deluded and infatuated King, who was determined to strengthen the bonds between Scotland and the 'Duke of York'. Before many days the enraptured Warbeck was given a bride, the lovely virgin, Lady Catharine Gordon, daughter of the Earl of Huntley, head of the great Clan Gordon. Her mother, Princess Annabella, claimed close kinship with the Scottish kings. The bridegroom was given a white damask robe for this wedding. It required fourteen ells of silk for its manufacture and cost £28. A newly-styled, sleeved, velvet coat for him was also supplied by James, and cost £21.

The King acceded to 'Prince Richard's' request for military aid, and with great enthusiasm, for he loved war, flung himself into the necessary preparations, instructing three of his sheriffs to muster men. Early in 1496, guns, armour and supplies were being produced and collected up.

Whether the Scottish nobles opposed this needless war, whether the levies were slow to assemble or the munitions less quickly manufactured than had been anticipated, one cannot say. For one or other or all of these causes, the proposed early attack on England was delayed. Possibly the ten months intervening between Warbeck's arrival and the first advance across the border had a more romantic explanation—Warbeck's love for his beautiful bride and his desire to have at least six months of peace and happiness with her before riding off to war.

In one of his letters he wrote that her face 'bright and serene, gives splendour to the cloudy sky, whose eyes, brilliant as the stars, make all pain to be forgotten and turn despair into delight; whosoever sees her cannot choose but admire her; admiring, cannot choose but love her; loving, cannot choose but obey her'. She was, he said, 'not born in our days, but descended from heaven'. Poetic and high-flown language, no doubt, and perhaps inspired by nothing deeper than his wife's high rank and wealth. Nevertheless, let us give him the credit for sincerity and an unusual power of self-expression, and leave the two of them enjoying their first months together in Scotland, as lovely a place for their honeymoon as the best of men could have desired, Warbeck relieved of all financial anxiety and his wife holding him all the closer in the certain knowledge that soon he must leave her, perhaps for ever.

[9]

On the 21st December, 1495, Henry lost his uncle, Jasper Tudor, Duke of Bedford, who had been ill for some time and was sixty-five years old. A strong link with his unhappy past was severed for the King, but there is no indication that he and Jasper were ever emotionally close. Jasper's wife was Catharine Woodville, youngest daughter of Earl Rivers and widow of Henry Stafford, the second Duke of Buckingham. Though legally childless, he had an illegitimate daughter, Ellen, who is reputed to have been the mother of Stephen Gardiner, Bishop of Winchester, a great statesman of the succeeding reigns. He may, however, have felt for Henry some of the affection and pride he would doubtless have felt for a son of his own. He was responsible for building the northern tower of Llandaff Cathedral.

During this same year the King also lost his third daughter, Elizabeth. European intrigues continued to preoccupy his mind, and he moved with extreme caution. The arrival of Warbeck at the Scottish Court offended Maximilian, jealous and touchy as ever. He now explicitly discarded this pawn of his, but still made no move to resume his friendship with Henry, nor made overtures of peace to France.

John Ramsay, Earl of Bothwell, who had accepted money from Henry for services rendered in an earlier unsuccessful attempt to kidnap James IV, had been living in England. Now, however, he went back to Scotland, presented himself once more at Court, and won the trust of the King, ever generous to those who, as he believed, spoke fairly. Bothwell was, however, a scoundrel without principles. Once more in Henry's pay, he sent back to him every scrap of information he could pick up concerning James's plans and Warbeck's movements, and even told the English King the proposed date of their invasion of England, the number and kind of guns at Edinburgh, and the unrest prevailing among the Scots at the thought of war. His treachery did not end even there. With James's brother, the Earl of Ross, the Earl of Buchan and the Bishop of Moray, he conspired to rise for Henry as soon as conflict began.

This trio were engaged also, it is said, in a scheme to kidnap

Warbeck and hand him over to the English. Bothwell, always acting in character, tried to persuade Henry to strike first and invade Scotland, but failed. Meantime the King went on watching events, having no intention of being branded as the aggressor. Bothwell revealed next that the French were seeking to win James over to their side, Charles having sent ambassadors to Scotland with an offer of 100,000 crowns for the handing over of Warbeck.

This would have suited the book of the conspirators admirably, yet they did not wish Henry to join the other European powers. The French ambassadors put forward, also, the proposal of a Scottish alliance with them by matrimony, suggesting that James might be willing to marry a Princess of France.

Bothwell also told Henry that the Earl of Ross was ready to support him against James and Warbeck, even though James was Ross's own brother.

In their turn the Spaniards, eager that nothing should interfere with Henry's joining the 'Holy League' (see p. 176), suggested to James an illegitimate daughter of Ferdinand's as a spouse, but this proposal was scorned by his Scottish advisers. His dignity would be impaired, they held, by marriage with any maiden of rank lower than an Infanta. Ferdinand and Isabella agreed to provide an Infanta, but only if the Scots did as they were told—handed over Warbeck to Henry and abandoned all idea of making war. The Pope added his papal authority to these stipulations.

His spies in Scotland reported all this to Henry. James, however, an honourable man, was too chivalrous to accept a bribe for the surrender of a royal guest, and made instead a firm agreement with Warbeck that if the war were won, Berwick should become Scottish territory and he himself be paid £50,000.

[10]

The obstacles Henry himself had placed in the way of trade with Flanders were now harming both countries and causing great distress among the people. The English had left Antwerp and set up their trading centre in Calais. Economic factors played always an important part in his calculations, and for this reason, when, in December, 1495, Philip of Burgundy proposed a new commercial agreement, the King agreed to receive Burgundian representatives in London, letting it appear as if he did so reluctantly and in response only to the Duke's entreaties.

The meeting with the Flemings in February, 1496, was important. The King was represented by Fox as Lord Privy Seal, Viscount Welles, Kendal, the Prior of St. John's, Warham, now Master of the Rolls, the ubiquitous Christopher Urswick, and Riseley. Philip, shaken by the feeble exploits of Warbeck, was convinced that the adventurer 'Richard IV' was doomed to fail, and this influenced considerably his attitude to the matter in hand.

The negotiations ended in complete success, and on the 24th February, 1496, a famous treaty, known in after years as the 'Intercursus Magnus Treaty', was signed. This restored the free flow of trade between the two states. No specific mention was made of Warbeck, but a clause provided that neither should shelter or support rebels against the other. Philip agreed to oppose Margaret of Burgundy if she attempted this. This new treaty effectively severed one of the last links between the Pretender and his European sources of men, money and supplies. The Burgundian mission, headed by Lord Beures, met the Englishmen in Crosby Place, a great house built by Sir John Crosby, a grocer and wool man. It was then but thirty years old and of stone and timber, being when first erected the tallest building in London. The negotiations lasted nearly a month.

When the terms of the new treaty were announced, however, the traders of the city of London were in a ferment. Protest was loud, and much persuasion needed before the dignitaries would set their seal upon it. A formal declaration of its acceptance had indeed to be sent by the Mayor of London to other cities, particularly Southampton and Canterbury.

In June the Burgundians strengthened the dislike of the London merchants for the treaty by openly violating it, the traders of Antwerp slyly clapping a customs duty on English cloth.

A few Yorkists in arms had already crossed secretly and joined 'the Duke of York'. Another tiny contingent came in from Flanders with a couple of ships. At last, in September, 1496, Warbeck hoisted his splendid standard embroidered in gold, and with a mixed force of various races, numbering no more than 1,400 all told, crossed the border and entered Northumberland. As was the custom, he issued a proclamation in which, as 'King Richard IV', he offered a reward of £1,000, together with a considerable revenue from lands, to whoever brought him the head of the English King, undertaking that his army should not harm the inhabitants of the districts they entered.

Unfortunately, as a modern writer has said: 'Hell knows no fury like a Scotsman on the make.' The Scots of Warbeck's army did what they had been doing to the hated English for generations. They sacked, pillaged, burned, killed, and destroyed whatever they could not carry away. In short, this invasion was little more than another savage border raid, ill-planned and ill-led.

No sympathetic English rising took place. A sullen silence met the Scots everywhere. After three days of this miserable business, the army halted. Warbeck, sickened by the ferocity and lack of discipline of the Scots, implored James to spare the English, whom he hoped one day to make his subjects, but James refused, believing a 'scorched earth policy' essential to the conquest of Britain. He might perhaps have advanced more than the four miles which he had covered, but his men refused to go on, not wishing to abandon the booty they had won, and having heard a rumour that the English were marching on them from Carlisle, though in fact they had not yet set out. The Scots feared that if they went further into England the men of the locality would turn upon them—with good reason—and cut their throats by night when they slept. They had done little more than 'cast downe two small towres or pyles', and rather than be massacred, withdrew at top speed. On the 21st September Warbeck was back in the little town of Coldstream in Scotland. His expedition was in ruins and he was farther from the throne of England than when he started.

The fiasco of the Scottish raid relieved Henry's anxieties. Although the snake was scotched rather than killed, he could afford now to return to the continental chessboard. The pressure on him to join the 'Holy League' was strong, but before coming to any decision he weighed carefully the advantages and disadvantages, his one desire being still for peace.

Nevertheless he felt that he was now a force to be reckoned with in the councils of Europe. His seat on the throne was firm, his people industrious and content, his navy, army and treasury stronger than for years. He had gradually built up his merchant fleet, and made a new departure by constructing three fine ships, the 'Great Harry' (Harry Grace à Dieu), the 'Mary of Portsmouth' and the 'Sovereign', with greater fire power and seaworthiness than any of their predecessors. He no longer relied upon hiring or seizing foreign ships, or on exercising his legal right to use merchantmen for the national service. (Despite this, however, he had failed to appreciate the value of a great fishing fleet, and had done nothing to encourage the English fishermen.) The continuous angling by one potentate after another for his friendship or support was gratifying because it demonstrated that England was once more powerful and esteemed.

At last, making up his mind, he sent an able negotiator, Robert Sherburne, to Rome. On the 18th July, Sherburne arranged on his behalf that England should become a member of the 'Holy League', consisting of Spain, the Emperor Maximilian—'Max the Penniless' as he was called—the Duke of Milan and the Pope, with Venice as a fifth member. By patient diplomacy aided by a strong will Henry wrested from his allies terms remarkably favourable to himself.

By this time Poynings was back in England as Warden of the Cinque Ports, and the King, pardoning Kildare, restored his Deputy Lieutenantship, and let him sail back to Ireland on the 28th August. After an appalling voyage, the Earl arrived in Howth, taking the oath of allegiance on the 21st September.

England's admission to the League did not bind Henry to make immediate war on France, nor was he asked for money. The treaty would be regarded today as one of 'benevolent neutrality' rather than of military alliance. That such terms should have been conceded revealed to him his great prestige among his fellow-princes. At Windsor on the 23rd September he confirmed his accession to the alliance.

On the 1st November, the Mayor of London and the civic worthies met the 'people's orator', who had the duty of announcing this, at London Bridge. Every street from the foot of the bridge to St. Paul's was gay with the standards of the Companies and the liveries of their members. Public rejoicings took place, with the glad ringing of church bells, great bonfires and much making of speeches. The morning after All-Hallows Day, Henry went in solemn procession with his prelates, nobles and principal courtiers to St. Paul's to give thanks. At the hands of the Papal Nuncio, acting for Pope Alexander, he received a hallowed sword and cap of maintenance borne before him, took a seat in the choir and heard a long oration from the Archbishop of Canterbury reciting his great deeds and commenting on the rarity of the honour conferred by the Pope. He was held to have built by his alliances 'a wall of brass about England'.

Early in the new year the treaty of marriage between Prince Arthur and Catharine of Aragon was signed, and ratified by Ferdinand and Isabella. Henry sent the Infanta Catharine the gift of 'a blessed ring' in gold and silver, with a letter from himself.

[11]

The King now decided that Scotland must be tamed. Calling a Great Council—an assembly almost as important as Parliament—on the 28th October, he notified them that James had violated the truce, and the two countries must now be regarded as at war. Vigorous action in providing the means to sustain an army, which would have the task of punishing the Scots, was requested.

The deliberations of this Great Council—which included merchants and burgesses from every city and town of size—lasted for twelve days, at the end of which the Council gave the King leave to ask Parliament for a grant of £120,000. Some Council members themselves offered to lend Henry money. He took advantage of this to raise about £58,000 at once, and began his military and naval preparations. On the 15th December, for example, he ordered Henry Fyner to hire 'founders and labourers' to build workshops for the making of iron for guns, and a week later advanced him money for 'wrought iron'. When ready, both iron and guns, made at Newbridge in Ashdown Forest, were taken to the Tower.

Henry also bought blast furnace iron and sent it to Simon Ballard, a Tower gunner, to be made into shot at Newbridge. The shot weighed 5 lb. each for 'serpentines', a form of small cannon, and up to 34 lb. for medium-sized cannon. Large 'bullets' for mortars weighed as much as 225 lb. each, and for hand guns, bullets weighing less than $1\frac{2}{3}$ lb. were made.

Calling Parliament on the 16th January, 1497, he invited them to ratify the decision of the Great Council and allow him the stipulated amount. Morton, the Chancellor, addressing the members, recited the misdeeds of the Scots, and dwelt on the burned towns and villages, the shattered homes, the stolen property, of the border districts. The members responded by granting a subsidy of two fifteenths and tenths out of the revenues to be paid on the 31st May as to one half, and by the 8th November as to the other.

The King had already sent out his commissioners to raise the balance of the promised money, and Parliament now legislated for additional heavy taxation to meet the cost of the coming war, while ensuring that the burden should not fall upon the poorest citizens.

The navy was now strong. Henry's big new warships were afloat, and had been reinforced by two more, recently acquired by purchase, and a third seized from the Scots themselves.

The 'Harry Grace à Dieu', which had cost the King £14,000 to build, was a fine ship with four masts, each with two round tops, three of them carrying three square sails. She had a built-up poop and forecastle and about seventy guns. Her tonnage was about 1,000 and her crew numbered seven hundred officers and men.

The King did not regret having paid heavily for the navy, for it brought in money. Merchants used his ships to carry their goods overseas, for which privilege they paid him a fee. It is on record that the 'Sovereign' visited the Levant like an ordinary merchantman. The increase in the number of ships available owed much to the special allowances Henry made to the boatbuilders. As long as the vessels on their stocks were for use in battle or naval work, a bonus of 5s. a ton on their costs of construction was given. Moreover the big guns of the royal ships were made in English foundries, something no other king had achieved, while a large new warehouse for naval munitions and stores had been constructed at Greenwich. It is significant that during 1497 the galleys of Venice ceased to visit England.

He had also trained more and more gunners. Armourers were brought in from Flanders, Spain and France to work at Newbridge. The gunners cast their own guns and designed their own shot. The technique of casting bullets and guns came originally, it is thought, from France.

Other great guns were stationed in the Tower batteries. The King had seen for himself the power and worth of heavy ordnance, and had made sure that his cannon were amply supplied with powder. The days when trained archers alone could win great battles were over. From now on, massive bombards and the thundering guns of naval warships must inevitably triumph. He could henceforward face both rebellion and invasion with confidence, though wishing for neither. His anxieties regarding France were lessened when the French King, seeing himself encircled by hostile powers, signed an armistice with him to take effect from the 27th February, 1497.

In March Parliament broke up. The clergy had made the King a grant of considerable size. James, alarmed by the news his agents sent him, paralleled the English preparations by making links of his gold chain into coinage to pay for his own supplies.

In England, nevertheless, trade was suffering from the continued piratical raids of the French and Bretons upon English shipping. This was partly caused by their exasperation with the commercial treaties, so cleverly and cunningly worded that the principal benefits fell to the English. Though both countries protested strongly, they could not move the single-minded, dominant Tudor King, who spurned or ignored their objections. They alleged also that the English took advantage of disputes between Spain and France to steal their commerce. In the end Ferdinand barred English ships from using Spanish harbours before sailing to destinations in France.

These troubles did not prevent the King from mustering an army under Lord Daubeney, and in early June sending them northwards to shatter the Scots.

Ever watchful of his traders' interests, he had also succeeded in obtaining from the new masters of Naples, the French, on the 24th May, 1497, an order for the restoration of original and old-established commercial privileges. A customs duty imposed at the

French port of Bordeaux was abandoned and the amounts charged refunded, while a new treaty was drawn up to regulate trade between the two countries. Moreover, in July, as a retaliation for the duty imposed on English cloth by the government of Flanders, Henry once more took his traders away from Antwerp and set up his own market centre in Calais.

CHAPTER ELEVEN

The Cornishmen Come to London

[1]

AMONG THE GREATEST WEAKNESSES of the Kings of England in the fifteenth century were the imperfections of the fiscal system. The taxpayer could never forecast what sums he would require to meet his obligations. Parliament met infrequently to vote money for the King's needs, and taxation came, therefore, in fits and starts. Not only this, the basis of assessment was a constant source of irritation. While the general levy on a specific area or town might in itself be just and reasonable, within that area there were many anomalies, and particular persons might be most unfairly assessed. John Morton, the Chancellor, had once to pay £15,000.

Moreover, entire groups were granted special concessions, which outraged the rest. For example, the clergy were often completely excused from paying taxes. The guilds were so powerful that through their influence the demands made upon them by the commissioners were much lower than those on less effectively organized bodies. This, too, was a cause of exasperation. Bacon himself referred to the guilds as 'fraternities in evil'.

However, one minor trouble was rectified. New standards for the gallon and the bushel having been wrongly made, Parliament ordered their return, and arranged for their replacement.

The harsh new taxes imposed by the Parliament of 1497 had created extreme discontent in Cornwall, described by some of its inhabitants as a land 'sterile and without all fecundite'. Those affected went about 'lamenting, yelling and crying', and blaming the King for this 'polling and shaving'. They resented being 'grounded to powder' for the sake of 'a smal commocion made of ye Scottes, which was asswaged and ended in a moment'. Seizing what they thought was their opportunity, two men, Thomas Flammock, a lawyer, and Michael Joseph, a smith and farmer of Bodmin, a notorious, vain, stump-orator, fomented these disturbances, declaring the new taxes unjust, if not illegal. They denied that the King was responsible, accusing his councillors, Morton and Bray, of having given him bad advice on which he had acted.

It was useless, they insisted, to grumble and groan. So grievous a burden could not be endured. They must take up arms, march to London *en masse*, and present a petition to the King to dismiss these evil councillors, while assuring him of their own loyalty. Joseph and Flammock would themselves lead the march until men more able and experienced in military matters took over, as would soon, they hinted, be the case.

The Cornishmen, 'stout of stomach, mighty of body and limb', were tough and tenacious, miners working underground in everlasting peril, cold and damp, to bring tin ore out of the earth, or sturdy labourers on farms. They were only too glad to leave behind their subterranean miseries, their toil in the fields, and snatch up bows, arrows, bills, scythes, staves, whatever crude weapons they could find. Out they poured in their hundreds, the two agitators at their head, and marched out of Cornwall into Devon and Somerset, doing harm to and robbing none until, because Bristol had refused them admission, they raked out there a hated, over-officious commissioner for taxes whom they called 'the Provost of Perin', and also, at Taunton, in a burst of fury, a 'rover', James, with his rascally followers, and put both to death.

They proceeded to Wells, and there James Touchet, Lord Audley, with whom the two ringleaders had been in secret correspondence, and who may have taken over command, joined them. A man of rank and good family, Audley was one of those turbulent, ambitious Englishmen, so often thrown up by the medieval era, who subordinated everything to their personal grievances, only to be blown down, as when Nature in winter strips trees of their weakest branches.

The Cornishmen tramped on unopposed through Salisbury to Winchester and there demanded that their leaders take them into

Kent. Flammock had told them the freest, sturdiest, most independent and least conquered people of England resided there, and would surely come to their aid; but in Kent they found no sympathy, for the British nobles and esquires exercised firm control over their people, who in any event were tired of revolts, which had caused them great loss and suffering during the preceding reigns. Disconcerted, they came to a halt, camping at Farnham on 13th June.

The Earl of Kent had meantime gathered together a force to meet them, and a preliminary skirmish between advance parties of spearmen took place on a down near Guildford, ending in the rout of the ill-armed rustics, a few of whom were killed and a couple captured. The fainthearts among them promptly slipped away unobserved and made their way homewards, foreseeing disaster now that Kent had proved unsympathetic and a reverse had been sustained. Others, however, encouraged by the absence of any large royal army, were all for marching on London. Altogether they numbered about 15,000 men, many more than the Earl of Kent had mustered, so that he presented, it seemed, no obstacle.

On the 14th, these sullen men from the south-west came over Banstead Down in Surrey to Blackheath, that broad, hilltop camping ground used by almost every English rebel in his final pause before assailing London. There where the tall elms cast dark shadows to cool and screen them they pitched their tents. At the base of the hill a footbridge, over which any force attacking them would have to pass, crossed the Deptford brook towards the west. This bridge they made ready to hold.

[2]

News had reached Henry of the rising soon after it began, but his hands were tied by the expedition against Scotland, and he had no army near London to send against the Cornishmen, marching impudently and unchallenged across his southern counties. Taken by surprise, he had some justification for fearing that if he recalled Daubeney and sent him against the rebels, the Scots and Warbeck would repeat their previous incursion, this time with greater resolution and success, while the dissident Yorkists in England might be encouraged to take him in the rear.

Swift in decision when emergencies arose, however, he accepted the smaller risk, ordering Daubeney to bring his army back to London without delay. The Queen and the 11-year-old Prince Arthur were sent for safety from Cold Harborough to the Tower, and the city of London was put on watch. The Earl of Surrey moved northwards with what local troops he could muster to defend the border against any new Scottish advance. Henry himself left Sheen and took up his abode at Woodstock, near Oxford.

London was, as usual, in a state of confusion and fear, but alarm ended when Daubeney, after forced marches, arrived in the city on the 12th June. He, with 8,000 to 10,000 mounted men and many footsoldiers, rested on Hounslow Heath. A cartload of food and wine was sent to them by London's Mayor. The King, having left Woodstock on the 10th, came to Kingston on Thames. Some envoys from France were at that moment on their way to the capital via Dover, and Urswick was sent to meet them and make sure they did not learn of the revolt.

In the city sentries and guards were posted at every point and the populace called upon to arm. The great gates were strengthened, and on the 13th Daubeney received Henry near Henley on Thames, where the King had been collecting reinforcements. Daubeney was shown messages from treacherous Cornishmen offering to betray their commanders in return for a pardon. All now moved to St. George's Field on the 15th. Henry, who had taken up quarters in the Bishop's Palace of Lambeth, addressed the troops there, and the following day, leaving the Field, all moved off towards Kingston, sending out a small reconnoitring body of about five hundred spearmen.

[3]

The Cornishmen, learning of their approach, held a council of war, and were 'in greate agony and variance'. Many would have thrown themselves on the King's mercy, but Joseph, the smith, stubborn as the iron he once hammered, urged them to resist.

Daubeney attacked at dusk on Saturday, the 17th. He had divided his army of 'about 35,000 men' (surely an exaggeration), both horse and foot, into three bodies. One, under the Earl of Oxford, with Essex and Suffolk as his lieutenants, consisted of horsemen and a good number of archers. These moved quietly round the base of the hill on which the rebels were camped, placing themselves across their line of retreat. Daubeney himself led the vanguard, aiming to seize the footbridge over which the Cornishmen would have to pass to reach London. The King commanded the rear, ready to bar the way if the other bodies were defeated. The Welsh claim that their medieval hero, Sir Rhys ap Thomas, was at this fight also, and he is said to have taken the leaders prisoner. Perhaps he was, and perhaps he did, who knows?

The Cornishmen had not expected attack so soon, so the assault achieved tactical surprise. At first they gave way before Daubeney. The royalists took the bridge, climbed the hill, came out on to the plateau, and charged their enemies recklessly and with daring, but they had been too impetuous. The main body of the Cornish forces resisted fiercely, giving their comrades time to collect themselves. Daubeney, slowly advancing over the plateau, was suddenly assailed by superior numbers and captured, many of his men being slain. Perceiving that the battle was in danger of being lost, Oxford attacked the rebels in the rear and on their exposed flank. Fighting without guns or cavalry, outnumbered, underarmed and outfought, the Cornishmen were first routed, then massacred, both in battle and as they fled. They are estimated to have lost 1,000 men killed, Daubeney a mere three hundred. Their leaders were all taken and the rest surrendered, handing over those weapons that had worked the greatest havoc among the King's men—their great bows with yard-long arrows.

The King knighted some of his commanders on the field of battle, and also the Mayor, John Tate, the Recorder and Sheriffs of London, in St. George's Field at 2 p.m. on his return to London via the Borough High Street, where he was enthusiastically received that same day by citizens happy in the knowledge that no hungry Cornishmen would plunder their city and their town houses. After a service of thanksgiving in St. Paul's, Henry rejoined his family in the Tower.

The property of the captives was awarded to their captors, either in cash or in kind, Audley's captor being given only £1, which does not suggest Rhys ap Thomas. Audley himself, in a coat of paper showing his arms reversed, was carried through the streets in sham procession with Flammock and Joseph to London, jailed in Newgate, tried, taken to Tower Hill and beheaded. Flammock and the smith were hanged, drawn and quartered at Tyburn on the 26th. Joseph is said to have vaingloriously proclaimed from the hurdle or sledge on which he was drawn to execution that he hoped to be remembered one day. For what good it may do him, so he is, in these and earlier pages.

The heads of the three leaders were exposed on London Bridge, Flammock's quarters being set over the four city gates, and Joseph's distributed between Devon and Cornwall. All the executed are said to have died before they were hanged.

The King had intended to let the two Cornish ringleaders dangle from gallows in Cornwall till they rotted, but changed his mind, or was dissuaded, as it was unwise to fan the anger of the people there still further. For the same reason he was lenient with the captives, allowing them to buy their pardons for such sums as his officers thought they could afford. His leniency had a double motive—to calm their fellows at home, and to distinguish between rebellion constituting an act of treason and momentary insurrection caused by hunger and need. Nevertheless the general impression created by the executions was bad. The English were no longer so fond of judicial murder as they had been.

Now that all was over Urswick brought the French envoys to London, where they pressed the King not to continue his membership of the 'Holy League'. A reconciliation with the Burgundian traders was also effected in July.

[4]

To prevent a Scottish invasion Henry had not only sent Surrey forward with a hastily-raised force, but also Bishop Fox of Durham, William Warham and John Carrington, to suggest to the Earl of Angus a marriage between James and Princess Margaret, his daughter. Two years earlier he had suggested one of his mother's female relatives, but without result. Fox, his present emissary, could not, however, arrest James's headlong plunge towards war. Consequently the King again ordered all Scots within his borders to remove themselves or be heavily fined. He also endeavoured through his ambassadors to have Warbeck turned over to him, but made no offer of peace. That must come from James.

Nevertheless, Fox had leave to agree to a meeting between the two monarchs if this would do good. All efforts and tentatives were, however, unavailing. James had decided on war, and the more Henry tried to avert it, the more the Scot interpreted this as weakness. Moreover, Warbeck was proving costly to keep—it is not certain that his pension was always regularly paid—and James wanted a quick return for the money he had already spent on him. He ignored the appeals of even Ferdinand of Spain, who sent his special envoy, De Ayala, to dissuade him.

For his part, Henry, also the subject of an appeal by Ferdinand, had no wish to go cap in hand to Parliament for money to support a new campaign. Taking advantage of the Cornish troubles, however, James decided upon a two-pronged attack. He himself would invade England by land, while Warbeck, descending upon her southern shores, probably in Cornwall, would raise a force and take Henry in the rear, or else join the Yorkists first, in Ireland. They had already invited him to come. In any event the war would prove an excellent opportunity to get a parasitic 'Richard IV' off his back.

Accordingly Warbeck, accompanied by his wife, proceeded to Ayr, Andrew Forman, later Archbishop of St. Andrews, being deputed to escort him there. He boarded the only ship, 'The Cuckoo', James could afford to give him. In the port by good fortune were, however, two daring freebooters, the brothers Andrew and Robert Barton, with a ship of their own. They decided to sail with him (though it is not established that Andrew did). Another volunteer was a trader from Brittany, also in his own vessel. James gave Lady Catharine, Warbeck's wife, $3\frac{1}{2}$ ells of tawny cloth from Rouen with which to make a gown for the voyage.

On 25th or 26th June a landing was made at Cork in Ireland,

chosen by Perkin because the Yorkist Irish had promised that many there would join him.

[5]

Early in August James attacked, aiming this time for Norham Castle on the Tweed, ravaging as he went. Having failed to take it by storm, he besieged it, 'Mons Meg' being one of the great guns used for the purpose. Those men not needed for the siege laid the surrounding country waste as before. Norham had become a difficult nut to crack, for Fox had spent £12,000 on strengthening its fortifications and building up supplies. He had expected a short, brisk assault rather than a siege, but his garrison was composed of experienced and physically powerful men, while all livestock and property in the surrounding areas had been carefully hidden away. He appealed to the King for help, and having no further need to keep his army in the south, Henry sent it northwards under the Earl of Westmorland and other lords to reinforce Surrey, while Lord Willoughby de Broke took a squadron of ships to raid the Scottish coast.

James had not expected so swift and vigorous a response. No message had reached him from Warbeck and he feared the worst, so without more ado he packed up his tents and ignominiously retreated a second time, recrossing the border into Scotland. Before the month was out Surrey, with many thousands of men, was hard on his heels, and nearly caught him at Ayton, a powerful fortress, north of Berwick, using his new cannon to blast the walls to pieces. The fortress promptly surrendered. James, but a mile away at the time, saw what was happening, but made no attempt to save the stronghold.

Realizing that he could not defeat Surrey in the field, he sent him instead a challenge to a hand-to-hand duel, the prize to be Berwick. Surrey rejected the proposal, saying Berwick was not his to give, but his master's. During the night, therefore, James slipped away with all his men, leaving many guns behind.

Surrey's force destroyed Coldstream Castle, but was suffering from a shortage of food. In addition the weather turned foul and stormy. In winter and wet weather the border marshes were virtually impassable, so after a few miserable days he took his men away from 'that tempestuous, infertile and barayne region' back to Berwick, where he disbanded them, convinced that James would not dare to attack again.

He was right. At Ayton on the 30th September, 1497, James gave in, and with the Spaniard, De Ayala, acting as mediator, signed a treaty of peace to last for seven years. Though its terms were not altogether to Henry's liking, he agreed that the points of difference should be left for later discussion.

[6]

On his return from the defeat of the Cornishmen, Henry stayed at the Bishop of London's residence in the centre of Hornsey Great Park, part of the large forest of Middlesex, whence he was later escorted by the Mayor and citizens of London to the city. On the 17th August he and his Court went to Woodstock, 'a sorry village', to assemble a new army. While here he welcomed on the 7th September the ambassador of Venice, Raymondo de Raimond, in his robe of crimson damask 'with a most rich collar, full of great pearls and many other jewels in four rows, and in his bonnet a pear-shaped pearl, which seemed to me something rich'. As this dignitary came into a small, tapestry-hung hall Henry, upright, was waiting for him, resting against a tall, straight-backed chair, beautifully gilded and draped with cloth of gold. Magnificent in a gown of violet lined with cloth of gold and with a collar of miniver, the King listened attentively to the pompous address in Latin delivered by his guest, but did not once take his seat. Later, the ambassador visited the handsome Queen, whom he found dressed in cloth of gold at one end of another great hall.

Finally, the King embarked upon a royal progress through Cirencester, Malmesbury, Bath and Wells. His wealth at this stage had increased to such an extent that the Milanese ambassador estimated it at £6,000,000. His personal bodyguard did not number more than one hundred men even when, as at Woodstock, he lived in a palace lacking formal defences and situated in the heart of thickly wooded country. His favourite residences at this period were still Greenwich and Sheen.

[7]

Warbeck had anticipated being met in Cork by James, Earl of Ormond, now openly hostile to Henry, but Ormond had been killed shortly before in a quarrel with Sir Piers Butler. John Walter and his son received him in his stead, but although Warbeck once more raised his standard as 'King Richard IV', he received little popular encouragement. Poynings, who had returned to Ireland in the early part of 1496, had the country well in hand. Though the Pretender was joined by an old campaigner, Don Pedro de Guevara, a Spaniard, Kildare and Desmond, whose aid was essential, were now submissive to England and too scared to foster his attempt. At the end of four vain and profitless weeks he was deeply discouraged, but at this moment, messages came from Cornwall, still seething, to the effect that he had only to land there and they would rally round him to a man. This seemed his most profitable course, and he decided to set sail at once.

Between them the Walters obtained a boat and hurried him to Kinsale, where three Vizcayan trading ships were lying. De Guevara may have persuaded the San Sebastian captain of one of them to give Warbeck passage to Cornwall, for when ready these merchantmen left harbour with him aboard one. Having learned of this plan through spies, Waterford notified the King, on whose orders they now despatched seven fast armed vessels to seize the Pretender. Catching up with the Spaniards, they halted them, searched them thoroughly, but without result. The sailors had hidden Warbeck in an empty wine cask, and stoutly denied his presence on board although they could have gained 1,000 marks reward by betraying him.

On the 7th September, Warbeck landed safely at Whitsand Bay near Land's End on the south-western tip of Cornwall. On the advice of his supporters, among whom were a mercer wanted for debt, a tailor and a 'scrivener' or notary, he made his way to Bodmin at the head of about one hundred and forty men, mostly Irish, who had traversed heavy ground and marshes to get there. An array of 3,000 'rude people assembled' cheered him warmly, and delivering the usual address, he attacked Henry and his Council, declaring himself 'King Richard IV'.

A council of war advised him to seize some fortified city to serve as both assembly and jumping-off point for an advance on London. This would also be a rich prize for the hungry Cornishmen, thirsting for revenge and loot. Furthermore, if he lost an engagement he could always shut himself up within its walls until relieved by well-wishers outside. Exeter was suggested as the most suitable place.

The Cornishmen were not in the least grateful for their royal pardons, many of which they had sold for 12d. or 2s. each, and sneered that the King had let them go free only because if he hanged all those in England who agreed with them, few would be left. Flocking to Warbeck's standard at Bodmin they marched on Exeter under his leadership. According to a Milanese report, he displayed three standards, one showing a little boy emerging from a tomb, one a boy issuing from a wolf's mouth, and a third a red lion. The little boys represented the Wisdom of Man about to defeat the enemy.

He left his wife at Penrhyn, and arrived at the gates of the city at 10 p.m. on the 17th September. Everywhere the Devonians had welcomed him, providing supplies to his hungry army, who had therefore no need to rob and steal.

[8]

The King was not displeased that Warbeck had landed in England, believing he could now dispose of him once and for all. Having had ample warning, he promptly proclaimed rewards for all who helped to defeat this troublemaker. Men came in fast to the assembly point at Woodstock. Daubeney and Sir Rhys ap Thomas were mustering a relieving force of Gloucester men and Welshmen to march on Exeter, while he himself prepared a more powerful army with which he would shortly join them. Though he had not ordered them to do so, the Earl of Devon and other Devonshire nobles and knights raised their levies and set off at top speed to beat Daubeney's men in the race to relieve the city. The Duke of Buckingham and others also came to Henry with their arms to receive orders. Sir Willoughby de Broke had already departed with the fleet to intercept the rebels if they tried to escape by sea, and to guard against any further landings from Ireland. As Bacon wrote: 'Every saint did help'.

Warbeck at first made no attempt to take Exeter by storm. Finding its gates closed against him, he ordered his men to howl and rage beneath the town walls to frighten the defenders, then addressed the citizens guarding the battlements, urging them to admit and unite with him, and saying he would make their city a second London for being the first to acknowledge him.

His words were ignored, the men of Exeter carrying on with the strengthening of their defences. They could see that their besiegers had no cannon, little strength and no great discipline. After dark, in secret, they sent men down rope ladders or by ropes from the walls with messages to the King that they were stoutly resisting, but urging him to come to their aid as quickly as possible.

All his appeals having failed, Warbeck ordered an assault on the east and north gates. Ladders were swiftly placed at various points against the walls, and while the defenders were throwing back or combating those who mounted them, a picked body risked their lives in a desperate effort to force one of the gates. Having no guns and no special assault devices, they used battering rams of heavy logs, and when these failed to break down the massive timbers, endeavoured to prise them open with crowbars and iron rods.

Still the strong wooden barrier held firm. Time was slipping by, and Warbeck knew that a relieving force could not be far away. He had already lost two hundred men in these abortive attempts, and therefore ordered the gates to be set on fire. Brushwood and other combustible material was set against them. They caught, and the cheering attackers waited impatiently till they were burned sufficiently through to be smashed down, when they would storm over the smouldering remnants and slaughter the defenders they had protected.

Seeing their danger, however, the citizens had not been idle. In their turn they had piled great heaps of logs and timber and whatever else would burn quickly behind each gate, while desperately digging trenches and throwing up earthworks behind each pile. When these had been completed and the moment was opportune, they set the heaps alight so that the attackers bursting through the charred and crumbling gates would be confronted by an impassable ring of fire.

Meanwhile Devon's guns thundered at the besiegers from the town walls, and when the assault came, it was everywhere repulsed, though Devon himself was wounded in the arm by an arrow. Warbeck's men, when at last they surged through the smoking, flaming gates, were forced back by the roaring fires before them, and driven outside the walls again by showers of stones.

Another attempt was made next day, with no more success, and Warbeck asked for a six-hour truce to bury the dead, which was granted. Not daring to risk more lives, he abandoned the siege and made instead for the village of Taunton. His onslaught had failed because his men were untrained in siege warfare, had no or negligible body armour, and knew themselves incapable of withstanding the relieving army his scouts advised him was on its way.

He had not covered many miles before his weary troops, who had left behind four hundred dead and were carrying with them many of the badly wounded, learned that a large body under Daubeney was near at hand, and that the King in person was moving with a second force to take them in the rear. Daubeney was, in fact, already a few miles to the north of Glastonbury.

Warbeck and his followers spent the night at Minet, reaching Taunton on the 19th. What happened next is a matter of doubt. Many writers assert that he slipped away by night from his wretched, unfortunate men, leaving them shamelessly in the lurch. It is more probable, however, as another account suggests, that when he knew the size of Daubeney's force, he put plainly to his council the impossibility of victory, asking their leave to depart so that the enemy should not gain a valuable prisoner. Fully believing his claim to be their king, they agreed.

They eventually clashed with Daubeney's advance guards at Taunton, losing twenty-four men in exchange for a mere handful of his. The thunder of his new guns convinced many of them that their cause was lost, and deserters were numerous. Warbeck stayed with them till the 21st, then departed at 5 a.m. with only three of his friends and a few horsemen. Taking the high road, he came to the river Exe, the bridge over which he found cut, so that he was compelled to change course and turn rightwards into the New Forest, hoping perhaps to reach Southampton and find a ship either there or off the coast.

Daubeney, discovering that he had flown, sent a few hundred horsemen after him, but they failed to overtake him, and he reached Beaulieu Abbey in Hampshire, where he took sanctuary. When at last his pursuers came up, they mounted guard over the abbey to prevent his escape, as was now their right.

Those Cornishmen who had not already fled remained behind in Taunton, having sworn not to abandon the 'King' while a drop of blood remained in their veins, but realizing this was useless, they left the village at 3 a.m. hoping to get away undetected. Daubeney was on the watch, however, and they were quickly surrounded. Their leaders surrendered, 'holdyng up their hands in asking mercy, offering and promising him' their loyalty and submission. The ringleaders alone were taken into custody, the King once again allowing these deluded and miserable men—miners and ploughmen for the most part, more used to 'the spade and the shovell' than to arms—to go home. The ringleaders, on the other hand, were put to death in Exeter 'in sacrifice to the citizens whom they had put in fear and trouble'.

A troop was sent post-haste to St. Michael's Mount in Cornwall, in the castle of which the Lady Catharine had taken refuge a little earlier. The reason for this swift move was that she might be pregnant. A male child of Warbeck's could mean a future Pretender to trouble Henry's own sons. She was captured and conducted to Exeter by Robert Southwell, who on the 15th October was granted £7 13s. 4d. for the horses, saddles, etc., he had used for this purpose.

[9]

Warbeck, having disguised himself in the garb of a priest to make his escape, soon saw the attempt would be futile, for the King's men had ringed the abbey and were constantly on watch. Called upon to yield himself up and placing his trust in the King's mercy he agreed after a brief parley, emerging with his three companions—Hero, Skelton and Ashley. All four were carried back to Taunton. In Wales his captor is said to have been Sir Rhys ap

Thomas again, but the Welsh are not always to be trusted where their heroes are concerned.

The King, who had once again played no part in the fighting, came into the village from Wells on the 4th October, and on the following day Warbeck was ushered into his presence. Kneeling, the Pretender humbled himself and confessed his crime. The King, observing his intelligence and good speech, told him to rise and treated him with courtesy. Having been dressed in cloth of gold, the Pretender was taken to Exeter in the wake of the monarch, who presented his own sword to the Mayor of the city to be carried before him on all future occasions. Warbeck's noble wife was brought to the King, and in her presence her husband repeated his confession.

Where ladies of high birth were concerned Henry was a 'gentleman'. He was not only gracious and kind to the unfortunate young Scotswoman, but gave her £20 and issued instructions that she was to be escorted to Sheen and lodged there as a member of the Queen's household. Catharine was known as 'The White Rose' because of her dignity and beauty, and for years afterwards was so-called by the common people.

With her 'sad matrons and gentlewomen' she was sent to London, and abandoning her married name reverted to that of Gordon. On the 1st December she was allowed a small pension or 'dole' of £2, her clothing being provided free by the King. Her later history is interesting. She remained in the Queen's service for eleven years, then during the reign of Henry VIII married James Strangways, a gentleman usher of the Chamber. Henry VII had settled on her in 1510 some estates in Berkshire once the property of the Earl of Lincoln, on condition that she did not return to Scotland or enter any foreign land. When she married Strangways, she gave up some of this property, a new grant of similar character being made in 1512 to her husband, or to Catharine if she survived him. In 1517 she became a widow for the second time, and was immediately given Lincoln's Berkshire property on the original condition. Barely a month afterwards she married Sir Matthew Cradock, and settled in Wales with her third husband. Cradock, an influential man of Glamorganshire, had not been knighted, but had won the regard of Henry VIII by providing a 240-ton warship bearing his own name for the navy, with a complement of one hundred and ninety-five men and under Cradock's own command. After his death in 1531, Catharine married *yet* again, this time Christopher Ashton of Fyfield, near Abingdon. She must have been a woman of considerable charm. She lived till 1537, and in Herbert's Chapel in Swansea Church effigies of her and Cradock are shown, but in fact her interment took place in Fyfield Church, where 'Lady Gordon's Monument' will be found.

[10]

The repentant Devonians threw themselves on the King's mercy, coming in each day 'in their shirts, the foremost . . . having halters about their necks', and were treated as leniently as the Cornishmen, but many wealthy men in Devon and neighbouring counties who had assisted or supported the rebels were heavily fined, no less than £13,000 passing into the King's coffers as a result. Sir Amyas Pawley and Robert Sherburne were the chief collectors of these fines.

While in custody in Exeter Warbeck in a letter to his mother finally and effectively revealed the truth about himself. 'I am your son and no other,' he wrote. 'I left you with Berlo to go to Antwerp. You wept when you said goodby, and my father took me as far as the Mavis gate.' He begged her to send him money, possibly to bribe his warders.

When Henry returned to London Warbeck went with him. From Lambeth they were carried on the 27th November by barge. Warbeck was then taken on horseback through Candlewick Street and Cheapside to Westminster, where he was called upon to repeat to the Mayor and his council, as well as to eighty citizens wearing their liveries, his confession of false pretences.

The following day, at his own command, no triumphal greeting awaited Henry when he came from Westminster by way of the Borough High Street to London. Modestly he explained that he had not deserved any such reception, having merely subdued a mob of rustics. His own city rapscallions rushed after him to gape at Warbeck.

Warbeck, though lodged in the Palace of Westminster, was not allowed to sleep with his wife. Henry was determined he should have no chance to beget an heir. Each day he was taken on horse-back through the streets of the city and exposed to the common view. The lords who conducted him subjected him to open ridicule, while the London louts swarmed round, hooting, jeering, taunting, cursing, reproaching, commenting on his looks, staring rudely into his face and expressing scorn and contempt. Through Cheapside and Cornhill he came to the Tower, then returned to the Palace of Westminster. Behind him rode a man in chains, a sergeant farrier, who had deserted the King's service, joined Warbeck, served on his council, and when his leader took sanctuary, put on monk's dress, posing as a hermit until caught, being executed at Tyburn on the 4th December.

Meanwhile the Queen, at Walsingham, learning that Henry was returning victorious to London, re-entered the city, being welcomed at Bishopsgate by the Mayor and his aldermen on fine horses. They escorted her to the King's Wardrobe at Blackfriars, where she spent the night, moving thence to Sheen to receive the Lady Catharine and formally welcome her into her service.

The great strength of Warbeck's position and its awkwardness from the King's point of view was that technically he was a *foreigner*. Consequently, his actions could not be legitimately regarded as treasonable. He was therefore treated with surprising restraint, and allowed to remain at Court. His confinement was by no means close, for he rode out on horseback each day for exercise. The King appeared to ignore and almost forget him.

Henry, steadily pouching 500,000 ducats a year, was now being courted by all. Warbeck's surrender had made life easier for him by removing one of the most effective weapons his enemies abroad possessed. Foreign ambassadors reported to their masters: 'The kingdom of England has never for so many years been so obedient to its sovereign,' and 'the kingdom is perfectly stable.' They praised Henry's knowledge of affairs in their countries, his wisdom and his wealth.

Every nation wished England to remain internally strong so that she should continue to be a powerful ally. Now that she was a member of the 'Holy League', the Spanish King in particular was anxious to bind her to him, wanting no hitch in the marriage of his daughter to Prince Arthur. He also favoured the proposed union between Princess Margaret, Henry's daughter, and James IV of Scotland.

[11]

Success would have left the King serene and content but for a calamity. The Surrey countryside was suddenly alarmed by billowing smoke, rolling and fraying out over the trees and meadows, the farmhouses and villages. Flames leaped high into the air and tossed gobbets of orange into the rising wind. There was a stench of burning, and the scamper of hurrying feet. Men looking out of their cottage windows saw that the splendid royal palace of Sheen had caught fire and was fiercely burning.

The Palace had recently been extended by the Prior of Sheen at Henry's cost, but by the time the last few flames of a charred and smouldering mass had died down it had been burned to the ground, together with most of its expensive furniture and rich draperies and the large library Henry had collected. The ancient manor house was gone for ever.

The King at once gave orders for the construction of a completely new palace, which was put in hand. Taking four years to construct, it was not occupied till 1501, the former palace having perished on the 21st December, 1497. When finished, it was so extensive that it covered some ten acres. Henry would not repeat the original name, which he disliked, christening it instead the Palace of Richmond, Richmond being his own name when he won the crown. The name has persisted, but the palace no longer exists, except for an old gateway in the west corner of Richmond Green which still carries the King's arms and forms part of a Gateway House. Here, on the Green, tournaments, contests and pageants were held throughout the reign.

The discovery of the New World by Columbus and John Cabot, as well as the continental trade on which so much of his realm's prosperity depended, had led Henry to interest himself increasingly in maritime matters. He perceived at last that there was indeed treasure in the New World which might be his. In March, 1498, he authorized and backed a second voyage by Cabot, and as an investment which he hoped would yield good profit, allotted sums of money to those who sailed with him. This expedition, unfortunately, met with no success, and some maintain that Cabot died at sea with it, though this has never been proved and is disputed. At all events his failure put America temporarily out of the King's mind, all the more because the Spaniards, regarding the New World as their own, resented the English voyages and suspected Henry's intentions.

In February Prince Arthur's betrothal to Princess Catharine was celebrated at Woodstock and ratified in due course by Ferdinand and Isabella at Alcalà.

The Cornishmen and Devonians were still paying dearly and slowly, if at all, for their pardons, some being still in default $3\frac{1}{2}$ years from the date of their rising. The Irish town of Waterford was recompensed for the display of loyalty she had made by being granted special privileges.

About this time the Pope issued condemnations of certain men reported to him as having poisoned grain waiting to be brewed and the brew itself, and publicly declared the King under the protection of the eternal Lord.

A third son, Edmund, was born to the King in March, while as the result of an accident, Charles VIII of France died on the 7th April, 1498. Anne, his wife, immediately set off for Brittany and once more assumed the title of Duchess. She even introduced a new coinage there. The new King of France, Louis XII, that same Duke of Orleans who had been so unruly and cunning in her province, now divorced his wife, and to ensure permanent hold on Anne's territory, himself married the widowed girl, recognizing her as Duchess of Brittany. By right of a female ancestor, he also claimed the Duchy of Milan.

Immediate alarm was felt in Europe. The new king's reputation as a wily, unreliable man was known, and although the 'Holy League' had not collapsed when Ferdinand signed his armistice of February, 1497, or when Henry signed his own, disturbing tremors ran through the edifice of trust it had built.

An important advance was made in the April of this year, for Philip of Burgundy invited the English to a conference at Bruges to discuss the trade situation. No agreement was reached, but a further meeting in London was to be held.

CHAPTER TWELVE

The Infanta Comes

[1]

AT THAT PERIOD things were bad again in Ireland. Continual fighting between the clans took place and showed no signs of coming to an end. The injury and destruction caused by these conflicts were weakening the economic life of the island. Crops were scanty, cattle infected with disease and feeble, and good land lay untilled for lack of men, money and energy. The inhabitants had become politically apathetic, striving only to keep themselves alive, yet were still expected to send the King of England his annual cash tribute. However, his rule was not excessively harsh and as he was, on the whole, cautious and just, no concerted revolt took place, however much the hatred of alien authority might slumber in the areas outside the Pale and sometimes within it.

The Irish having been subdued, the manners and customs of the English were imposed upon them. They were compelled to wear English clothes and carry English arms. Wealthy Irish families could no longer ride barebacked, but had to adopt the saddle 'after the English fashion'. This applied, of course, only to those living inside the Pale. Those outside it were still regarded as barbarians. The dress and habits of the 'civilized Irish' were designed to differentiate them as much as possible from these untutored, primitive dwellers in the bogs and mountains, with whom all trade was prohibited, horses having to be sold exclusively to the English, and none to the natives.

In May, 1498, the King obtained £5,000 from the city of London in exchange for certain privileges, and during the year the drawbridge of London Bridge was made higher so that the King's new warships could pass safely under it.

Although Warbeck's confession had been printed by royal order and distributed throughout England, the Pretender, having tasted adulation and notoriety, craved for more of this insidious drug. By some means, possibly bribery, he eluded his two keepers, who slept one on each side of him in the Wardrobe, and getting through a window, escaped at midnight on the 9th June, 1498, 'without any reason' except a passionate desire for freedom and the faint hope that all was not yet lost. He intended to ride to the coast and take ship for the Continent, but his absence being quickly detected, all roads were promptly watched, and men set out on horseback in pursuit of him. Losing heart, he gave up the attempt, and took sanctuary once more at the Carthusian monastery of Sheen, where he threw himself upon the mercy of the Prior, imploring him to intercede with the King for his pardon.

Although many advisers urged Henry to hang him, the King was not vindictive, granting Warbeck his life, though not letting him go scot-free. On the 15th a scaffold was constructed out of 'pipes and hogsheads' and the Pretender was set in the pillory, first in the courtyard of the Palace of Westminster, where he stood for most of the morning, then, on the 18th, in the stocks at the Cross in Cheapside, where he sat from 10 a.m. to 3 p.m. At both points he was made to repeat his Taunton confession and to endure the insults, vituperations and peltings of the vulgar. This done, he was taken to the Tower and imprisoned in a cell so dark 'that he sees neither sun nor moon, in such fashion that he will never, with God's help, be able to play such another trick again'.

This close confinement visibly affected his health, and when he was shown to the ambassadors from Flanders in July, they thought he had not long to live. Yet even now this high-spirited young man was to trouble the waters. It was later rumoured that the leniency of his treatment and the negligence of his original guards were deliberate so that he might be caught in the act of escaping and executed, but this is improbable.

The traders from Flanders had come to London with the Bishop of Cambrai at their head to carry on the negotiations begun at Bruges, but again nothing was decided, and the delegates were courteously dismissed.

Henry now turned back to his European problems. Not having

15—H VII

made war on France, he as well as his officials were continuing to draw their pensions from that country. Charles's death had, however, created a new situation. The King believed there might be uprisings against Louis XII, and through the Spanish ambassador, De Puebla, hinted to Ferdinand and Isabella that he might raise an army with a view to invading France and recovering England's former French provinces. Hearing of this, Maximilian lost no time in urging him to seize the opportunity and launch an attack without delay. Henry was too old a hand now and too wise to be jockeyed into once more pulling Maximilian's chestnuts out of the fire for him. Sardonically, knowing the man, he replied that he would prefer to see the Emperor himself make the first move, 'but only by way of witnessing his wonderful feats', he ironically intimated. This, of course, Maximilian dared not attempt without much more support than he could then muster.

[2]

The Antwerp traders having removed the offensive duty on English cloth in July, the English traders returned to that city, receiving a magnificent welcome amid collective delight expressed in the usual manner. Despite this there was still no final trade treaty, but a new conference was planned to be held in Calais early in the following year.

Alarming events had been taking place in Europe. On the 5th August, 1498, Ferdinand had shattered the 'Holy League' by signing a treaty of peace with Louis XII, known as the Treaty of Marcousis. At the same time, Maximilian, following suit, took away his army. This led Henry himself to draw a little closer to the French, to which he was all the more inclined as the Venetians had also come to terms with Louis. Nevertheless, no disaster followed. The Dowager Duchess Margaret of Flanders wrote to him expressing regret for her support of Warbeck, begging his forgiveness and promising to have no more truck with rebels. There was an easing of tension everywhere, as if a shadow had passed.

[3]

The League of the Hanse was still at odds with the King, who, irritated by their grumbles and complaints, suggested that they discuss their grievances with his representatives at Antwerp in June. The Hanse men arrived, and were asked to show their authority to undertake firm treaty obligations. This they could not do, and sent to Lübeck for it in a great hurry, but the English emissaries, either weary of dawdling in the Flemish port or to show their lack of enthusiasm for the meeting, went home before Lübeck's consent had been received.

In retaliation for the Hanse's too vocal protests, the King set out to capture their trade in those areas they monopolized. He made overtures to Danzig and once more to Riga in the Baltic, which had become almost a private lake for the League. Danzig refused his terms, but Riga made a pact with him, so breaking the closed circle linking the Hanse towns.

Finally, in November, 1498, at a conference in Westminster, the Hanse conceded that the Treaty of Utrecht should be interpreted as the King wished. The new agreement was to be ratified by both parties in Calais within five months. Further bickering and bargaining went on for some time, however, Henry refusing to give way. It seemed as if the agreement would be cancelled, but although a compromise was reached in the end, the King never quite broke the Hanse hold on northern trade, though he gave them many bad moments.

The new conference with the Burgundian traders began in Calais in March.

[4]

Once more internal troubles disturbed the King. In the early part of the year, Father Patrick, an Augustinian friar from Suffolk, having learned no lesson at all from the fate of Richard Simons and Lambert Simnel, persuaded his best pupil, Ralph Wulford, a London shoemaker's nineteen-year-old son, to play the part of the imprisoned Earl of Warwick. Wulford's father lodged at 'The Bull' in Bishopsgate, but his son's personation began in Kent, where it met with no success, the conspiracy being discovered almost as soon as it was born. The youth was hanged in his shirt on Shrove Tuesday, the 12th February, 1499, at St. Thomas a

Watering, and dangled from the gibbet for four days. Patrick, after torture, was imprisoned for life.

This affair was probably instigated by someone near or dangerous to the King, for he was alarmed to a degree one would have thought absurd but for what followed. Henry came, in fact, to the dark and bitter conclusion that he had blundered in keeping Warwick alive in the Tower. While ever he lived, the fanatical Yorkists and the ambitious priests would give him no peace.

In the following month he went, it is said, to a soothsayer who had earlier predicted the deaths of Edward IV and Richard III, to ask when and in what way he himself would die. Answer was made that throughout 1499 he would be in great peril from plots and treason. Although ordered to keep this conversation secret, the soothsayer babbled to a friend, and it leaked out. When one to whom the story had been told revealed it and was imprisoned, the soothsayer and his friend made themselves scarce.

Coming on top of Warbeck's attempted escape, the new personation appeared to the King to confirm the soothsayer's prediction. This, however, is not why he later punished Warwick. What is true is that de Ayala, Spanish envoy at his Court, remarked that the King had come to look twenty years older in a single fortnight and had grown exceedingly pious, listening to sermons each day of Lent.

Henry was rendered uneasy again by the flight of Edmund de la Pole, Earl of Suffolk, who one day in the summer of 1499 left the country without permission and by way of Calais and Guines joined the Dowager Duchess Margaret in Flanders. This Earl was the younger brother of the Earl of Lincoln, supporter of Lambert Simnel, who had been slain at Stoke. Suffolk, a Yorkist, had nevertheless fought well at Blackheath in 1497 against the Cornishmen, but in 1498 had killed a man in a fit of temper, and been convicted by the King's Bench instead of the Star Chamber. The King pardoned him; nevertheless, he resented what he regarded as a humiliation, and as Edmund was legally heir to both his brother's estates and his claim to the succession, Henry could not regard his departure to Flanders with equanimity, for it smelled of disaffection. He sent Sir Richard Guildford and Richard Hatton to the Archduke Philip to meet the Earl at Guines, near Calais, which was

English, and persuade him to return, having also put his spies to work and ordered a careful look-out to be kept at the ports for any hostile fleet with Suffolk in command.

They were successful in obtaining the Earl's return. In September the fugitive came back, and was in no way penalized for his flight, though since it had been without his sovereign's permission it was a punishable offence. He had indeed crossed into foreign territory at St. Omer after a month in Guines Castle as guest of the Governor, Sir James Tyrell. Soon afterwards, a strange character, Sir Robert Curzon, gave up the captaincy of Hammes Castle near Calais and went into Tournai, to join the Court of Margaret of Burgundy. It is believed that he was sent there to spy for the King.

As arranged, a further trade conference with the Burgundians took place in May, and a settlement of their differences was reached at last. The King had won the right to sell gold or wrought noble metals in Flanders and to sell English cloth duty-free. The agreement rankled with the Burgundians, however, and led to a political coldness.

Henry was eager to conclude the marriage of Prince Arthur to Catharine of Aragon. On Whit Sunday, the 19th May, 1499, after Mass at about 9 a.m., the Spanish ambassador, de Puebla, acting as proxy for the young Princess, met Arthur at his country residence at Bewdley in Worcestershire. In the presence of the Bishops of Lincoln, Coventry and Lichfield, in the Chapel of the Manor House, each laid his right hand in the other's, exchanged vows, and declared that Arthur and Catharine were now man and wife.

Richard de la Pole, Suffolk's brother, the Prince's chamberlain and a Knight of the Garter, was at the ceremony. The two young people now wrote their first dutiful letters to each other, expressing love, yearning and the hope of frequent messages, yet they had never seen one another.

[5]

There was trouble again on the Scottish border, always turbulent, while James IV was hypersensitive and irritable. Some of his lairds came over the Tweed on two successive days, ostensibly as sightseers, to look at Norham Castle. They 'made merry' with the garrison, but their being fully-armed suggested that their explanation of having come merely for an outing was untrue. When challenged to explain themselves, the Scots, standing on their dignity, refused with some show of temper, possibly telling their questioners to mind their own business. Their continual peering at the castle walls soon led to their being accused of spying; high words and a brawl followed in which they were severely mauled, some being wounded and others killed. They fled back over the river, demanding vengeance.

James sent heralds with an indignant remonstrance to the King, grumbling to his courtiers that 'by sweet St. Ninian' one could not trust an Englishman. Annoyed by this breach of the truce, Henry undertook to inquire into the disturbance and punish his men if they were to blame, sending Bishop Fox, his experienced negotiator, to do what was necessary.

Fox quickly put himself on the right side of the Scottish King, who invited him to Melrose Abbey, home of the Cistercians, where he was then in residence. James accepted Fox's declaration that Henry sincerely wished to keep peace, and before the Scottish council the Bishop apologized for the brawl at Norham.

James privately inquired of him what was the surest means of ensuring good relations with England, and Fox seized this opportunity to revive the plan that James should marry Princess Margaret, then but nine years old. On his return, the Bishop advised Henry to replace the truce by a firm treaty of peace and proceed with the betrothal. At first reluctant, the King finally agreed, and the truce was replaced in July, 1499, by a treaty of peace to endure while either King lived and for at least twelve months after the death of the survivor. No Englishman was to enter Scotland and no Scot to enter England without royal permission from the country entered. This proviso was designed to seal off the border. Furthermore, on the 11th September a commission was appointed to arrange the marriage ceremony.

[6]

Warbeck's friend, Thomas Astwood, pardoned in 1495, had been appointed one of his jailers. On the 2nd August, 1499, he and another man, Robert Claymound, who may also have been a jailer, met the Earl of Warwick in his prison chamber and offered to help him claim the throne of England as the legitimate Yorkist successor to the Princes murdered in the Tower. They would bribe servants, murder Sir Simon Digby, Lieutenant of the Tower, steal his keys, raid the royal treasury and explode the powder store of the Tower artillery, so causing fire and chaos. In the confusion all three would slip away, take horse with as many gems and coins as they could carry, find a ship and sail to Flanders, where they would hide until the hue and cry had died down. Then they would use their wealth to suborn as many as possible in England to join them.

Claymound was obviously the leading figure in all this, but we do not know his true identity or antecedents. The name may have been an alias. Claymound left a short sword with the Earl to use in his own defence, undertaking to remove him and Warbeck and ensure their safety. What followed is fantastic.

Warbeck's dark cell lay directly under the Earl's. Claymound, with Warwick's permission, knocked on his floor to establish communication with Perkin and indicate that something was afoot. Unquestionably Warbeck came to know what was being proposed, and clutched at any straw that might restore his freedom. Warwick, told by Claymound that he would soon be executed whatever happened, thought he might as well seize what chance of freedom he could. Secretly a hole was bored in his cell floor so that he and Warbeck could communicate. According to their later statements, their conversations amounted to little more than greetings and words of comfort. The Earl, a mere innocent in the hands of the worldly Claymound, agreed to give the man a wooden image he possessed, to prove that he was truly concerned in the plot. Claymound explained that this would help him to claim sanctuary in Westminster through Thomas Ward, one of his friends. This claim was necessary, he later declared, because Warbeck had betrayed their proposed escape to the King and given their names.

The story may sound absurd, but stranger transactions occurred in medieval times. Most historians and many chroniclers believe that the plot was a deliberate attempt by the Crown to implicate Warwick and Warbeck together so that they could be accused, the one of high treason, the other of attempted murder, and put to death, but this has not been proved. The plot was evidently discovered or betrayed, for on the 16th November, Warbeck, John Taylor—back from France—and John Waters, the former Mayor of Cork, were all tried in Whitehall before Sir John Sigley, the King's Marshal, and a colleague. Their guilt having been established, they were sentenced to be dragged on hurdles to Tyburn, hanged on a low scaffold, drawn and quartered, with the usual disgusting mutilations. Eight other men were also accused, tried and sentenced, two to be hanged, Astwood being one of them. Warbeck 'took his dethe meekly' and was executed on the 23rd November, at Tyburn, where he once again read out his public confession that he was a foreigner and no prince, and swore to its truth. His body and those of the others were brought to the Augustinian Friary and buried, the heads being set up on the spikes of London Bridge. Bacon was later to write: 'on the first grain of incense sacrificed on the alter of peace at Boulogne, Perkin smoked away'.

The Earl of Warwick was arraigned in the Great Hall of Westminster, the Earl of Oxford as High Constable presiding. He was charged with conspiring with Warbeck to cause sedition and destroy the King. Claymound's 'confession', in which he claimed to have received a cloak and velvet jacket from the Earl, damned the unhappy Warwick, who confessed and was condemned to be beheaded. On the day of execution, the 28th November, he walked out of the Tower between two men to the scaffold on Tower Hill. Afterwards, his body was placed in a coffin and between 2 and 3 p.m. returned to the Tower. When the tide rose it was conveyed up river by barge to Bisham Abbey, near Windsor, and buried beside Warwick's ancestors at a cost, the accounts show, of £13 18s. 3d. After years of incarceration the last of the male Plantagenets was dead. 'Thus,' it was said, 'did the winding ivy of a false Plantagenet kill the true tree itself.'

[7]

From this time onwards a change came over the King. That narrow-chested, ascetic figure of his lost spring and resilience. His self-confidence had been shaken by this plot, and there are indications that he suffered from remorse for his treatment of the young Earl, which had brought him a temporary unpopularity with his people, a further source of distress.

The soothsayer had scared him, the executions had troubled his conscience, the latest revelations had worried him, and the moves taking place on the European chessboard were intricate and alarming. Some of his wise and statesmanlike tolerance now deserted him. Moreover, he was over forty, which in medieval times was almost middle age. He knew only too well from symptoms that showed themselves that he was not the man he had been. He may even have felt his physical powers waning and seen the dark hull of death coming up on the horizon. All these things occurring together may have accounted for his savage reactions and his 'touchiness' in the following months.

For example, he was at loggerheads with the Flemings again over new duties they had imposed on English cloth, but on the other hand the Spaniards were rejoicing at Warwick's death, which they said, meant that 'no doubtful drop of royal blood' remained in England. The young Prince Arthur, betrothed to the Infanta Catharine, could now have no legitimate rival.

In later days Henry, it is said, was inclined to blame Ferdinand for Warwick's execution. The Spaniard, he argued, seeing first one man, then another, strive to throw him down, had feared his hold on the crown might not be strong enough to guarantee the succession to his son, and had continually impressed upon him the danger of allowing the Earl to live, until he had felt compelled to act on his advice.

[8]

A new century was on the way. It led to a general assessment of Henry's reign and character as so far manifested. One chronicler wrote: 'from the time of William the Conqueror . . . no King has reigned more peaceably than he has; his great prudence caused him to be universally feared . . . His crown is unassailed and his rule strong in every respect.' According to Polydore Vergil the King himself wished that 'he might not wrongly be called a ruler, but be one who would rule and not be ruled'.

Prince Arthur being now fifteen, there seemed no reason why the Infanta of Spain should not come to England, the betrothal treaty having specified that her departure should be deferred only till the Prince's fifteenth birthday.

For England the new century had dawned in radiance and hope. Whatever his private feelings, Henry was now one of the most experienced kings in Europe. Faction was virtually dead. Peace reigned everywhere, no potentate threatening England with war. The King was about to bind two royal families to him by marriages.

Nevertheless, no year but has brought its troubles. This time, in 1500, it was the 'sweating sickness' again, which broke out first in London, then throughout England.

Concerned for his and the Queen's safety, Henry moved from one residence to another, then made an unexpected departure with his spouse to Calais to receive an anticipated embassy from Philip of Burgundy. They landed on the 3rd May. Philip, who was at St. Omer, had arranged to meet them on the 9th June outside the town in St. Peter's Church, which no longer exists, and which stood on English soil, the Archduke not being willing to trust himself to the English within the fortress walls. With the royal pair were the Duke of Buckingham, the Earls of Surrey, Suffolk and Essex, Lord Daubeney—at that period Lord Lieutenant of Calais—the Bishop of London, Lord Burgavenny, Lord Dacre, Lord William of Suffolk and his cousin, Richard de la Pole, and Lord Zouch. The Archduke, knowing he had blundered in backing Warbeck, did his best to regain Henry's friendship, making to hold his stirrup as he alighted, which Henry would not allow, and embracing him with every appearance of goodwill, which Henry reciprocated. All dined at the church, which had been draped with cloth of arras for the occasion, while to split up the various 'committees' or 'offices' into convenient sections for their discussions, the interior had been partitioned, again by hangings or screens of arras cloth.

Such a glitter of nobles would not have come together but for the weighty deliberations anticipated. Indeed, when Ferdinand learned of the conference he was distinctly alarmed, suspecting that the King was secretly planning to give the Infanta Catharine the go-by and affiance Prince Arthur to a daughter of the Archduke.

The discussions were protracted and serious. When they were over, a gorgeous banquet was served, followed by dancing, the Archduke honouring the English ladies by taking them as his partners. (Next day the remains of the feast were distributed to the local inhabitants.) After this he bade the company goodbye, mounted his horse and rode back to Gravelines. The general result of the meeting was the revival of the original trade treaties and the removal of the fetters on commerce between the two states. It was also proposed that marriages should be arranged between Prince Henry of England and Philip's daughter, Margaret, and between his son, Charles, four months old, and Princess Mary of England.

The royal party did not leave Calais till the 16th June, and landed at Dover. Almost certainly they returned because of the death of the King's third son, the infant Edmund, born in the March of the previous year, who had died on the 12th June. He may have been a victim of the 'sweating sickness', prevalent again, though his death took place at the mansion of the Bishop of Ely at Hatfield.

On the 22nd his body was carried back to London through Fleet Street. The Duke of Buckingham acted as chief mourner, and in the funeral cortège were many nobles. The Mayor and representatives of all the crafts, arranged in strict order of precedence, lined the street as the bier passed to Westminster, where the prince was buried at the shrine of St. Edward the Confessor.

[9]

The French, still eager to keep on good terms with England, sent the Governor of Picardy and the Bailiff of Amiens to pay Henry their respects and notify him that he had greatly strengthened his position in Europe and their own country's as well. The King reported this courtesy with pride to the city fathers of London, whose favour he sought and cultivated, without, as Bacon remarks, achieving the affability of Edward IV, nor, one may add, that monarch's intimacy with the wives of these worthy men.

The year was marked by a Jubilee in Rome, and the Pope was making great play with 'Indulgences'—remissions before God of the temporal punishment for those sins forgiven in the Sacrament of Penance. At this period these remissions were regarded as of great financial value because they could be sold, the money going towards the construction of St. Peter's in Rome. His Holiness now sent a Papal Nuncio, Gaspar Pons, to distribute them to those in England who, unable to visit Rome, would make a compensating payment to cover what their visit would have cost. These particular monies were to go towards a crusade against the infidel Turks, who, having crushed the Venetians, were threatening to extend the Ottoman Empire in Europe. The Nuncio also brought a plea from his master that the King should lead an army to this crusade and send a strong fleet to join the Venetians in taking Constantinople.

Henry had no objection to the papal sale of indulgences, but was by no means enamoured of the crusade, saying Turkey was too far off and the crusade would cost him too much. In any event, he added, his warships were not big enough and he had no pilots for those distant waters. Even if the Turks came into Italy he would not lose any sleep. However, he gave the Nuncio £4,000 towards the cost, having first asked Ferdinand of Spain whether the money was likely to be embezzled in Rome. Some who bought indulgences maintained that Henry took a commission on their sale, but this was untrue.

Henry's gift to the Papal Nuncio brought him the title of 'Protector' of the Order of the Knights of Rhodes, occupants of a great fortress on the island of that name who had firmly held an area of the Mediterranean against the infidels.

Money for the Pope's war did not all come out of the King's own pocket. The Prior of Canterbury, for example, was called upon to pay a tax of $\frac{1}{10}$, but compounded this by a down payment of £12,000. A similar lump sum was obtained from York. After handing over his £4,000, doubtless with much reluctance, the King said he hoped to hear no more of the crusade. This hope was, however, unfulfilled. Throughout the waning year he was badgered by the Venetians and the Hungarians with requests for money and men, but refused to listen to their envoys, snapping that they would do better to make peace with the Turks than war, but in the end he grudgingly sent money to King Ladislaus of Hungary, though he took his time about it. Ships and men, however, he refused once more to send.

The months went by, but still the auburn-haired Princess

Catharine of Spain did not set out for England. The King, nagged by new anxieties—his overriding superstitious fear of death, his haste to establish his son in an impregnable position—began to agitate for her departure, making the excuse that she would need time to learn both the English language and the English mode of life, though the Queen would have preferred her to learn French first, which would be easier for her. The ladies of the English Court, she pointed out, spoke neither Latin nor Spanish, the only two languages the Infanta knew. The King suggested that Catharine should bring in her train wellborn ladies only, with good looks. He wanted, he told his intimates, no ugly faces at *his* Court. The number of servants Ferdinand proposed she would bring seemed to him excessive, especially as he would, if the Spanish King had his way, have to pay their wages himself.

There were reasons for Catharine's continued delay. First, Ferdinand was suspicious that Henry was planning an alternative bride for his son, then he was disturbed by a rising of the conquered Moors at Ronda. Next, the Infanta herself fell ill, and he hesitated to let her risk the long sea voyage to England until she had fully recovered. Henry was therefore forced to agree to a postponement.

[10]

The King now lost one of his right-hand men, the Chancellor, John Morton, Archbishop of Canterbury, who died at the age of eighty at Knole, near Sevenoaks in Kent, on the 12th October, 1500. Morton, a Dorsetshire man, born in 1420, had been educated in Cerne Abbey and at Balliol College, Oxford, where he read law. Coming under the notice of Thomas Bourchier, then Archbishop of Canterbury, he had rapidly climbed the ecclesiastical and political ladders, but when Edward IV came to the throne his fortunes changed. After the battle of Towton, at which he is believed to have been present and at which the Lancastrians were routed, he fled to St. Mighel en Barrois in France, where Henry VI's exiled Queen, Margaret of Anjou, was still holding her Court. Later, making his peace with Edward, he became one of his ablest ambassadors, and even an executor of his will. His later career has already been narrated.

Sir Thomas More had a high regard for him, and in his 'Utopia' drew a character sketch of him in his later years: 'He was of meane' (medium) 'stature, and though stricken in age, yet bare he his body upright. In his face did shine such an amiable reverence as was pleasante to beholde. Gentill in communication, yet earnest and sage . . . In his speech he was fyne, eloquent and pitthye. In the lawe he had profound knowledge, in witte he was incomparable, and in memory wonderful excellente . . . the Kynge put much trust in his counsel, the weale publyque also in a maner learned unto hym, when I was there.'

A practical man of broad outlook he had been responsible when Bishop of Ely for draining the fens between Wisbech and Peterborough, and had also constructed a dyke and waterway to the sea for barges and small craft. It is doubtful if he devised 'Morton's Fork', the discredit for which should, it is said, more properly go to Fox, but he had a reputation for severity and was not easy to approach, which made him enemies among both nobles and populace. Nevertheless, he was a loyal servant of the King, who trusted and respected him.

Though an opponent of the House of York, he had worked hard to quell the strife between the two Houses, was a good speaker and could keep the King's secrets. They had been together in adversity and prosperity alike, and indeed, but for him, Henry might have been even more autocratic and tyrannical, for the Archbishop disliked injustice and was always more of an ecclesiastic than a statesman.

In 1493 Morton had been made a Cardinal on the personal appeal of his sovereign, and two years later became Chancellor of Oxford University. He was buried in the crypt of Canterbury Cathedral.

On the 9th November, the ancient charter of the Merchant Adventurers was confirmed, and thirteen days later another important event took place. At Ludlow Castle Prince Arthur was 'married' to Catharine of Aragon for the third time, the Bishop of Worcester performing the ceremony. This was at the insistence of Ferdinand, still afraid lest his daughter should be jilted in favour of Philip of Burgundy's daughter.

The year faded and died, and 1501 was nearly halfway to the

churchyard when at last, on the 21st May, having recovered from her bout of fever, Catharine left Granada and began her long journey to England. At that date the roads across Spain were barbarous and methods of transport slow, while the summer heat was barely supportable. She did not reach Corunna in her litter till the middle of July. There she waited, either for a ship or for favourable weather. On the 25th August she boarded a vessel bound for Gravesend, though her mother would have preferred Southampton or Bristol as less dangerous harbours. John Paston and others had already been deputed by the King to receive her there. She had not been long afloat when a savage storm tossed her ship wildly hither and yon until, terrified of losing the Princess's life and his own as well, her skipper ran for safety into the harbour of Laredo, south of Corunna, where the Infanta went ashore. Here she had to wait once more, but sailed again on the 27th September, meeting more wind, rain and thunder in Biscay. This time, however, the wind was a following one and drove them not into Gravesend, but into Plymouth, where she landed on the Hoe on the 2nd October, 1501.

Plymouth hated the French, who not long before had savaged and burned the port. They were enchanted by the thought that Spain, that great Christian maritime power, having expelled the Moors, would now be their permanent ally and protector against their neighbours and enemies across the Channel. At the head of her wretched train of seasick maids and men, Catharine walked to the church to offer up thanks for her safe deliverance and successfully accomplished landing. It was crowded with the common people of the town, sating their eyes with the sight of their future Queen. They knew what she had just been through, guessed the terrors and anxieties that must have been hers as she tossed on the seas in her little wooden tub—for that is all it was—and were sorry for her, while recognizing and admiring her courage and royal dignity, visible and preserved, as slender, erect and grave, she came up the aisle to her seat. They loved her at once.

As soon as her arrival was known to be imminent many knights had ridden in to welcome her. She was handed a letter of greeting from Henry himself and her reception was warm and sincere. One of her suite wrote with feminine exaggeration that 'she could not have been received with greater rejoicings than if she had been the Saviour of the World'.

She had been told by her parents to accustom herself to drinking wine because English water was undrinkable, and even if it were not, the climate would make it an impossible liquid for refreshment.

Catharine waited a month to rest and prepare herself before being finally conducted to the Palace of the Bishop of Bath and Wells at Dogmersfield, thirty-five miles from the capital.

[11]

In the Palace of Lambeth the King was busily organizing the festivities and procedure for her anticipated arrival in London. Not until the first few days of November was he ready to set off to receive her. Then he and Prince Arthur with the ministers of state and an escort of some hundreds of armed men rode towards Dogmersfield, only to be met at Winchfield, four miles west of Farnborough in Hampshire, by the Spanish envoy, de Ayala. The Spaniard, having paid his respects to the King, was consulted as to the etiquette to be observed at the forthcoming meeting, and Henry was courteously told that Spanish custom forbade any meeting of the King, Arthur and his betrothed until the day of the wedding.

This touched Henry on a sore spot. That might be the rule in Spain, he said irritably, but Catharine was in *England* now, and would have to learn to do as the English did. He rode off at once, Arthur with him, and arrived at the Bishop's house, into which he strode just as he was without apology. Arthur went off to remove his damp and miry garments and change into clean ones, but the King would not stop even for this, and demanded to see the girl at once, saying: 'I'll see and speak with her even if she were gone to bed.' These words and their peremptory tone indicate clearly that Henry was as much a Tudor as the son who succeeded him. Catharine was compelled to greet him, and after him his son.

Their conversation was halting and awkward, Henry and Arthur speaking English, the Bishop turning their words into dog-Latin, and a priest translating the Latin into Castilian so that Catharine should understand. Arthur seems to have confined himself to comments on dogs and birds.

After resting at Dogmersfield for three further days to recover from her long and trying journey, the Infanta was taken to London. Meantime Henry returned to Richmond and from there to Baynard Castle, where the Queen joined him. He then moved to the King's Wardrobe in the City and lodged there. The Prince returned to the capital with his father.

Catharine was now sixteen years old and her husband-to-be little more than fifteen. Over a coif or close-fitting cap, similar to that worn by a cardinal to hide his tonsure, she wore a hat with a wide brim, and displayed the colours of Spain. She did not actually pass through the city gates, but made on the 9th a detour to Lambeth, where she stayed for a few days, setting out again on the 12th to be ceremonially received by the King. Having traversed London Bridge by way of Southwark, she encountered the habitual pageant, in which representations of St. Catharine and St. Ursula welcomed her with long speeches, and in which many young girls participated. Passing quickly through Bruges Street, she came into Gracechurch Street, where, at its widest point a magnificent mock castle smothered in red and white roses and other decorations, appeared before her. From the walls of this castle poetic eulogies were delivered by figures signifying Policy, Noblesse and Virtue.

The procession now turned into Leadenhall and thence into Cornhill. Here the Princess was greeted by a remarkable mechanical model of the planetary and zodiacal systems, relative motions of which were provided by clockwork. According to the chronicler 'the twelve signs moved off the zodiac and the moon showed her course of light and darkness'. An archangel, St. Raphael, dominated this pageant, and with him were 'Alphonso X of Castile', one of her ancestors, Job and Boetius, all eloquent in verse.

It was much the same in Soper Lane and Cheapside. Here at the 'Sphere of the Sun', opposite to a lane now Queen Street, was a man seated in a chair of gold. This was the legendary King Arthur of Britain. At the Standard in Cheapside was yet another pageant entitled 'The Temple of God', ornamented by an enormous red rose, and tenanted by ancient prophets, among whom the 'Father of Heaven' Himself was represented and even addressed the

Princess. Here the Recorder also addressed her windily on behalf of the citizens of the neighbourhood.

The King and Queen, with a consideration one would hardly have expected of those distant days, did not interfere with this essentially civic occasion, being present merely as unofficial observers from the near-by residence of William Geffrey, a haberdasher of means. With them were courtiers and nobles.

Now came the great moment. The Mayor, aldermen and representatives of the crafts and guilds, came forward on their horses and reverently welcomed Catharine, who was conducted through the rows of mounted dignitaries on both sides of the street to the Conduit at the end of Cheapside. Here the befurred Mayor, Sir John Sha, richly clad, wearing his chain of office, and with the pomp for which he was notorious, presented to her a gift of plate from the City. A final pageant was revealed showing the seven Virtues accompanied by a charming array of virgins dressed in white, who ranged themselves under a series of fine seats, the central one of which was occupied by 'Honour', the others accommodating figures carrying sceptres and coronets as normally held by the Prince and Princess.

On the way she had been joined by Prince Arthur and followed by a grand parade of nobles, knights and esquires. Everything had been done to match the occasion. Indeed, the city seemed to have flowered overnight, being ablaze with banners and streamers. Gaily-coloured silk hangings dangled from windows and swayed in the breeze, while hundreds upon hundreds of cheering folk endured the stench of refuse and the dribbling waters of the narrow, crooked, cobbled streets to shout her name and call down blessings on her head in a language she did not understand. Stands had been erected from Gracechurch Street to St. Paul's. Everywhere were the vivid surcoats of heralds, shining gold chains and sparkling jewels, the gleaming body-armour of escorting soldiers, the rich robes and furs of nobles and their companies, the embroidery worn by the ladies, and the trappings of the horses with their bells and spangles of gold, while the water conduits once more 'ran wine'.

The pageants were the medieval equivalent of such modern spectacles for state occasions as firework displays and the trooping of the colour, and were presented as much for the enjoyment of the populace as for the delectation of the Princess. The 'noises of loud instruments'—trumpet and clarion—were notable on these occasions and as greatly loved and indispensable as the military bands of a modern procession. Grave and self-satisfied scholars mouthed Latin verses from stages erected for the purpose, and little boys piped the translations in thin unbroken voices. However accurate, these were far from poetical.

Throughout her grand parade the Princess, her maids of honour, the nobles and the rest, were entertained also by ballad music produced by the instruments of the period—rebeck, harp, zither and pipe—sounding from every street, until they came finally to the Palace of the Bishop of London, near St. Paul's. Here after a time came, too, the King, the Queen and the King's Mother, the Countess of Richmond. So ended Catharine's glittering memorable day.

Two days later, on the 14th November, 1501, the wedding took place. Already a great concourse had gathered in and around St. Paul's. A huge raised platform specially erected ran out from the west door of the choir. On this the bride and bridegroom, who had been conducted with magnificent display to the cathedral, stood clothed in white satin. The Archbishop of Canterbury celebrated Mass before the high altar, and here, too, assisted by fifteen prelates, he solemnly performed the marriage ceremony. The Prince of Wales publicly declared Catharine's jointure to be one third of the revenues of Wales, Cornwall and Cheshire. When the time came, she was to be treated as earlier Queens of England had been. Thereupon one half of her dowry was carried in in massive chests and handed over by her to the King as an 'act of renunciation'. The other half was to be paid later in two annual instalments, partly in jewels and gold plate. Two Welshmen acted as sponsors for the Prince. After the wedding, Catharine, Prince Arthur and the Spanish ambassador went back to the Palace of the Bishop of London.

Ten days of jousts, feasting and good cheer followed, the first great occasion being a banquet in Westminster Hall given by Henry, who had spent £14,000 on jewels alone for the wedding, and now had his gorgeous, gleaming gold plate placed before the numerous wedding guests, including the Archbishop of Santiago,

Count de Cabra, and the Bishop of Majorca, representatives of Ferdinand and Isabella, to all of whom the King did honour and showed esteem. He and the Queen began the dancing.

During these ten days tournaments in the grounds of Westminster Palace were staged, and in the great Hall, hung with the costliest cloth of Arras, dancing went on hour after hour. On one occasion the King danced in the dress of a Spanish grandee, he and the Queen leading off, followed by Arthur and Catharine. At this affair Prince Henry, finding he could not otherwise move freely enough, flung off his state robe and capered about in his doublet. The company were delighted by this princely informality.

Over this dazzling parade of beauty, colour and graceful movement, through which the notes of music threaded themselves like gold wires, shone a tremendous 'lanthorne' carrying 'a hundred great lites and twelve goodly ladies', which was greatly admired. Various scenes were represented, the most ingenious being, perhaps, a device showing two mountains symbolizing England and Spain, mounted on wheels, united by a chain of gold, and drawn through the streets. One of these mountains was verdant and adorned with a shawl of trees, with rocks cropping out of the sides. Wild beasts appeared and on the summit a lovely maiden sat, head uncovered and hair flowing free. The other was a barren, parched rock from whose flanks issued streams of molten metal, while glimpses of ores and unmined gemstones could be caught. This, too had its attractive occupant. Both maidens sang sweet songs.

There were also imitation mermaids, games of bowls and archery contests at the butts at Richmond, where also the royal party watched with delight the skill of a Spanish acrobat. Indoors the guests played cards, threw dice and went on dancing. The Princess endured the tedium of still more elaborate astral conceits in which she was compared to Hesperus and her husband to Arcturus. Alphonsus, an ancient King, was introduced as a soothsayer who had foretold the marriage. Even King Arthur of Britain was dragged in effigy out of the tomb, so to speak, and a choirboy sang 'sweetly with quaint harmony'.

In charge of all these ceremonies and festivities was Fox, the able Bishop of Durham. All agreed he had done magnificent service, and that Henry had given his daughter-in-law a memorable wedding. In fact, this man, so commonly regarded today as parsimonious, shabby and grudging, was, on the contrary, a great lover of elaborate displays, the sparkle of gems, the rich flowing shimmer of cloth of gold, the brilliant colours and gay fluttering of banners, flags, draperies, and robes. He particularly loved jewels, on which he spent considerable sums, and any opportunity of displaying them. Something in his otherwise austere character needed these occasional splashes of light and colour to offset the monochromatic cares of state.

[12]

After the banquet the young couple returned to their bedroom at Lambeth Palace. In medieval times royal wedding nights were public occasions. Arthur and Catharine cannot have been surprised when they found their room gleaming with the light of many candles and chock-a-block not only with gaudily-clad barons and suave, sonorous priests intoning Romanist prayers and blessings, but also with those whose duty it was to remove the garments of bride and bridegroom till they were mother-naked, anoint their bodies and perfume their skins. Ceremonial demanded that they should kneel at this moment of final revelation, pray, and drain a goblet or bowl of mulled wine, spiced and sweetened.

Even this did not satisfy the Church. The marriage bed itself had to be given a solemn benediction. Only then was the room vacated and the pair left to themselves, knowing all the while that in a chamber beyond, their attendants would pass the night, alert and ready at any moment to obey a summons.

When the festivities had ended, Arthur and Catharine were sent off to Ludlow Castle. Catharine rode there pillion behind her Master of Horse, followed by eleven Spanish ladies of her household mounted on palfreys. Here the Prince kept a Court modelled exactly on that of his father at Westminster. Edward IV had abolished the office of Warden of the Marches, and the Prince's Court was made up of the President and members of his Council. Governor and Treasurer to the Prince was Sir Henry Vernon, who had fought at Bosworth. The Prince nominally guarded the Welsh border. He wrote to Ferdinand and Isabella that he was happy, and promised to be a good husband. He had been given able advisers, and as tutor had the blind Bernard André, one of the few contemporary chroniclers of the reign, though not one of the most trustworthy.

Henry had conceived the plan of letting the young couple *use* the plate and gems Catharine had brought, then writing to Ferdinand that these could not be accepted as part of her dowry, since they were now virtually second-hand goods; but De Puebla protested: 'If the Princess uses all this now, and you afterwards refuse to accept it, my sovereign lords will be ashamed to take from her what she has already used as her own on her person as well as in her household.' (He was referring to her plate, jewels and tapestries.) 'They must then leave it to her, and fulfil their obligations to you.'

Henry understood from this that his son would be entitled to keep for his own use all this rich treasure, while he himself could then claim the equivalent in cash to make up its value, as well as the balance of her dowry. However, when De Puebla demanded first a formal acknowledgement by the King that he accepted these goods at their face value, he smelled a rat.

'I see now there is a crafty design,' he told the Spaniards, 'and I shall not consent that it be attributed to me. I should not like to be held for a person who asks what is due to me before the time. God be praised, I am not in want, and, if it were necessary, I could for love of their highnesses and you, my senora daughter, spend a million of gold without contracting a debt.'

It was partly for this reason that Henry had decided Catharine and Arthur should live at Ludlow Castle, where the Prince could make full use of what his wife had brought with her, thus putting him to no additional expense in furnishings.

CHAPTER THIRTEEN

A Daughter's Dowry

[1]

ALL THIS REJOICING had not lightened the King's spirit. He had not lost courage, but his energy had declined. The signs of incurable disease were showing themselves in a stiffening of his fingers and a bending of his back. He was hoarding not only money, but also relics by which he set great store, such as a piece of the Holy Cross and the leg-bone of a Saint, which figured eventually in his will. He made gifts of money to deserving priests to offer up prayers for his soul. He had an alchemist working for him in the Tower, and is said to have been tormented again by sombre dreams connected with the House of York. He had already shown signs of a sterner, less humane spirit.

There arrived in England during this year a remarkable scholar named Polydore Vergil, who was to write a history of the reign. He came originally to collect 'Peter's Pence', the annual papal tribute of one penny from all who possessed at least thirty pence in the value of their 'quick or live stock'. Becoming a favourite of the King, he decided to stay on and was given high ecclesiastical office, living at the Court. His history was begun when Henry was still alive, and with his approval, and is one of our best sources for the period.

In 1501 also the King appreciated that his original neglect of overseas exploration had lost opportunities for Britain. He now made amends for this by granting Richard Ward, John Thomas, Hugh Eliot and two Portuguese, John Gonzales and Francis Fernandez, permission to go on a voyage of discovery. The merchants of Bristol were also allowed to set up trading posts in newly-discovered lands.

In this year Margaret of Burgundy repudiated the Treaty of Intercursus Magnus and agitated for a new one, and there was also an attempt by the Bakers' Guild to corner the market in bread. Although the price of corn had not markedly increased and there was no shortage, the bakers cut down their output, so producing a shortage of bread in the cities to force up the cost of their loaves. Parliament countered by ordering all guilds to obtain royal permission before issuing by-laws, and to submit themselves to government inspection.

Princess Margaret was now about eleven years old, and not only poor in health, but also far from bright in mind. This was one reason why Henry had not too enthusiastically welcomed the proposal that she should marry James IV of Scotland. Both the Queen and his mother, the Countess of Richmond, believed that marriage and separation from her family might set the child back still further. Moreover, James was so much older than she that they would have a long time to wait before they could be married, the girl being so young, so there could be little genuine affection between them. Would it not be better to affiance her to some younger man, such as the Crown Prince of Denmark? James himself was reported to prefer a daughter of the Emperor Maximilian, another Margaret.

However, the marriage had been agreed upon and Scottish envoys came to London on the 20th November, 1501, to arrange its terms and share in the rejoicings over Prince Arthur's wedding. They were entertained and given by the Mayor a banquet, rendered memorable by a ballad composed on the spot by a Scottish cleric named Dunbar, expressing his affection for that city upon whose 'lusty Brygge of pillars white been merchauntes full royall to behold'. It was, he said, 'the flour of cities all'.

The festivities had still not ended when the year closed, for when all was favourably settled, Henry feasted the Scots magnificently and compelled them to listen to verses singing their praises. On the 24th January, 1501, the treaty of marriage and alliance, consisting of three separate documents, was signed. At Richmond the following day the Earl of Bothwell, as proxy for James, 'married' the Princess, the Archbishop of Glasgow performing the ceremony, which was attended by the usual constellation of 'establishment' and foreign personalities.

According to the treaty she was to go to Scotland on or before the 1st September, 1503. A jointure of £20,000 was promised and her dowry was to be 30,000 English nobles (gold coins worth from 6s. 8d. to 10s. each), to be paid in three yearly instalments, and stop at once if she died within this period or failed to bear a child. James was to provide £1,000 a year for the expenses of her establishment and as part of the agreement, to admit her twenty-four English servants.

The second result of the negotiations was a treaty of alliance whereby each King undertook to assist the other if attacked. Trade between the two kingdoms was to be promoted and the border to be firmly controlled against raids and theft, which would be heavily punished. The peace was to be kept, and in the regrettable event that both Prince Arthur and his brother Henry should die without issue, James was recognized as having a just claim to the kingdom of England.

The 'marriage' was witnessed and celebrated not only by courtiers, but also by the Spaniards, the French, and the representatives of Venice and the Pope. After a fanfare had sounded, the Scottish nobles and plenipotentiaries were entertained to a meal at the King's table. Feasting, jousting and revelry took place. The marriage was proclaimed in St. Paul's and in cathedrals and churches throughout the realm. The bells rang out and bonfires with great casks of wine beside them sent small boys and topers into raptures and normally sober citizens into a seventh heaven. Te Deums were sung, and Henry wrote a description of all this to Ferdinand and Isabella, promising at the same time to be a second father to Catharine. The Scots went back to their native land, this time with legitimate booty—the presents bestowed upon them in parting.

Some feared that if anything happened to the two young Princes, England might come to great harm if a Scottish King acquired the crown, but the King, with his dry wisdom, replied that the greater would absorb the less, and the marriage was therefore safer than one with a French princess.

At twenty-eight James, an amorous King like Edward IV before him, had already had several mistresses. His latest, a beautiful woman, Lady Margaret Drummond, by a curious coincidence, died a strange death in this very year of the marriage. He also had an illegitimate son, Alexander Stewart, by Margaret Boyd, this boy being tutored in 1508 by Erasmus.

[2]

Suddenly, like a cold knife piercing the wineskin of rejoicing, came calamity. On the 2nd April, 1502, Prince Arthur died at Ludlow. The suite of rooms in which he reached his end now lacks a roof, and the castle walls are tufted with random vegetation. The young couple had been together little more than three months, and there was some doubt, revived in the following reign, whether these two young people had genuinely consummated their marriage.

The King and Queen were at Greenwich at the time. Henry's Father Confessor came to the palace and craved admission. From him they learned of their eldest son's death. The friar quoted Job: 'If we receive good things at the hands of God, why may we not endure evil things?' The Queen was consoled by her husband. She said: 'God is where He was, and we are young', retired to her room, and gave way to grief. When Henry heard of this he went quickly to comfort her again as best he could.

The Prince lay in state, and on the following Friday a funeral procession by torchlight took place at Ludlow, the bier being covered with 'rich cloth of Majestie'. Burning candles encircled it, and over it stretched banners showing the arms of England, Spain, Wales, Chester, Normandy, Guienne, Poitou and Cadwallader. In the church of every parish a solemn dirge was sung, with a requiem Mass on the Sunday. All parishioners were summoned to attend and offer up their prayers.

In London the Mayor and city officials in black attended another solemn dirge in St. Paul's, and offered at Mass. The Prince was buried at Worcester, the ceremony being performed before the high altar of the cathedral. The total expenses of the funeral came to £566 16s. Tradition has it that Jean Gossaert of Maubeuge painted a portrait of Arthur, his father and his sister, but this is by no means certain.

It was commonly believed that the storms that had delayed and shaken Catharine on her voyage to England had presaged this disaster, considered national as well as royal. Though the young Prince has left little mark on history, he appears to have been better educated than most royal sons, and was also a skilled archer. His reputed learning may have been acquired precisely because he had never been robust. A contemporary writer described him as 'of remarkable beauty and grace' and 'taller than his age would warrant'.

The position of his younger brother, Prince Henry, had now become of the greatest possible importance. He was the unquestioned heir to the throne of Britain—unless Catharine were pregnant, but until this could be known, he could not be given the title of 'Prince of Wales'.

[3]

As if taking advantage of the royal bereavement, in July or August, 1501, the Earl of Suffolk once more fled the country, taking with him his brother, Richard de la Pole. This time, possibly at the instigation of Curzon, he went to Maximilian at Imst in the Tyrol. In 1491 the Earl had signed away his right to the title of Duke and agreed to pay £5,000 for that portion of his father's estates returned to him by the King, to raise which sum he had been obliged to mortgage the property. Smarting under his punishment and his real or imagined humiliations, and burdened with overwhelming debts, he set off with little knowledge and less sense, but with recommendations from Sir Robert Curzon, to persuade Maximilian that with his help he could depose the King. Henry suspected him of having made a similar appeal to Philip of Burgundy when he escaped to St. Omer on his first flight from England. There is no reason to believe that at that time Philip encouraged him, and indeed he was probably instrumental in sending him home when Guildford and Hatton arrived.

Maximilian, though nominally in alliance with Henry, was ever ready to acquire an extra string or two for his bow to be used if necessity arose. The Spaniards had already told him that Suffolk might be a lever with which to move Henry more briskly away from the French and towards himself. Consequently the Emperor did not flatly reject the Earl when they met in the autumn, but held out vague hopes to him of men and cash, while keeping him waiting idly at Imst for six weeks, saying he would help any man with Edward IV's blood in his veins to claim his rights. He eventually advised Suffolk that until the time was ripe for an attempt on the throne he should settle down in Aix (Aachen), a free city of the Empire, to which town he sent him with introductory letters to the authorities. Despite this duplicity, he had no hesitation in asking Henry, with whom he was once more friendly, for a handsome contribution towards his latest war—with Turkey.

Suffolk, though a dashing man in the lists, was a vain, illiterate swaggerer whose bravura appealed, nevertheless, to quieter, more retiring men such as the King of England, who had given him the Garter and been a guest at his residence. On learning of his flight, however, Henry reacted violently. Sour and disillusioned, he threw into prison in November, 1501, all who might at some future date help the Earl to create a new disturbance. Among those seized were the Marquis of Dorset, Lord William de la Pole, one of Suffolk's cousins, and Lord William Courtenay, son of the Earl of Devon, who had married Suffolk's cousin, Catharine, one of Edward IV's surviving daughters. Others impeached were Sir John Wyndham and Sir James Tyrell, Governor of Guines when Suffolk arrived there during his first escape. Tyrell was suspected, not without cause, of being in league with the Earl, having earlier been a loyal follower of Richard III, and of having been instrumental in the murder of the Princes in the Tower. De la Pole and Courtenay were kept in that grim fortress under indefinite sentence, and later sent to Calais.

It must not be assumed that men sent to the Tower were always kept in grim and wretched dungeons. Many were given comfortable quarters and had special privileges.

Tyrell shut himself up in Guines Castle and was besieged there. He emerged only on the assurance of a safe-conduct. Leaving his son behind in charge of the castle, he took ship for England with his captors, but once out of sight of land he was offered a grim choice. He could either be drowned in the Channel there and then, or send his son a 'token' to admit the besiegers into the fortress. Tyrell chose to send the token, and in this somewhat shameful way

Guines was surrendered. Wyndham and Tyrell were both tried at the Guildhall and executed on the 6th May, 1502. None regretted Tyrell, and there was vindictive satisfaction when it was learned that he had been imprisoned in the selfsame cell as that of the young Princes whose murder he was believed to have arranged.

Naturally, Henry would give Maximilian no money while ever he harboured a traitor, but in June offered him 10,000 gold crowns if he would surrender Suffolk. Not finding this adequate temptation, Maximilian refused. A long squabble ensued, but on the 19th June, 1502, the two potentates agreed that in exchange for this sum as a contribution towards his Turkish war, Maximilian would withdraw support from all rebels against Henry, and undertake to expel them, treating as criminals any who resisted.

Throughout this bargaining, the French, aware of the enmity of Spain, were appealing to Henry for help in persuading the Emperor to turn against the Spaniards. Brushing aside this plea, Henry played his own careful game, and continued to flatter Maximilian

Until the treaty with Henry was ratified, Maximilian kept Suffolk dangling on the hook, telling him through his Treasurer that he would buy ships from Denmark to take him and a force of 1,000 men to England, but whenever the Earl asked *when*, he was fobbed off on some pretext. When in October the treaty was ratified and the cash handed over, the Emperor's tone changed. It might be better, he hinted, for Suffolk to apply to Louis XII for aid, or even ask Henry for a pardon. Despite the new treaty he did not have him expelled from Aix, but left him there, hard-up, fretful and increasingly in debt, with the cold suggestion that he ought to rest content with having found shelter and not cadge money as well, there being no obligation on Maximilian himself to finance him, since he had made no promises.

During this year the Tailors' and Linen Armourers' Guild received their formal charter from the King, and were henceforward known as the 'Merchant Taylors', being described as 'men of the misteries . . . in all quarters and kingdoms of the world' who 'used all and every wares and merchandises whosoever and especially woollen cloth, as well wholesale as retail throughout our realm of England'.

This Guild, having given the King loyal support in his disputes with the Burgundians, now received their reward, and later a shield.

Increasingly driven by his feverish desire to accomplish quickly before death could strike him down all the plans he had formed, the King decided that the marriage of Princess Margaret to the King of Scotland should now take place. He himself escorted her from Richmond all the way to Collyweston in Northamptonshire, a new residence belonging to the Countess of Richmond. He had carefully seen to her trousseau and supplies himself. On the 9th July he handed her over for good to a large number of maids of honour and attendants, having spent £16,000 on her jewels alone. From Collyweston she was borne in her litter through Newark, York, Durham and Newcastle, at all of which cities their functionaries, including the Mayors, welcomed her. Church bells rang in her honour and the streets were furred with cheering crowds. Music poured into her ears from many minstrel troupes.

She herself came riding in at a walking pace on her small thoroughbred horse, followed by a train of magnificently-clad nobles and an escort of 2,000 horsemen. Leaving Berwick behind, she crossed the border on the 1st August, and was met at Lamberton Kirk by the Archbishop of Glasgow on James's behalf. James himself came to meet her at Dalkeith on the 3rd, and doffing his cap, embraced her, paid his respects to her followers, then retreated with her into his private quarters, where they dined together. Later, music was played, and Margaret danced with the Countess of Surrey. Lady Grey, one of her maids, is said to have playfully shortened James's long beard for him.

The following day was spent in similar fashion, James delighting his betrothed by a performance on both the lute and the clavichord, a primitive square pianoforte with keyboard and strings. Margaret spent some time playing cards with her ladies-in-waiting. James then ordered his horse to be brought, alighted on its back in one bound, scorning the use of stirrups, and made off.

The Princess arrived in Edinburgh on the 7th in garments plentifully sprinkled with the sign of the red rose, to add which many embroiderers had worked hard. She now rode pillion on James's horse. The same emblem was displayed on the cushions of her original litter and the trappings of her horse. The marriage 'of the Thissal and the Rois' was completed with great pomp and dignity in the Abbey Church of Holyrood Palace. The wedding procession was brilliant in its display of wealth and splendour. The treaty of permanent peace between England and Scotland was then confirmed, and the festivities that followed were bright and cheerful.

Tournaments were held, and the entire proceedings are said to have greatly depleted James's treasury. Barely fifteen, Margaret had the reputation of being haughty, changeable and fond of amusement, but was later described as 'decent, urbane and wise', being said to unite wisdom and modesty. Tall, with sparkling eyes, she is said to have had a smooth skin, beautiful hands, golden hair and a rosy complexion. She could speak several languages. These contrasting descriptions suggest that on becoming a Queen she had acquired the usual circle of flatterers. Her husband showed no signs of abandoning his amorous adventures, and many dour Scots' heads wagged and tongues clacked over this unsuitable union.

Earlier, the English King had taken good care to ascertain by special emissaries the worth of the jointure to be given to his daughter.

[4]

During 1502 the treaty of 'Intercursus Magnus' was renewed, though its course had never been smooth. There was now further dispute, and once again the English shifted their headquarters to Calais. Now, however, a meeting with the Burgundians took place in that port in May, 1502, and produced a new treaty, signed on the 18th, representing a slight concession by the English, who agreed that their traders would not send cloth into Flanders entirely free of duty; but in return for this, they obtained the right to ship coinage or precious metals abroad.

Throughout the summer of 1502 Queen Elizabeth was ill, being once more pregnant. Early in October, Henry finally conceded that Princess Catharine of Spain was not in the same condition as Elizabeth. At the start of the New Year, therefore, he gave Prince Henry the title of 'Prince of Wales, Earl of Chester and Flint, and Duke of Cornwall'. The Prince was only eleven years old, and from this time on his health and welfare became of the greatest importance to his father and the kingdom. In a country rarely free from epidemic diseases his life was bound to be precarious and his marriage of considerable consequence. It had already been suggested that he might become affianced to Margaret, daughter of Philip, Archduke of Burgundy, but so far this had not been agreed by either party.

Elizabeth had been the guest in August of Sir Walter Herbert, younger brother of the Earl killed at Danesmoor, who though exiled for not actively supporting Henry's landing at Milford Haven, was back in favour again. She and her household came to Raglan Castle, the King's old refuge, bringing with her her 'mynstrelles' and buying while there a pair of clavichords for £4. When she left, returning through Chepstow and across the Severn by ferry to Berkeley, her 'stuf of the wardrobe of hur beddes' was transported 'from Ragland to Abyndon' and thence to London by her servants. Eight days were required to reach Abingdon, and from there the royal beds and luggage probably went by river to either Greenwich or Richmond.

[5]

The King sent Sir Thomas Brandon and Nicholas West to Cologne to represent him when the Emperor arranged to take the necessary solemn oath of ratification of their new treaty. However, having received his golden crowns, promised in June, Maximilian was in no hurry to swear. Although the envoys arrived in Cologne in January, 1503, he was not there to meet them, having gone to Antwerp, where they had to travel to find him. Eleven days later, however, on the 1st February, the ceremony was performed in the church of St. Michael, and a service of thanksgiving held. Later, bonfires were kindled at suitable points in the city, and great junketings took place. Probably few of the inhabitants knew the precise terms of the treaty, but they seized the opportunity to rejoice while they could.

There should have been an accompanying ceremony, the formal investiture of the Emperor with membership of the Order of the Garter, but Maximilian waived this as needless, saying it could be performed later by proxy in England. The treaty being now ratified, the English envoys naturally asked if Suffolk had been banished. Maximilian gave no direct answer, still playing for time. As he would have to send envoys to England, he said, to witness and receive Henry's own formal ratification, the banishment could wait till then. The Englishmen returned home suspecting they were being bamboozled and the Emperor meant to keep Suffolk in his hands as long as possible.

[6]

The King's political affairs receded temporarily into the background, however, when during the night of the 11th February, 1503, at the age of thirty-five, the Queen herself died in the Tower after a premature childbirth. The birth should have taken place at Richmond, but the infant, christened Catharine, was born ten days too soon. The Queen's body was placed on a bier in the St. John's chapel of the Tower, close to the room in which Edward and Richard, her two brothers, had met their death. There she lay in state.

Elizabeth had been popular and seems to have been sincerely mourned. Afterwards she was carried through the streets in a funeral cortège, her coffin surmounted by her crowned effigy wearing her robes of state. The pall displayed her coat of arms with the motto 'Humble and Reverent'. She was interred in Westminster Abbey in the centre of the unfinished Chapel of Henry VII. The burial cost £2,000. Her infant daughter died shortly afterwards.

Elizabeth had been a careful, economical Queen, quietly influencing her husband towards careful management of his royal income and the preservation of solvency. From her father, Edward IV, she had learned the advantage to the kingdom of a thriving trade, and the strength its master would derive from paying his way. Doubtless she conveyed this lesson to Henry.

On the other hand, in matters of high policy and statecraft she was always subordinate to her mother-in-law, older and more experienced, but the King had great affection and respect for her. He never inflicted upon her injuries such as her father's open and unashamed love affairs had inflicted upon Elizabeth Woodville, his

Queen. There is ample evidence that the Queen deferred to Henry in all matters not directly concerning her, receiving in return courtesy and friendship, if little more. His behaviour on the death of their eldest son revealed his genuine fondness for her. Nevertheless, kingship mattered more to Henry than love, and inevitably Elizabeth had had to endure frequent absences and inattentions, while his domestic measures had to be accepted even if at times harsh and unreasonable. She had suffered many devastating blows, such as the deaths of her children, Elizabeth, Edmund and Arthur, and had recently surrendered Margaret to James IV. These sorrows, robbing her of the will to live, may have hastened her death.

The chapel in which she was buried had been built on the site of the crumbling and ancient Lady Chapel and an inn contiguous to it. The foundation stone had been laid by the King himself assisted by the Master of Masons on the 24th January, 1502, but the chapel was not completed till 1519. The fan vault is considered by some a supreme example of medieval masonic craftsmanship and Gothic architecture. Leland later called it 'the miracle of the world'. Its cost to Henry was £14,000. To its altar he bequeathed 'one grete piece of the holie crosse, conveied, bought, and delivered to us from the isle of Cyo in Greece, set in gold and garnished with perles and precious stones', given to him, he said, by Louis of France when he captured Milan, and brought to him by the Cardinal of Amboise.

Elizabeth had loved the chase. She danced, played cards and games of chance, paid a jester to make her merry, took part in those entertainments that eventually developed into masques, and was especially fond of the royal gardens. She and the King showered small gifts on one another, and she was usually at his side on state occasions. He for his part never stinted her for money, and she repaid him by wifely services, such as embroidering with her own hands his mantle of the Garter and setting gems upon his helmet. Essentially she was a wise and kindly woman, pious, economical, yet so generous to those in need and in her service that when she genuinely wanted money, not merely for herself but for others, she is said to have shown Henry her mended, relined and refashioned robes in proof. She did not appeal in vain.

The King made sure that whenever she appeared beside him at

Court she was dressed as became her position, and if at times he showed a little jealousy of her personal popularity, he suppressed it. Erasmus considered her intelligent and even 'brilliant'. As far as can be judged, she inherited her father's good looks combined with a charming expression.

Her guiding hand had left him, and in August of this same year another valuable member of his Council died—Sir Reginald Bray—'a very father of his country, a sage and grave person, and a fervant lover of justice', who 'had with the King the greatest freedom of any counsellor'. Bray had a great love of architecture, and is said to have supervised the construction of Henry's Chapel at Westminster, and also the completion and ornamentation of St. George's Chapel at Windsor, towards which he contributed much money out of his own pocket. He was buried in it himself.

Like Morton he was unfairly blamed for the heavy taxation of the reign, but like Morton again, was a moderating rather than an inciting influence on the King. He had devoted his whole life to his master, who trusted, consulted and rewarded him, making him both a Knight of the Bath and a Knight of the Garter.

It was with men of this kidney that Henry had originally surrounded himself, which speaks well for his judgement and wisdom. These deaths had taken from his side three of the most experienced and able advisers he possessed. His mother remained, but was no effective substitute. Her influence, though always strong, was often uninspired and harmful. She was 'stiff and starchy', competent enough within narrow limits, and possessing much vitality and charm or she could not have secured and held no fewer than three husbands, but although a religious woman, she was rather too fond of rich living. She had so thoroughly mastered the art of Court ceremonial that she was the acknowledged authority on royal etiquette. However, it is to her credit that she established chairs at both Oxford and Cambridge.

From now onwards, Henry, approaching fifty, had to rely on new counsellors. Bishop Fox remained, but of him it was unkindly said that 'to serve the King's will, he will not stick to agree to his father's death'. He was not the man, it is clear, to steer the King as firmly and well as those who had gone.

Poynings had recently been in disfavour with the King, perhaps because Warbeck had eluded him in Ireland, which the suspicious monarch did not like. He had been recalled, and after a rigorous examination, compelled to leave his son, Gerald, behind before returning to his work—as a hostage, perhaps, for his father's future behaviour. He had come back to England in 1503, possibly for the Queen's funeral, and when he went to Ireland once more, took his son with him, having evidently regained the King's friendship. Being out of the country, however, he could not exert any strong influence at Court.

The new men of the Council were of lower calibre than their predecessors, being ruled by rather than ruling their master. To add to Henry's difficulties, Margaret of Scotland was by no means happy. She missed her father, her country, her family and the Court, and kept writing sorrowful letters to him. More than ever thrown back upon himself the King took complete control of the affairs of state, moving along ways whose course was often difficult for others to follow. He was obsessed by the need to act quickly, for his health was becoming increasingly bad. The throne, he felt, must be made secure for his son by strong matrimonial ties.

This brought him into renewed contact with his old opponent Ferdinand of Spain. Both men were skilled and wary bargainers. Hardly was Prince Arthur cold in his grave than Ferdinand and Isabella claimed through their envoy, the Duke of Estrada, the return of Catharine's dowry, together with her jointure of 100,000 crowns. In the past there had been sordid squabbles over her marriage settlement, squabbles that weary the historian who regards them from this distance of time and scarcely deserve to be recorded. Now they were resumed.

Henry had no intention of returning money already received, nor did he consider himself bound, either legally or morally, to part with it. Through the Spanish Duke he said so bluntly, asking, indeed, for the unpaid balance to be sent at once.

Queen Isabella herself now entered the fray. Showing no excessive concern for her daughter's wifely distress, she devoted herself while she lived to this sordid dispute, seeking primarily to secure for her a firm foothold in England. Without hesitation she told Henry through her representatives that the Princess must be married to the Prince of Wales as soon as he reached the proper age.

If this could not be arranged, then Catharine would have to come home to Spain.

Henry was too far-seeing not to have had the same idea long before, but was also too clever to snatch greedily at the tempting bait. Catharine was not now the prize she had once been. Unless the Spaniards formally abandoned their clamour for the return of her dowry, she should stay where she was, a bird in his hand. No one appears to have cared much what the bereaved girl herself thought of these proposals. Princesses and Princes obeyed their parents without question. Isabella and her advisers, Henry and his, pondered whether such a marriage would be legal. A woman could not then marry her deceased husband's brother nor a man marry his deceased wife's sister. If, however, Catharine's marriage had not been consummated, this might put a different complexion on the matter. The Pope could be asked to grant a special dispensation. But had it been consummated? Who knew?

Courtiers who had 'bedded' the young couple on their wedding night were discreetly questioned, but all that could be ascertained with certainty was that the morning after, Arthur had asked for wine, saying: 'My masters, marriage is a thirsty pastime', and when a cup was brought to him, proudly proclaimed through the hangings of the bed: 'Last night I was in Spain.' The informants were ready, they said, to swear to this. On the other hand, by Catharine's leave one of the Princess's maids in waiting had resolved the doubt and declared her 'as intact as the day she came from her mother's womb'. But who could be sure she spoke the truth?

Henry determined to insist that the marriage *had* been consummated, and did so. There had already been an attractive proposal that Prince Henry should be betrothed to a French heiress, sister of Francis of Angoulême, but another and better notion now came into his mind. Much might happen before the Prince of Wales reached the legitimate age for marriage, whereas he himself was, as of this moment, eligible to re-marry. Who more suitable for his royal bed than the young Spanish widow herself?

The mere suggestion scandalized Isabella. 'It would be an evil thing,' she wrote, 'the mere mention of which offends the ears.' She said also that if the King of England felt he must have a new wife, Joanna, the Queen of Naples, then residing in Valencia, would 'console him in his deep affliction'. This young Queen, Ferdinand's sister, twenty-six years old, had a pleasing character and plenty of money. Henry did indeed consider this suggestion, but when Isabella put the proposal to the lady, Joanna quickly dismissed it. She had no wish to marry a man of fading vigour and go to live in a cold and foggy country.

[7]

Spain was having one of her periodical wars with France, and badly needed England. Rather than lose her, Isabella gave way at last. She and Ferdinand would no longer ask for their daughter's dowry to be returned nor for the 100,000 crowns of jointure. They would, as Henry had requested, persuade Maximilian to have Suffolk banned or hand him over, strengthen the existing treaty of alliance between their two kingdoms, and in addition Catharine should retain her right of succession to the throne of Spain. The marriage to Prince Henry should be celebrated as soon as he was fourteen.

The King, though rebuffed as a suitor, had won the major battle. The bargain now offered was one he could not resist. On the 25th June, 1503, Prince Henry and Catharine were officially affianced at the mansion of the Bishop of Salisbury in Fleet Street. The Princess was eighteen and her future husband twelve. Her parents confirmed the betrothal on the 24th and 30th September. On the 26th December Pope Julius despatched his dispensation to Isabella. This Pope, Giuliano della Rovere, had succeeded Alexander VI in that year, being then sixty years old. It was he who laid the foundation stone of St. Peter's in Rome. He died in 1513.

Isabella, herself failing fast, had just enough strength left to read the dispensation when the copy was placed in her hands.

[8]

The absent Suffolk was now preying on the King's mind. On the 5th March, before noon at St. Paul's cross, Henry caused him to be excommunicated 'with bell, book and candle' and his estates confiscated. The same treatment was given on the same occasion to Suffolk's 'friend' Sir Robert Curzon, an old opponent of the King's, who as governor of Hammes Castle had sheltered the Earl when he first escaped. Curzon had returned to England in 1499 ostensibly to fight against the Turks. He is said to have received his knighthood through the good offices of the Earl, and had joined with him in tournaments. There had been discussion between them, the King's spies reported, regarding the succession to the throne, and Suffolk, familiarly known as 'The White Rose', had been mentioned. This Henry could not ignore. He asked both France and Spain to use their influence with Maximilian, whom he wished to issue an edict preventing the Earl from finding refuge in any big city or town. On the 5th March he asked Maximilian to have a proclamation, on English lines, issued against traitors and drew up suitable wording, but Maximilian was not to be rushed.

In fulfilment of his promise to Henry, Ferdinand asked Maximilian to expel the Earl from his territories or else put him on a ship for England. So did Louis of France. Maximilian told Aix to refuse him further assistance, but his continued duplicity is revealed by his sending Suffolk 1,000 gold pieces, followed by a further 2,000 in July, 1503, so that he could pay his debts. On the other hand, this may well have been because Aix refused to let him go until those to whom he owed money had been repaid.

As promised, the Emperor's representatives came to England led by the Margrave of Brandenburg. They reached London in March, 1503, lodging in Crosby Place. The envoys were received on the 30th March by Henry in person at Baynard Castle. On the 2nd April came a procession to St. Paul's, and after Mass Henry took the oath of ratification and a Te Deum was sung. The usual popular enthusiasm followed, with the customary flaming bonfires and the broaching of numerous casks of wine. Maximilian having been invested by proxy with the Garter, Henry gave £20 of his own money to St. George's Chapel at Windsor. He was later to give the same chapel a golden image of St. George, weighing over 8 lb., with diamonds, rubies, pearls and sapphires surrounding it.

Whether secretly warned by Maximilian or by his own friends, Suffolk took fright and bolted, leaving his brother Richard behind to look after his affairs and endeavour to pay off his debts. He did not tell Maximilian of his flight and left his creditors to whistle down the wind for their money. Henry was now in so strong a position, however, that Suffolk found himself welcome nowhere. He sought assistance from the Count Palatine, who ruled over a powerful and extensive district of Germany to the west of the Rhine and whose ancestors had been royal officials. At the request of the French the Count rebuffed him, so Suffolk went on into Guelderland, a province in the Low Countries, meaning to take refuge with Duke Albert of Saxony in Friesland. Despite having a safe-conduct for Friesland, he was arrested by Duke Charles of Guelderland, who had him imprisoned at Hattam on the Yser the moment he crossed the border. Suffolk offered to pay 2,000 florins for his freedom. When Duke Charles showed some scepticism, he explained that this would be lent to him by a Spanish trader in Antwerp. The Duke, unconvinced, insisted on five hundred florins at once on account, but when he got them, though he set Suffolk free, he still refused to let him leave the country. The Earl had to stay at Wageningen in Guelderland for a time, owing money right and left, and borrowing on the strength of half-promises of men and money made to him by the Duke.

He continually importuned Charles for help, obtaining little response, tried to leave the country surreptitiously, was arrested again in the neighbourhood of Tiel, and put under close guard in a suitable prison, being allowed only a single manservant. Despite a reinforcement of his jailers, he managed to smuggle messages out to his friends begging the Archduke Philip of Burgundy to secure his release. Philip, however, was unwilling to quarrel with Duke Charles. Suffolk would be the first to suffer in such a case, he was roughly told.

Nevertheless, Philip and Charles both considered the Earl potentially useful as a means of extorting money from Henry for his surrender, and for some time bickered continually over which of them should have him.

CHAPTER FOURTEEN

Despair of an Earl

[1]

ON THE 10th August, 1504, Princess Catharine, then at Richmond, went with the King to Windsor, where they stayed nearly a fortnight. Each day, when the weather allowed, they hunted deer and other game in the Great Park, then returned to Richmond for a further week. A light is thrown on Henry's character by an incident that occurred on one of his hunting excursions. A poor labourer named Taylor had become the father of triplets, a rare occurrence in those days, and was presented to the King, who, charmed by the event and perhaps by the man himself, undertook to have all three boys educated at one of the public schools and afterwards sent to Oxford, all at his own cost.

One of them eventually read Civil Law at Oxford, studied at a foreign university and, it is said, became Master of the Rolls. He was John Taylor, also a famous canonist. Henry is believed to have had a chapel erected on the site of his father's house. Taylor died in 1534.

Catharine now had a touch of 'ague' or malaria, and was confined to the palace for three days. Henry went off to Westminster, taking Princess Mary and the English court ladies with him, but leaving his son's widow behind. From there after a few days the royal party proceeded to Greenwich, the Princess joining them for a week. She suffered here a much worse attack, having to be sent into Kent to recover, after which she returned to her original English mansion, the Manor House in Kennington Road, once the refuge of John of Gaunt and sometimes used by the King himself.

Her health remained uncertain. Each day she experienced alternating extremes of cold and heat. Her complexion became sallow and unattractive. Henry had also left Greenwich and wrote to her frequently, always in the politest style, saying he would visit her if she wished, and would get together every doctor in England to find a cure for her ailment. The Prince of Wales was with him at this time, which was unusual, for he rarely took the boy with him lest his studies should be interfered with. He was fond of the Prince, and sought to have him thoroughly prepared for his future role as King of England. Shortly after they had left Greenwich, news came that the dispensation for Catharine's marriage had been granted by the Pope. Henry notified Catharine at once.

[2]

The European chess-masters were forced to rearrange their pieces and prepare for new games when on the 20th November, 1504, Isabella, Queen of Spain, died. New strategy, new openings, new tactics and new moves had to be thought out. Castile, Isabella's own inheritance, passed now to her eldest daughter, Joanna, wife of Philip of Burgundy. Unfortunately Joanna was losing her reason. Her husband's fondness for other women and her own excessive jealousy were reputed to have turned her mind and she was liable to become violent. Ferdinand, though appointed Governor of Castile by Isabella's will, was now merely King of Aragon again. The Dons of Spain, of whom he had hitherto been master, would have preferred Philip of Burgundy as their overlord, and all Spain held its breath, waiting to see which of these two Princes would prevail over the other.

Henry had quickly to reconsider his own and his son's position. Fortunately, a chance came to discover what power remained to Ferdinand in Castile. The Spaniard had been pressing him to strengthen their alliance against France, but a hitch seemed to have occurred in the already granted dispensation from Pope Julius for the Prince of Wales to marry Catharine. This should have arrived in July, 1504, but the King had been warned by Robert Sherburne, Dean of St. Paul's, that the Pope, uncertain of Henry's policy concerning the 'Holy League', was holding it back. When Isabella lay dying, however, the Pope had been persuaded to send it to her so that she might 'depart out of this life with a quiet mind'. He had told her to keep its arrival secret, but after her death Ferdinand swept aside this instruction, and to the disgust of the Vatican made sure that Henry knew it had come. The official dispensation could therefore no longer be withheld, and the Pope, his hand forced, sent it himself to Henry early in 1505 by the hand of the Bishop of Worcester, Sylvester de Giglio.

It covered Catharine's remarriage, whether the first had been consummated or not, and was carefully antedated to the 26th December, 1504, so that it should not seem to have been deliberately delayed. Henry sent Francis Marsin, James Braybrooke and John Stile to Spain, ostensibly to discuss the proposed new alliance, but in reality to report confidentially on the strength or weakness of Ferdinand's position there. They were to travel to Madrid by a roundabout route so as to take in Valencia, where they should study Queen Joanna of Naples and bring back a full account of her height, age, deportment, girth, hair, features, limbs, complexion and other physical and temperamental attributes, as well as a portrait of her and the whole truth about her finances. She was still much in his mind.

The report when it came praised the virtues of the 'amiable, round and plump' young widow, but offered a poor opinion of her wealth, for her jointure had vanished into the coffers of the French in Naples. Henry promptly dismissed her from his mind.

As for Ferdinand, the three gentlemen reported that he was governing Castile in his daughter's name as administrator, both his and her signatures appearing on documents, Philip's being carefully excluded. Ferdinand was hoping to continue along these lines, but if not, meant to marry again and produce a son. A proposal had been put forward that the King's second daughter, Princess Mary, should marry Charles of Castile, which had considerable appeal for him.

On the whole, however, the envoys favoured Philip's rather than Ferdinand's prospects, a strong party in Castile being eager to break the King of Aragon's grip and hand the province over to the Burgundian. Indeed, the Archduke had already given himself in Brussels the title of 'King of Castile', and was preparing to take over the whole of Spain. He had been promised French aid, and his father, the Emperor Maximilian, was already his ally. What chance would Ferdinand have against such a coalition?

[3]

London was now growing and redeeming herself from filth and meanness by putting up houses more durable and seemly, some of stone and timber, some of timber and brick, in which the wealthier of her citizens could live rather than exist; but she was still for the most part a reeking girdle of slums about a cluster of palaces and mansions.

It had been evident for some time that that admirable institution, the Association of Merchant Adventurers, hitherto a loose grouping of traders covering the entire country, needed a tighter, more formal organization. Accordingly it was decreed that a Governor should be elected to preside over twenty-four 'of the most sad, and discreet, and honest persons', each elected by and representing a particular guild. This body would 'look to the good ordering of the brethren of the company everywhere', control the members and their activities, draw up ordinances and regulations, ensure that these were obeyed, and sit in judgement on any who infringed them, with power to inflict penalties.

The Merchant Adventurers now found it necessary to tighten up their organization still further. It was therefore enacted that the Governor and his Council could summon the members to meet at whatsoever place they appointed, and enforce their rules and regulations, with the proviso that nothing they did should usurp the authority or impair the prestige of the King.

This had two advantages. It gave the Adventurers a closely-knit and powerful administrative organ, able to address the King as a powerful body of influential opinion, while the King himself could more easily make his wishes known and prevent sporadic action by the members that would militate against his foreign policy. For example, when the Merchant Adventurers had strengthened their organization, but their efforts to shackle the trade of their English competitors had failed, their representatives in Flanders demanded that every English competitor should be compelled to pay £20 for the right to sell there. In this way they hoped to keep the cloth trade of the Low Countries in their own hands.

The other traders promptly left Flanders and took their grievance to Parliament, arguing that this would mean smaller sales of English cloth, and so the cost of imports would rise. Henry at once stepped in to repress the greed of these rich London merchants, and at his bidding Parliament reduced the fee to ten marks. The Merchant Adventurers were forbidden to do this sort of thing again, either singly or in association.

One other feature of the year 1504 was an internal dispute among the Adventurers, who were suffering severely from growing-pains. They had had difficulty in obtaining recognition of their authority by certain members of the Staple, and took the case to the Court of the Star Chamber. It was there laid down that any Guild member entering the trading field of another body must observe the rules appertaining to that field. Empowered by this decision the Adventurers immediately imposed a toll of ten marks on all members of the Staple who sold cloth as distinct from wool, declaring that the wares of whomsoever refused to pay would be impounded. It was obvious to those with foresight that sooner or later some stricter code of conduct for the Adventurers would have to be drawn up and given the power of law.

In June the King had once more to step in between them and the Staple. He interpreted the Star Chamber verdict as meaning that the Association could not confiscate a Stapler's goods, which on payment of the toll must be returned to him. Nor could they blackmail a Stapler or any other trader into joining their body.

The envy of the Merchant Taylors by the rival Guilds came to a head when an election for Sheriff was held, and the Merchant Taylors' candidate, Fitzwilliam, was kept out of this office by some means. Henry, aware of the jealousy, refused to accept Thomas Jonson, the successful candidate, ordering a new election. Stalking haughtily into the Guildhall, Edmond Dudley conveyed to the Mayor the King's insistence on Fitzwilliam as Sheriff, and after much objection, he was reluctantly elected. This was not the only occasion on which Henry stepped in to call a city or town authority to order.

When he did so, it was usually because these bodies had usurped royal privileges, or ignored the 'common law'. This was that largely unwritten code, supposed to have come down from ancient times, which governed the 'liberty of the subject' to behave as he thought fit as long as he did not interfere with the liberty of his fellows, break the laws, or offend the morality of his day as established by common consent. The guilds and corporations were eventually debarred from carrying out any ordinance not previously sanctioned by the Lord Chancellor, the Lord High Treasurer, and two or even three chief justices. If these were not available, then two justices of the circuit, including in their scope the particular body concerned, could be consulted. The jails were placed under the full control of the Sheriffs.

On the 25th January, 1505, with these and other grave issues in mind, Henry called his first Parliament for six years. William Warham, now Lord Chancellor and Archbishop of Canterbury, opened the session. The legislation enacted was aimed at rebels and rioters. People were forbidden to assemble without formal permission. Guards conniving at or negligently allowing the escape of prisoners were to be severely punished.

The Parliament of this reign was much different from that of today. It was not neatly divided into a House of hereditary Lords and a nationally elected House of Commons. The lords were not simply the inheritors of titles acting as national legislators, competent or otherwise, but men already holding important administrative or courtly positions about the King. They included the King's Council, the Law Lords, among whom were the law officers of the Crown, the judges and the masters in Chancery. These men had proved themselves in one capacity or another, and in common possessed years of practical experience, a knowledge of men and of the affairs of state.

The King's Council, including the Lord Chancellor, constituted in effect his Cabinet or governing body and secretariat, and wielded executive power under the King, whom they advised. They sat in Council with him in the Star Chamber, whose records they kept in the form of 'rolls' produced by those expert calligraphers, the clerks.

The Commons met in a different place altogether, the Chapter House in Westminster Abbey, and came to the 'other House' on important and infrequent occasions only, primarily to hear the Lord Chancellor's opening address. There they waited, mute and attentive, at the bar, beyond which they could not advance, on most occasions having to kneel. If they had proposals of their own to put forward, they could do this only through their Speaker, and had to obtain the royal leave or that of the lords, whose decision was conveyed to them by the same officer. The Speaker was the only other person allowed to address the King in the Parliament House when he presented their petitions.

Like the purely titular lords the Commons had minor importance. Many were 'knights of the shire', representing particular country districts, but even they were administrators. Some served as confiscators of lapsed property, some were virtually tax collectors, and some sheriffs, but the majority were local magistrates.

Parliament was, in fact, not the representative 'democratic' body of today, but a blend of men from carefully chosen and superior classes, the heads of Church and State, the Church being the more numerous and predominant. Essentially it was an upper-class institution. The King, though he seldom called it together, knew better than completely to ignore or dismiss it. Whatever new law or modification of old ones he and his Council proposed had eventually to be submitted to and approved by Parliament. Normally, opposition by individual members brought no penalty (Sir Thomas More's father (p. 259) was an exception), but the King could veto any Act of which he disapproved.

The members considered that 'what is pleasant to the prince has the force of law'. They were largely compliant, yet despite this were being steadily steered by the King, little though either he or they realized it, towards a new rôle in government, the expression of the popular will.

Henry was less tolerant of the cities, the guilds and their governors. He made no bones about shearing off, with the sharp edge of his authority, the shoots of provincial or commercial self-interest and narrowness if in his view they conflicted with the national interest.

A devout and orthodox churchman, he accepted the tenets and disciplines of his faith, yet was aware that its practitioners' predominance in political life might threaten his personal position. He was like a man with a tame lion in his quarters. As long as he kept it fed and satisfied, he could move freely and without fear, but one accidental painful tweak of its tail, one snatching away of an anticipated tit-bit, and he was doomed. In consequence, he left the ecclesiastics free, not curtailing their powers or weakening their authority in matters spiritual, but at the same time not allowing them too much latitude in purely temporal matters. He kept on the right side of the Pope, while not hesitating to differ from him when necessary. He promoted, flattered and listened to archbishops and bishops, and whenever the offences of priests were reported to him—as they were—he left chastisement to their ecclesiastical superiors. Clerical misconduct in taverns, in honest mens' bed-chambers, in monasteries or nunneries, were their concern, not his. Indeed, at that time much loose living and lawlessness prevailed among the clergy. Some were topers, others gambled and forni-cated, others again let their hair cover their tonsures and discarded their priestly clothing the better to taste the delights of ordinary life. They even embezzled the funds of their own institutions.

On the other hand, Henry would never allow even the highest ecclesiastics to ignore his regality. In all his relations with them he maintained great courtesy, but insisted on their treating him with equal or greater respect. In return he brought the ablest of them into his Council, and when needing a new bishop, picked an Englishman, unless some illustrious person from overseas had earned or needed special recognition, as with Polydore Vergil, whom he made Archdeacon of Wells.

In all his dealings with the Church, however, he never forgot the interests of his kingdom.

[4]

In this session Suffolk and his adherents were the subject of an Act of Attainder, and all traitors, dead or alive, were legally deprived of their offices and property. This included the Earl and was one of the main causes of his destitution, but it did not include Curzon, whose exemption from these penalties the King allowed. Bacon held that Curzon was an *agent provocateur* and spy, reporting all Suffolk's doings to the King while pretending to be his friend, but this has been questioned. It does seem, however, as if there were some justification for the belief.

New taxes were proposed. For instance, Henry argued that when the King's eldest son was knighted or his eldest daughter needed a dowry, English law entitled their father to claim certain monies from his people. Thomas More, then a young Member of the House, strongly opposed this argument, which so enraged the King that, unable legally to imprison More himself, he had More's father thrust into a cell in the Tower until he paid £100 for his freedom. The House granted Henry £40,000, but in fact he took only £30,000.

Henry had tried to have Suffolk proclaimed a traitorous rebel throughout the Holy Roman Empire, but believing it useless to appeal to Maximilian, the Emperor, he went behind his back to his old rivals, the Hanseatic League. To this end Parliament enacted a removal, both immediate and for all time, of the trading restrictions upon these fortified market towns as long as they did not attack the livelihoods and liberties of the citizens of London. This was a considerable concession in exchange for the proscription of a needy noble, and shows how large the Suffolk affair bulked in the King's imagination. Possibly he meant the concession to last only until the Earl was in his hands or out of the way. Whatever his purpose, the consequence of this decision was that the industries of the country were soon called upon to meet and withstand competition from an energetic body of merchants overseas. It was, in fact, a surrender, which he afterwards regretted and did his best to remedy.

At this juncture the King, resenting the lack of care for the user shown by many home producers and their eagerness to make money out of their own countrymen by charging excessive prices, kept a tight hand on the guilds. The pewterers and braziers of London and York had been quick to protest that in rural districts some men of their craft were fraudulent, pilfered raw materials, turned out shoddy wares and used false weights. In consequence it was enacted that the standards of the London guilds should be everywhere observed, and inspectors, locally appointed, sent round to ensure that this was done.

[5]

Henry was still in a highly advantageous position. He had no wars on his hands, and on the whole peace still reigned. Friendly with and bound by ties of marriage to Scotland, in league matrimonially and politically with Spain, courted by Burgundy, on better terms with the Hanse, receiving an annual tribute from France, and not in dispute with the Pope, he had become one of Europe's senior monarchs, his only equal in experience and capacity being Ferdinand of Aragon, whose power was at last diminishing. All the great potentates courted and flattered him. The linchpin of alliances and regroupings, he could not be ignored. Soncino, the Milanese ambassador, reported to his master, the Duke: 'In the midst of this his Majesty can stand like one at the top of a tower, looking on at what is passing in the plain.'

He was no more remote, secret or awe-inspiring than other autocratic kings, but in the main was tolerant and considerate, rewarding good service with liberality and giving freely to the deserving. Quick to bestow gifts on those who served him or his household well, he aided the wives of Warbeck and Fitzwalter after their husbands' deaths, and assisted those who suffered in his wars or were injured in other ways, as when he gave 20s. to a man who lost a hand—a handsome sum for a commoner in those days.

Always a human being, he was cordial, even friendly, to his people, allowing them audiences and leave to present petitions, while refusing to punish them if they had been misled by their masters or manipulators.

When he and the Queen journeyed through the land they never hesitated to mix freely with even their less wealthy subjects. Records reveal that Henry quaffed beer under a farmer's roof, and having paused to watch men cutting corn, gave them a couple of shillings each. Humble folk came up with their offerings—a few young hares or perhaps a lump of almond butter, used on Good Friday when the ordinary kind could not be eaten, or a carp. Fresh-cheeked maids, timid widows, stout yeomen, children, sun-browned labourers, pressed forward to bring the King and Queen the pick of their produce, from apples to strawberries, from pheasants to quails, from rabbits to venison, from flowers to rose-water. With kindly eye the King received a pair of fighting cocks, a dollop of tripe, a clump of puddings, a flagon of cider. Wine, cheeses, spirits, spices, even musical instruments, were brought in by proud and loyal countryfolk. All these were graciously accepted. Once, out hunting and offered by a housewife water to quench his thirst, he gave her five shillings.

Every day some human problem brought to him was given grave and serious thought. He comforted the emotionally disturbed, and stepped in more than once to remedy injustice, as when a madman's wife was ill-treated. He remembered his old schoolmaster and the son of his former nurse, giving both small pensions. Above all, he avoided revengefulness unless the offence affected the throne or hampered his policies. His behaviour towards the acknowledged Yorkists, Northumberland and Surrey, was magnanimous, and in consequence he escaped much enduring hostility and bitterness.

He particularly loved the trappings and pomp of regality. He was never seen on great public occasions without magnificent robes, while he invariably behaved in a manner consistent with his position. He revelled in rites and ceremonies, and was a splendid patron of the fifty-two goldsmiths in Cheapside. If his courtiers did not wear dress he considered adequate, he would quietly present them with bales of suitable material, as when he gave the Earl of Oxford forty-one yards of fine satin for a gown. In 1504 he was still indulging his love of jewels, which he considered both beautiful in themselves and valuable as security. In this year he spent £30,000 of his own money in buying still more from abroad.

After the Queen's death, however, he began to rake in money by direct taxation with the object of amassing a splendid treasure for that son to be some day his successor. His new ministers, Empson and Dudley, were far more ruthless in this respect and far more subservient to him than Morton and Bray had been. They set to work with a zest and pertinacity that won them the title of 'horse leaches and shearers'.

Edmund Dudley, a man of forty-two, belonged to the great family of that name. Made a Privy Councillor in 1485, he was Speaker of the House of Commons and a clever orator, especially in debate, but his severity in executing the King's stiff and despotic financial demands made him hated.

Sir Richard Empson, who shared his unpopularity for the same reason, was a Towcester man, a trained lawyer, and Speaker of the Commons in 1491, knighted in 1504. He and Dudley threw men into prison until they had paid the sums demanded of them, and were said to summon men to appear before them not in a court of law, but in private houses, where they were condemned without genuine trial, irrespective of whether their offences affected the Crown or the Council.

A lack of scruple marked the work of these men, who were quick to see that if money could not be extracted from the wealthy by legitimate taxation, it could be extracted by fines. Informers were found to report offences, at first of no great moment, then, as rapacity in both respects increased, grave. Whether the accusations were true or not, the offenders were at once called before a magistrate, and unless they attended the hearing, convicted without any chance to defend themselves, their property being forfeited to the King and themselves consigned to the nearest jail.

As the victims often lived a long way from the court concerned, they frequently knew nothing of either charge or verdict until apprehended. 'Men thus condemned were marked for the future as outlaws, that is, deprived of every civil right which the law gives to man.' Freeholders with land worth £40 were expected to become knights. Enormous sums had to be paid to the Crown by its wards when they were twenty-one. Many old laws which had passed from men's minds were dug up, and those who had broken them heavily fined.

In fact, full advantage was now taken of the law of 1495 which allowed judges and magistrates to act on the accusation of private persons. The informers 'in their greed for money, paid too little heed to their duty, to their own danger, or to humanity, although they were often admonished by persons of importance that they should act with more moderation'.

Thus, in amounts ranging from £50 to £10,000, money flowed into the King's treasury, and it would be absurd to suggest that he did not know how it had been obtained. As he grew older he succumbed to one of the vices of monarchy and old age—avarice.

He accumulated cash as a bee honey. In comparison to many earlier kings he himself was moderate in tastes and habits. It was primarily for his son, and for that perpetual yearning to found a Tudor dynasty, that he heaped coin upon coin. He knew it could not come to pass and endure unless underpinned and buttressed by massive accumulations of gold and jewels.

Yet he was not wholly unrelenting, for in August, 1504, men who considered themselves unjustly convicted were allowed to appeal within two years, and assured of fair treatment. This promise was nevertheless largely ignored by Empson and Dudley, who were doubtless lining their own pockets as well as the King's. Polydore had no doubts about Henry's motive. He wrote: 'certain it is that the prince, so moderate himself, did not rob his subjects above measure, he who left his Kingdom in every respect in the greatest prosperity'.

The Hanse traders still grumbled that too high a customs duty was being placed on their goods. It had always been a sore point with them that they had to send their cloth to London to be dressed, and this cropped up again. They also complained that the merchants who did their business in England were inefficient and their probity suspect. These men, they protested, brought the League into disrepute by their over-elaborate dress, their wenching and tippling, and also enjoyed special advantages which they ought not to abuse.

The Hanse had always annoyed the King by their refusal to further his trade with Burgundy, so he paid no attention to their complaints, which he brusquely dismissed.

To remedy defects in the Act of 1497 relating to the wages of workmen, Parliament, having deleted certain sections, more strictly regimented both men and apprentices, who were forbidden to play cards, dice or ball except at Christmas, and then only if watched over by their employers. Any who broke this law could be put in the stocks for a whole day. Bad timekeeping also was made a punishable offence.

The currency question was tackled next. It was laid down that no person should carry currency, gold or silver, beyond the shores of the kingdom, while foreigners were debarred from acquiring it in the course of trade or barter, and taking more than ten crowns out of the country. To conserve the store of bullion, a route by which it was slipping out abroad was barred by law when those journeying to Ireland were prevented from carrying with them more than 6s. 8d. Every step was taken to ensure observance of this prohibition, and with the earlier restrictions it achieved the desired result. Not only did the King and his nobles now heap up large quantities of precious metal, but the Church and those who had the wherewithal accumulated great treasure in gold and silver utensils, plate and ornaments. The royal amassing of bullion, most of which came from the strongboxes of the wealthy, was designed to keep down prices. In consequence the goldsmiths flourished and in London was heard a constant brouhaha of chaffering merchants selling the precious metals their ships had brought in from their own countries.

Parliament also occupied itself with the problems of domestic currency. The coins then in circulation were badly made and lost a great deal of their substance in use. Nevertheless, however much they were diminished in size and weight, their face value remained the same. It became common practice, therefore, to clip bits off gold and silver coins, the clippings being then collected up, melted down and sold. To prevent this it was enacted that gold coins should be legal tender only if of their original weight. Any coin showing a clipped edge was rejected.

Silver coins had likewise been clipped, some were counterfeit, some from Ireland were imperfect or valueless, yet if any of these carried the royal stamp they had to be accepted, and in consequence people did not know where they stood. The new coins—groat, half-groat and penny—would, it was hoped, prevent this. Stable coinage began in this reign.

[6]

Bacon has a story that about this time the Earl of Oxford, Lord High Steward and the King's uncle by marriage, entertained him at Castle Hedingham in Essex, his powerful fortress. As Henry was leaving, the Earl's henchmen in their livery coats with the Oxford badge made a lane through which he passed. The King told Oxford that the noble and sumptuous hospitality he had received was 'greater than speech'. These handsome gentlemen were, no doubt, his menials. Smiling, the Earl replied that they were not there for his own ease, but were retainers who had come to help him out and see the King.

Henry 'started a little', thanked him for his 'good cheer', but added coldly that all the same he could not have his laws regarding the wearing of livery ignored. His attorney, he added drily, would speak to him.

Empson came, and it cost the Earl 15,000 marks. Bacon claimed to have seen himself an account book of Empson's with the King's notes in the margin of almost every leaf. For example, where Empson had written: 'Item, received of such a one five marks, for a pardon to be procured, and if the pardon do not pass, the money to be repaid, except the party be in some other ways satisfied', the King had written in his own hand at the side: 'Otherwise satisfied.'

Catharine of Aragon was becoming a perpetual nuisance to the King. She was eternally squabbling with members of her household, and they with each other, and kept nagging him to step in as umpire, which he steadfastly refused to do, since this would imply that he was their master and financially responsible for them. Privately, however, he put matters right by means known to himself alone, taking care that his daughter-in-law did not discover and take advantage of this.

He was, moreover, seriously afraid that Ferdinand might fall from power in Castile, in which case to go on with the Prince of Wales's marriage would be disastrous. Throughout his negotiations with Ferdinand he had taken care never to be trapped. Each move the Spaniard made had been countered, pawn exchanged for pawn, piece for piece, so that he should never be placed in a losing position. Now, in his perplexity, he did as good chess players often do to extricate themselves from an awkward position. He 'castled'. In other words, he wriggled out of his commitment to Catharine.

On the 27th June, 1505, in the Palace of Richmond, the Prince of Wales, just before his fourteenth birthday, declared before Bishop Fox and other witnesses, one of them Sir Charles Somerset, that his betrothal to Catharine had been made without his consent, and he refused, therefore, to confirm it. This declaration, he asserted, was made of his own free will, which assertion few accepted.

This purely formal and legal declaration was not publicly

announced, but was held in reserve for use if required, and kept strictly secret. The King was now free to consider once more his own remarriage. The theory has been advanced that he had become a lecherous old man, afflicted with satyriasis, and looking everywhere for a young woman to share his bed. This I do not believe. He was but forty-nine, and even in medieval times a man of that age was neither physically senile nor inevitably libidinous. When necessary a King's sexual needs could always be satisfied without difficulty, and Henry was far too wary to seek a royal consort solely for physical reasons. On one thing, however, he was determined. Either for aesthetic reasons, or because she would be unpopular with his people, he would have no ugly bride. What he wanted was a healthy, attractive woman young enough to bear him a son as an insurance against any mishap to the Prince of Wales.

He had been rejected by and had privately rejected the Queen of Naples. There still remained Margaret of Savoy, the eleven-year-old daughter of the Emperor Maximilian, whom either the Emperor himself or the Archduke Philip had proposed, not wishing Henry to nibble further at the Queen of Naples. Margaret of Angoulême, the French girl he had hinted to Louis XII he might be prepared to consider, was also a possibility, but was only thirteen and had originally been proposed as a candidate for his own son's hand. Her mother, Louisa, was suggested as more suitable, but it is doubtful if Henry seriously contemplated marrying any of them. They were bait to keep their princes friendly to him, and either too young, too poor or too raddled for his taste.

Instead, he went on arguing with Ferdinand. The balance of Catharine's original dowry had never been paid, and the King of Aragon still refused to pay it until the Prince of Wales was fully fifteen, though it should have been sent the previous year. Catharine was now in great difficulties, for although her father had given her a considerable quantity of gold and jewels for her personal needs, this had been entrusted to De Puebla, the Spanish ambassador, who refused in March, probably on his master's orders, to allow her to draw upon it except for food. Since her arrival in England Henry had had to maintain her. Now she was a widow, he considered her father should provide for her.

De Puebla is said to have been malicious, miserly, a moaner who stabbed his enemies in the back, a sycophant ridiculed for his lack of dignity and pride, and a shameless usurer. Though Henry liked him, his enemies at the English Court called him calumniator, boaster and 'show-off', declaring that he lived in 'a vile and miserable inn of bad repute' solely to cut down the cost of his food. Nevertheless, the King placed great trust in him, had much respect for him, and held him to be diligent, watchful and 'adroit in all negotiations trusted to him'—which as far as the King was concerned he certainly was.

Henry may have liked him because he was supple. He greedily swallowed the ambassador's blandishments, but kept from him all the same those matters he did not wish should reach the ears of his master. Indeed, Ferdinand and Isabella when she was alive had both preferred to entrust their private business with Britain and Scotland to a special envoy, De Ayala. De Puebla greatly resented this and made no secret of the fact.

In his own country the ambassador was accused of not paying enough attention to the affairs of the Spanish traders, though he had unblushingly accepted their private gifts. He was also blamed for not taking advantage of Henry's difficulties to obtain favourable trade terms from him.

Now, whenever the King saw Catharine he asked why her father did not fulfil his promise, complaining that his own kindness of heart alone made him go on lodging and supporting her, since she had as yet no genuine claim upon him. The poor girl could not even provide properly for her own servants, though they did not on that account desert her. Whatever harsh words she used concerning Henry when writing or speaking to De Puebla, the ambassador promptly repeated to him. In December, 1505, she tried to extract a remittance from Philip of Burgundy, but failed.

[7]

Like Henry, Ferdinand was thinking of a new wife. His eye fell upon the daughter of a French general, Gaston de Foix, a lively young woman of Navarre named Germaine, on whom he hoped to beget a son. It irritated him that letters from his daughter were full of grumbles such as: 'I have nothing for chemises, wherefore by your Highness's life, I have now sold some bracelets to get a dress of black velvet, for I was all but naked. Since I departed from Spain I have nothing except two new dresses, for till now those I brought from there have lasted me. On this account I beg your Highness to command to remedy this, for certainly I shall not be able to live in this manner.'

Ferdinand merely shrugged his shoulders. To send her money would be to concede victory to the English King. As was inevitable Catharine presently learned that the Prince of Wales had repudiated his betrothal. Her distress was so great that beside it her recurring ague was negligible. Other brides for the Prince were being considered, she knew, and her age—she was now twenty— her poverty, her sickness, the effect it had had on her looks, and above all her shame and humiliation, tormented her.

Her fulminations against De Puebla had no effect on Henry, who wining and dining him, flattering him and his country, pretending a warm friendship, consulting him, and letting him believe he was in his confidence, was using him to learn the minds of the Spaniards and their ruler. Nevertheless, he was not wholly ungenerous to Catharine, for he allowed her an annual sum, wrote her kindly letters, and in October offered her a house in Fulham which he thought better for her health—or any other if she preferred it.

[8]

Another chapter in Suffolk's life story was written in July, 1505, when he was handed over by Charles, Duke of Guelderland, to his conqueror, Philip of Burgundy, now openly claiming the kingship of Castile. The quarrel between these two rulers was over. It has been asserted that Charles had earlier offered the Earl to Henry in exchange for a ransom the King thought too high. In Antwerp it was also rumoured that Henry and Charles were privately planning to oppose Philip's claim to the kingship of Spain.

In the summer of that year, however, Henry seems to have been for once totally unaware of Suffolk's plight. Nonetheless, this rumour from Antwerp alarmed Philip, who tried to convince Henry that he had nothing to fear from the Earl. The English continued all the same to clamour for his surrender, calling him 'scullion' and 'runaway youth', but Philip, locked in his everlasting struggle with them over Flanders trade, a struggle chiefly hinging on customs duties, refused to let him go. Instead, he kept him prisoner in November, 1505, in the castle of Namur, to which he was conveyed. Suffolk's innumerable creditors at once besieged Philip with appeals for repayment of the sums his prisoner owed, or that the Earl himself should repay them, but a dismissive wave of the hand from the Archduke and yet more empty promises from the incarcerated debtor and his brother were all they received.

Richard de la Pole, his brother, had in fact remained quietly in Aix, doing his best to pacify them, but now they attacked him whenever he put his nose out of doors, howling that his brother was a cheat and a perjurer. So fierce was their demeanour, indeed, that the young man dared scarcely leave his lodging, being both humiliated and put in fear of his life. At any moment footpads might seize him, he believed, and whisk him back across the Channel to England. He had earnestly besought the Hungarians to receive the Earl, but this they were unwilling to do.

In his frustration and misery he was now accused unjustly by Suffolk of slackness in extricating him from his difficulties and of putting his own interests first, which so cast down the unhappy Richard that he wished he could die. He had done his best for his brother, receiving only cruel and unwarranted censure in return, but still he persevered. Suffolk's hopes were continually raised, only to wither before they had bloomed. Philip was busily assembling a fleet, which the Earl was told was for him. The Duke of Pomerania and the King of Denmark were also to be asked for aid. Meantime, immobile in his fortress, Suffolk had to depend on the charity of friends. While he buoyed himself up with the windy Burgundian words from outside, his movements were closely watched and his liberty scant. The 'White Rose', heir to the House of York, could but fume and wait. He did not know that as a bribe for his surrender Philip had been lent £108,000 by the King, followed by a second loan in the following month.

In October Ferdinand married Germaine de Foix, who had the royal blood of France in her veins. At the same time, Louis of France gave up his pretensions to the Kingdom of Naples and made a pact with the Spaniard against the bumbling Maximilian. The alliance between the Emperor and Spain was now hanging by a thread, soon to be cut.

Erasmus had been in England in the autumn, meeting many of her leading men, including Warham, Archbishop of Canterbury, Bishop Fox and Tunstall. The 'sweating sickness' had broken out again, but by now the proper treatment was known, and few died. So ended the year 1505.

[9]

The year that followed was remarkable. In England on the 15th January it was introduced violently by a great storm. Trees were wrenched up by their roots and tiles ripped off the roofs of houses. The wind seized the brazen eagle weathercock from its long pivot on the top of St. Paul's, and flung it the entire length of the cathedral—about a hundred paces. It came smashing down on 'The Black Eagle', the sign of a bookseller, outside his shop in the churchyard. As Philip of Burgundy's standards included one with a black Roman eagle, perhaps as a tribute to his father, the word sped round that he was a doomed man.

The weathercock was replaced, but with great difficulty, and after the storm came bitter cold. The Thames froze so that carts could travel safely over its surface. A heavy snowstorm followed, and lasted till the streets were choked.

In Europe a new grouping of states was taking place. Instead of the tremulous 'Holy League' against France a prospective coalition was suggested of the Duke of Guelderland, the Swiss, Spain and possibly England, against Maximilian and Philip of Burgundy. The task of bringing the English into this was left to Ferdinand. Once more a carrot, Princess Mary's marriage with Duke Charles of Guelderland, was dangled before Henry, and a personal meeting suggested between Mary herself and a maid of honour or other representatives of the two houses. Henry, however, turned a deaf ear. '*Aut Caesar, aut nullus!*' Either the Earl of Suffolk must be handed over and the obnoxious customs duties of Flanders removed, or there would be no marriage.

With the same motive, perhaps, the daughter of the King of Portugal was proposed as a bride for the Prince of Wales. Henry, hovering like a vulture over a battlefield, waiting for the pickings, was secretly flattered by the effects of the new alignment in Europe. All were competing for his favour, for Philip himself now offered his daughter, Eleanor, as the Prince's wife. Neither suggestion was taken up.

Suffolk had been reduced to a sorry state, and on the 24th January, 1506, his friends or servants, Killingworth and Griffith, left Namur for England with the self-endowed status of ambassadors to request his free pardon, the restoration of his estates and offices, and the liberation of his cousin William and his friends, in return for a solemn undertaking by the Earl that he would in future be a loyal subject. As if the King or anyone could have trusted the oath of a man so forsworn as Suffolk! Killingworth and his companion would probably never have set off had they known that at that precise moment Philip, Suffolk's jailer, was himself in England.

This was one of those extraordinary pieces of luck that have a remarkable habit of occurring whenever England is in danger, so that the resentful have declared that 'God is an Englishman'. Philip had been driven to the conclusion that unless he forcibly removed Ferdinand from Castile he would never become her King. He had been steadily assembling ships, soldiers and supplies in Antwerp, meaning to invade Castile, take Ferdinand by surprise, and send him packing. After a period of waiting for a fair wind at Middelburg in Zeeland, he and his wife, Joanna, went on board their ship at Ymuiden, taking with them Quirini, ambassador of Venice, and a host of servants and retainers. Charles of Guelderland should have joined them with his men, but did not appear.

The departure of the fleet was delayed till the full moon rose, but it remained invisible, and not until the early morning of the 10th January did they at last, with great pomp, set sail, forty ships putting to sea to the sound of music and of guns fired in salute.

It was a bad month in which to attempt the Channel and the Bay of Biscay. Calais was soon left behind, but Philip, warned that a storm was blowing up, declared that if cast ashore in England he would endeavour to obtain an unopposed voyage to Spain.

Two days of sailing down the Channel with a fair wind were followed by a dead calm. Then a terrific north-easterly gale sprang up. A 'hideous wind' made working of the ship with all sails set difficult, toilsome and dangerous. Canvas had to be reduced, but despite this the fleet was driven helplessly south. All day on the 12th the wind blew, forcing the flagship with the royal couple on board so deeply into the oncoming waves that she threatened to founder. She was lightened as much as possible by tossing cannon and whatever else was heavy and movable into the sea.

At one moment the force of the storm was so great that she keeled over and nearly sent the Archduke into the water. Not only this, but three separate outbreaks of fire occurred on board, and the mainsail was blown down while being lowered so that its weight made the gunwale go under. A seaman dived thrice into the sea to cut away the shrouds, but it took half an hour to right the vessel. After this a second calm set in, lasting till the evening of the 13th, when this time a south-westerly gale sprang up.

Driven wildly before it in the darkness the fleet was dispersed and, when morning broke, a third of the ships had disappeared.

Of the visible remainder of the fleet, four made harbour at Plymouth and three at Dartmouth. Only three Burgundian ships and one Breton vessel were lost, but most of their crews were picked up. Few had ever weathered a storm so terrible, and it was said that only experienced Dutch skippers and seamen could have done so.

[10]

News that a great fleet was approaching brought out the armed forces of the English in various localities. After the swell left by the gale had subsided and they had had time to recover, Philip's advisers recommended that the voyage should be resumed. Philip, however, to say nothing of Joanna, had had enough of the sea for one occasion, and promptly rejected their advice, believing it better to make for land, acquaint the King of their misfortunes and stay where they were till they knew his reaction to their unexpected appearance. If favourable, the correct course would then be to visit him and the Princess Catharine.

During the night hours the flagship's pilot, taking regular soundings to ascertain their whereabouts, conceived that they were being flung willy-nilly towards the coast of England. He strove to change her course by tacking, but the gale steadily intensified until by midnight owing to the fury of wind and wave they were little more than fifty miles from shore. In the pitch-black night not a thing could be seen. Old seamen swore there had been no storm like it for fifty years. Each ship sought her own safety, some trying to reach the nearest harbour, while others aimed to clear the Channel and risk the open sea. (This was the same storm as struck London and did great damage.)

At dawn the wind died down, but a thick fog now swallowed up the ship on which Quirini, the Venetian, was a passenger. He could hear the boom of waves breaking on massive cliffs, and knew that the eighteen ships, of which his was one, must be close to some rocky coast. He said his prayers, believing he would soon be drowned, but to his joy his portion of Philip's fleet came safely into Falmouth harbour, 'a wild spot where no human being ever comes save the few boors who inhabit it', was how he described the place. The Cornishmen, he said, were a barbarous people whose language was so different from that of the Londoners that these could grasp their meaning little better than the Venetian himself. The roads between Falmouth and London were too dangerous for him to travel, he explained, being frequented by robbers, murderers, bullies and the like, so that he would now remain where he was rather than risk his life by going inland.

Meantime, Joanna, who had put on her richest dress to ensure that her queenly dignity should be recognized and respected when her body was washed ashore, was being tossed wildly out at sea in the flagship with her husband throughout the 14th and 15th, there being only one other vessel in sight. Philip in his doublet went bravely about the deck, encouraging his sailors, until a wave dashed him down so fiercely that he was stunned and believed dead. He had given up all hope of survival, but to his joy on the 16th, the skill of captain and crew brought the ship into Melcombe Regis in Portland Bay, opposite Weymouth.

When he had sufficiently recovered he had a small boat lowered and went on shore.

CHAPTER FIFTEEN

End of a Reign

[1]

ON REACHING LAND Philip was met by Sir Thomas Trenchard, who believed he would earn the King's gratitude if he detained these uninvited guests until the news of their arrival had reached Windsor. By stealth, therefore, he despatched two small craft, one a short time after the other, with the message. This done, Sir John Carew and a numerous band of armed men joined the many fisherfolk and idlers gathered on the shore. Carew joined with Trenchard in urging the exhausted, battered, salt-stained Archduke not to depart, as the King would certainly wish to welcome him. They invited him to Trenchard's house.

At first Philip was reluctant, but finally, although treated with every courtesy, he suspected that if he continued to refuse he might be forcibly detained, so he gave way.

When the news of his arrival came the King was overjoyed. It was as if in absence of mind a chess opponent had allowed him to capture his Queen. Here were Castile and Burgundy combined helpless on his shores and in his power. He arranged to feast and entertain these royal castaways at Windsor, instructing the gentry of Dorset to wait upon them and see that they had whatever they needed. Splendid horses and litters were despatched for their use when travelling. Trenchard and Carew were commanded to see that the Archduke did not leave England, while the Earl of Arundel was sent to notify Philip that the Prince of Wales himself was coming to Winchester specially to meet him there. Arundel arrived by torchlight with great impressiveness at the head of three hundred mounted men.

When the Archduke and his party set off in due course for

Winchester they were accompanied by many English nobles, others joining them along their route. On the King's behalf Prince Henry welcomed them in Winchester, whence they proceeded towards Windsor. On Cleworth Green, two miles outside the town, Henry awaited them astride a bay horse whose trappings were of the finest needlework. It was 3 p.m. on the 31st January. The King was wearing a purple velvet gown and displayed a chain with a jewelled medallion showing St. George slaying the dragon, as well as a hood, also of purple velvet, which he did not remove, though he doffed his hat and bonnet, Philip doing the same. Philip's mount was a small, strong, sorrel horse, which the King had given him.

What sort of king did Philip encounter? With a new age had come a new man, one who had been a fugitive in his own land, a refugee in another, an exile, and was now an autocrat. Here, in fact, was a tough, tenacious, prudent, watchful monarch who had learned to shed illusions as a serpent its skin. He had lived the formative years of his life among the French and the Bretons, hard-headed, close-fisted folk loving the land. He had had to make do with little, been poor and pursued, hungry and athirst, made aware of the sharp turns of fortune and the existence of forces too powerful to be scorned.

He had learned in this way that a little could go a long way; poverty be endured and defeated by endurance; hunger and thirst be satisfied if one used one's wits and exercised caution and self-restraint; fortune be twisted in the direction one desired by courage and foresight; great forces be harnessed to one's own advantage by will and purpose, veiled but unalterable.

He had learned that the world of men was different from the world of dreams, that one had to use and manage those one met, to keep one's lips firmly closed and one's thoughts to oneself. Philip saw before him, indeed, no dashing Plantagenet warrior, no gifted and eloquent genius nor magical orator, but a king who had learned from the mistakes of others, and even better, from his own. In short, a *great* king, who had he not been so would have left his granddaughter, Elizabeth I, with neither a navy nor the money to build one.

In striking contrast to the King, Philip was dressed from his hat to his horse's harness entirely in black velvet. He told Henry that he had been truly punished for not accepting his offered hospitality when they met in Calais. As they moved towards the castle, the King offered to ride on the Archduke's left, but this honour was politely declined, nor would the Archduke alight from his horse until the King had done so, but waited a decent time before himself dismounting, a further mark of respect. When he did leave his horse, Henry would have taken him in friendly fashion by the arm, but Philip declined the courtesy and instead took Henry's arm and was led by him towards the castle, where a suite of rooms had been richly furnished with tapestries. Altogether seven separate chambers had been set apart for him and the Queen of Castile, all hung with cloth of arras into which the thickest possible gold wire had been woven. Three beds of estate were provided.

[2]

For more than five weeks everything was done to make the King of Castile, as he insisted on calling himself, enjoy his stay. He and his companions launched arrows at the butts, watched experts tease the bull and the bear, wagered money on the feathered combats of trained cocks, saw embryonic masques and morris dancing, tumblers, conjurors, men who swallowed fire. They were entertained by torchlight processions, while for Philip and Joanna's amusement fools and jesters flung their quips at all and sundry. Henry was usually missing when the fools appeared, for he could not bear them.

Banquets, hawking, horse baiting, hunting the deer and music passed the time. Princess Mary played the lute and the clavichord for them and song was provided by minstrels. Men wrestled with one another. Glorious notes issued from silver trumpets, from the diminishing strings of harps and the gut of fiddles. Recorders played sweet melodies, and even the bagpipes of Scotland stirred the blood of those who could endure them, while the sound of hunting horns vied with the songs of children. Music was one of the King's passions, and he himself had bought the instruments on which the Queen and his daughter performed.

He showed Philip and Joanna—whose state of mind was already

in doubt—the female giant from Flanders, the dwarfs from Scotland, the enormous babe, and other extraordinary freaks of nature, in all of which he himself was greatly interested. Entertainment with indoor and outdoor pastimes, such as tennis, was laid on with neither stint nor niggardliness. Once the fun was over, however, business began. The King said significantly to his guest: 'Sir, you have been saved upon my coast. I hope you will not suffer me to be wrecked on yours.'

Many conferences now took place in palace chambers. Under the gentle persuasions of overwhelming hospitality and with the knowledge that not only was he already in the King's debt, but also badly needed his support in his Castilian venture, Philip made one concession after another. A new treaty was proposed whereby the two potentates once more bound themselves to unite in defence or attack. Each, if asked, was to surrender up exiles, rebels and fugitives within his borders. Maximilian was included in the treaty, Philip undertaking to have it confirmed and signed by his father within four months.

His sister, Margaret of Savoy, might be persuaded, he thought, to become Queen of England. If so, Henry would be her third husband, because she had earlier been married to Prince John, eldest son of Ferdinand and Isabella, and Duke Philibert of Savoy, yet was still only twenty-seven. Lastly, Philip granted extremely favourable trade terms to England, and a new treaty was drawn up to embody these, known eventually as the Intercursus Malus Treaty.

Among its provisions were that English merchants should be relieved of custom dues payable in certain territories of Flanders. English wool could be sold wholesale without restriction in every part of Philip's dominions, and retail also anywhere in the territory. What this treaty did in effect was to remove the protection hitherto enjoyed by Philip's merchants and traders in the Low Countries. Castile, however, was carefully excluded from the treaty.

On the 9th February Mass was celebrated, all discussions came to an end, and the treaty was signed. A final banquet followed, during which Henry made Philip, as he had earlier sought to make his father, a Knight of the Garter, though in the end Maximilian was never installed, and as he refused the Oath, his investiture lapsed. In return, Philip conferred the Order of the Golden Fleece upon the Prince of Wales. A few days afterwards, on the 12th, Queen Joanna, Ferdinand's daughter, met Princess Catharine, her sister, and on the 14th, first Philip, then she, prepared to depart.

[3]

The provision in the new treaty for the surrender of rebels had inevitably brought up the matter of Suffolk, and it is said that on the 15th, Philip, although with some reluctance, offered of his own accord to hand him over to the King, sending a secret message to Namur to this effect. This done, Queen Joanna went with him to Romford in Essex, and from there she departed for Falmouth, where the Burgundian fleet was reassembling. On the same day Philip rode with the King through London to Richmond. Henry is said to have kept him in the country till Suffolk arrived, but this is unlikely, for after spending eight days at Richmond, during which period he agreed to Henry's marriage to his sister Margaret of Savoy, the Archduke departed for Falmouth on the 1st or 2nd March, whereas Suffolk did not reach England till the 24th.

After two days of his journey he was taken ill and rested for a few days at Reading, not arriving in the port until the 25th or 26th. He did not mention his illness to his wife so as not to alarm her, and told his entourage that the King of England could not have done more for him had he been his father.

The Archduke Philip, a man of average height, was not ill-favoured, though somewhat overweight. He was intelligent, courteous and free with his money, but found Falmouth a poor town and living there for four full weeks while his ships made ready extremely expensive. On the 23rd April he sailed. Before he went, Henry agreed to lend him a large sum of money, most of which he took with him, specified as 'for his next voiage unto Spayne'. The balance was to be remitted later. The King aimed to keep Philip and Ferdinand in opposition to each other, and it was therefore in his interest that the King of Castile should sail for Spain with cash enough to meet his needs.

On the 30th April the new trade treaty, drawn up in great detail by the plenipotentiaries of both sides, was formally signed, but when the Netherlands wool merchants knew its terms they rejected them, dreading the inevitable English competition. It soon became clear that final ratification, fixed for the 15th May by Henry and the 31st July by Philip, might never take place.

[4]

During Philip's absence from Flanders, Margaret of Savoy, appointed Regent, took up residence in Mechlin. Henry had settled all Philip's debts in England, and had also given him a few ships to make up for those he had lost. When Margaret was ordered to surrender Suffolk she was alarmed. The bargaining counter for better trade terms with the King of England was, she thought, being snatched from Flanders. Her brother's long stay in England might, indeed, be a veiled captivity. She refused to release the Earl until Philip was safely on his way again to Spain.

However, firm orders in her brother's own hand forced her to obey. Suffolk was accordingly escorted from Namur to Wageningen, and on the 16th March, a body of armed men brought him in to Calais. In strict secrecy he was shipped across the Channel and handed over to the Lieutenant of the Tower, who treated him with great respect.

Killingworth, who had tried hard to prevent this, was now so heavily in debt through his own generosity to the Earl that he had not the money to bribe anyone to assist him. He did, however, try to make life easier for Richard de la Pole by beseeching Maximilian to remove him to some town less dangerous than Aix. He need not have worried, however, for when Richard learned that his brother had been taken to England, he himself, fearing the same fate, slipped away without fuss in the autumn, and entered Hungary, where he was joined by Killingworth. Curzon did not return to England till Suffolk was safely in custody, where the Earl stayed till long after the King's death, being executed by his son in 1513.

Maximilian had agreed in March of that year to the marriage of Henry to Margaret of Savoy. The new treaty having already been signed by Henry and Philip, he ratified it on the 15th May. Margaret's dowry was to be 300,000 crowns, together with a yearly income of 70,000 crowns, her jointures from her earlier marriages. She was to have the sum of 20,000 golden nobles as her marriage portion from the King, while any children of the marriage were to inherit their mother's estates.

Now, however, the girl herself when told emphatically rejected Henry, realizing that once she became his wife he would be *de facto* ruler of all her estates, and what was left of her jointures after he had taken his stipulated share would pass to Spain and Savoy. Nevertheless she did not break off the negotiations with a definite refusal, but continually and cunningly introduced obstacles and objections from time to time which prevented their conclusion.

[5]

Philip having arrived in Corunna, Spain, on the 28th April, Ferdinand could no longer pretend to be the sole ruler of Castile. The relations between the Archduke and Joanna, his wife, had never been good, and over the years had become steadily worse, so that in June, 1506, there was talk of sending her to a strong castle and keeping her there.

Meantime, Henry's ambassadors were still patiently waiting in Calais for Margaret's signature to the marriage treaty and for the final ratification of the Intercursus Malus trade treaty by Henry and Philip, both of which appeared to be as far off as ever. Ferdinand and the Archduke were seemingly about to fly at one another's throats in Castile, having quarrelled violently at Remesal, near Pueblo de Senabria, and also at Renedo. Ferdinand had accused Philip directly of keeping Joanna, the Spaniard's daughter, locked up.

In view of this, Henry made ready to send troops into Flanders if Duke Charles of Guelderland took advantage of Philip's absence to attack the Regent, Margaret. The Duke had appealed to James of Scotland for aid in an onslaught on Burgundy, but James proposed that he should submit his grievances to arbitration. In his role as arbiter of Europe the King of England sent envoys to the Duke, the French King and the Netherlands in an effort to preserve the peace, while simultaneously trying to persuade Philip and Ferdinand to submit their dispute to arbitration. While he did not wish them to make friends with one another, he did not wish them to go to war.

All at once, on the 25th September, being too hot after a game of tennis, Philip had a 'stroke' and died at Burgos at the age of twenty-eight. (Some writers believe typhoid fever to have been the cause of his death.) Europe was once more in the melting pot.

To the Emperor, Philip's father, Henry expressed deep regret, undertaking to ratify the new treaty still hanging fire. Maximilian could never resist using an expression of amity as an opportunity to beg, and at once solicited a loan of 100,000 crowns for the support of Philip's children, for which he offered security, but the money was not forthcoming.

Margaret of Savoy also saw her opportunity. She had herself confirmed in the regency on behalf of her nephew, Charles, Philip's son, expressed a wish to trade with Britain on a firm footing, but ignoring the Intercursus Malus treaty initiated by her brother, went right back to the Treaty of Intercursus Magnus as the starting point for new negotiations.

Exasperated, Henry decided to humour her for the sake of their proposed marriage. He sent her six horses and some greyhounds, agreeing that trade should be resumed on the lines suggested, as long as certain safeguards were introduced. In May, therefore, he submitted a new draft treaty, insisting that this should be ratified and returned within a fortnight. She and her Council set their hands to it on the 5th June. In principle it reduced the proposed customs duties and cancelled the complete freedom of English merchants to sell their wool wholesale and retail in Flanders. On the 17th, however, it was agreed that the Merchant Adventurers could take their goods into the Low Countries and sell them there. As for their marriage, all that Henry could get out of Margaret, who was visiting Savoy, was that she had already had two husbands, and feared a third marriage. Moreover, she did not consider the dowry arrangements made by Philip satisfactory. Her father had suggested to Henry that the French were turning her against him.

The treaty of military alliance not having been ratified before Philip's death, the King, irritated, refused now to confirm it, releasing himself thereby from the explicit obligation to defend Margaret against the Duke of Guelderland, whose offer of arbitration was rejected early in 1507 by the Burgundians. This was a studied move on his part, for he knew now that Ferdinand, once more in power in Castile, had been annoyed by the treaty. With Philip's death, the Spaniard's friendship had all at once become essential again, especially as another notion germinating in his mind was about to burgeon and flower.

A tiff with the Pope occurred during this year. More ships from Italy had been captured with their cargoes of alum by the English. On a previous occasion, the King had undertaken to prevent this from happening again, but the Pope felt he was not fulfilling his promise. When a further case occurred the Pope insisted that the cargoes should be either destroyed or seized.

Maximilian now came back into the picture. Determined to make Castile a dependency of his own, he proclaimed himself heir to Philip in that country, asserting that Ferdinand had no right to the regency of a kingdom not his own by right of inheritance. He would become Regent himself, if necessary, on behalf of Philip's widow, Joanna, and her son Charles. For these grandiose plans he sought Henry's backing, and early in July his envoy, Andrea de Burg, came to London. A protracted meeting followed.

Briefly, Maximilian proposed that the King should marry Joanna, bringing both her and her son to England. He should then occupy Castile, for which action the Emperor would give him authority, since the child, Charles, would be in his care. He could then rule the kingdom as his own.

'This is all very well,' said Henry in effect, knowing the Emperor, 'but what will it cost me? Who will pay my expenses if I occupy Castile?' Maximilian was prompt to reply: 'You will pay your own costs, but you may keep a share of the Castilian revenues, sending the rest to me. In return, I ask only your support of my claims, and assistance, if necessary, against France.'

Henry was tempted. Ferdinand, with the tacit approval of the French, had virtually usurped Castile, but in his heart the King had no wish to offend either him or the French. If he annoyed the French, his annual remittances would cease, and while he had no objection to seeing Maximilian clip the Spaniard's wings in Castile, he was unwilling to use his own troops for the purpose. In consequence he temporized, suggesting that while England would not oppose the Emperor's legal claim to Castile, she would be better employed in keeping the French from allying with Ferdinand.

Meantime, Richard de la Pole, Suffolk's brother, had left Hungary and reached France, where he was welcomed by Louis as a potential threat to England and given a pension. Believing his brother in England had secretly been put to death, he took for himself the title of Duke of Suffolk, and was given command of a German contingent of the French army. When Louis discovered that Henry was negotiating with Maximilian and might at any moment declare war, he planned to send Richard with a powerful force into Cornwall. In the event, however, Richard was never needed, and died fighting at the side of Louis's successor in 1525.

Marriage to Joanna, the widowed Queen of Castile, would, in effect, if not in name, have made Henry King of that province. There had already been rumours that she was insane. After her husband's death the doubts became certainties. She had declared while he lived that he continually maltreated her, yet she would not leave his corpse, but sat watching it for days in the hope that he would return to life. Stranger conduct still was to follow, but even up to fifty years ago historians were not convinced that Joanna had truly lost her reason. That Henry knew of her condition is probable, though not wholly certain, but in any case, what she represented was more important to him than her sanity. He was supported in his determination to marry her by his Council, but they were so subservient that it does not follow they approved. The marriage in Henry's view had the advantage that if their union failed to produce a son, Joanna already had one in young Prince Charles, who, if the Prince of Wales died, would make an unchallengeable and powerful King of England.

Henry asked Ferdinand for her hand in March, and even persuaded the Princess Catharine and De Puebla, the Spanish ambassador, to write separately in support of his proposal. Obediently De Puebla wrote on the 15th April, 1507: 'There is no King in the world who would make so good a husband . . . whether she be sane or insane.'

Joanna did nothing to weaken the doubts about her. Wherever she went her husband's body in its coffin went with her, and she rejected every effort to have him buried. Moreover she was the victim of delusions and dementia. Henry and his Council may have accepted De Puebla's argument that she was not mad, merely weak-minded, but whatever the truth of this, she could still bear children, couldn't she? She had plenty of money, and whoever married her would be master of Castile. What else mattered? Once her obsession with her husband's body had been overcome, she might even recover her wits.

Philip now out of the way, Ferdinand did not welcome the prospect of another rival in Castile, but was still unwilling to annoy Henry, not wishing him to marry Margaret of Savoy. Accordingly on receiving these various letters he replied with his customary ambiguity: 'I shall never consent that she wed with any other than the King of England.' Nevertheless, he added, until she would bury Philip's corpse he dared not mention remarriage to her for fear of causing 'an unfavourable impression'.

Shortly before the Easter of 1507 Henry had suffered a devastating attack of 'quinsies' and for nearly a week had been unable to swallow. This attack had left him so feeble that for a time it was feared he might die. However, he made a slow recovery by taking regular exercise, and was soon on the mend. He spent a great deal of time in the open air, loving the chase, and indeed on many occasions envoys and ambassadors were compelled to hurry from point to point after him, only to be told when they caught up with him that unless their mission was urgent, they would have to wait. Almost the whole of September was spent in going from one forest to another, from one mountain to another, in quest of game. The King did not stay one day in the same place. Hyde Park was a favourite haunt. It belonged to the Abbey of Westminster, but Henry used it to extend his hunting territory northwards to give himself an unbroken run from Westminster to Hampstead Heath, then surrounded by a fence to keep in the deer.

By the autumn he was out chasing stags and bringing down birds with his falcons in the mellow October air. He was growing stronger every day and even putting on a little weight. His son accompanied him, and to his father's delight showed every sign of health and vigour, combined with a sturdy frame and limbs.

[6]

The King's recovery enabled the marriage of Charles of Castile, Joanna's son, to Princess Mary, Henry's daughter, to be concluded. The details of the marriage settlements had been fixed after months of tricky disputation, and in May agreement had been marked by the signing at Calais, by Bishop Fox and other plenipotentiaries of England and the Emperor Maximilian, of a preliminary treaty, followed by a definitive and final treaty of marriage dated the 21st December, 1507. This ensured that the couple should wed before Easter, 1508. The marriage was to be solemnized by proxy at both Courts after the little Archduke had attained the age of fourteen. The bride's dowry was to be 250,000 crowns, and if for any reason the wedding did not take place, the party responsible had to hand over an equivalent amount to the other. The treaty was welcomed in London, bonfires being kindled, tournaments held and public rejoicing encouraged.

By the match England and Maximilian came together, and as they were two of the great powers of Europe, this boded ill for Ferdinand, who was bitter, saying he should have been told before anything was done. Henry replied that the Spaniard had favoured the notion when first propounded, and ought therefore to countersign the treaty, since Maximilian, Henry and himself were all three nominally in alliance.

Ferdinand said he was willing to countersign the treaty if Henry would renew the marriage contract between Catharine and the Prince of Wales. This was tantamount to a refusal, for he knew very well that the King would do no such thing until the remainder of Catharine's dowry reached him, and this Ferdinand had no intention of sending.

Catharine, who, through De Puebla, knew the King's mind, or as much of it as he thought should be known, believed he had decided he could now ignore her father.

Friction between the two monarchs, fanned by Catharine, was so great that all Spain seethed with reports that Henry was assembling ships and men to invade the country. Though he did not attach importance to these rumours, Ferdinand guarded against surprise by himself preparing ships and men. At this period he was running out of funds, or said he was, a further reason for not transmitting the missing portion of his daughter's dowry.

He now angled for renewed friendship with France, convinced that the union with Mary and Charles was meant to blackmail him into handing over the unpaid part of the dowry, the first instalment of which had consisted of cash, plate, jewels and tapestries worth a great amount of money. He knew that Henry had been endeavouring to marry Prince Henry to Margaret of Angoulême, and now told the King firmly that Catharine's betrothal to the Prince of Wales could not, as he supposed, be arbitrarily set aside by the Prince's one-sided declaration.

Catharine was down to the last 30,000 crowns of her original dowry, half of which had been secretly conveyed out of the country so that Henry should not lay hands on it. Ferdinand blamed Philip for his shortage of money and her misery, saying that the balance of the sum had been all ready for shipment to England until 'he prevented it'. So, at least, he wrote to his daughter.

No doubt Catharine was anxious to have her future secured and a husband found for her. It was in her interest to allay the ill-temper of the two Kings. She had recently acquired a new Father Confessor, Friar Diego Fernandez, a young Spanish priest, who took up her grievances with fervour and taught her not only how to dissimulate, but also how to use the King for her own ends. Under his influence she was led to support Henry's marriage proposals.

Though she and the Prince of Wales were on many occasions housed in the same palace, they were forbidden to meet, and when she complained, she was told that this would be so until her father had settled his debt. Writing to Ferdinand she declared that no girl in England received such treatment as she, and that Henry himself had told her bluntly he no longer regarded her as affianced, the dowry money not having been paid. Nevertheless she 'played along' with him, telling Joanna that if she, her sister, married the King, she would become 'the most noble and powerful queen in the world'.

[7]

The Scots had given little trouble since making their pact with

England, but the general ferment was affecting their King, who made menacing noises, vowing that he would break the treaty and take up the claymore if Henry attacked Duke Charles of Guelderland. Secret negotiations were going on between James and the French, and Henry early in 1508 discovered that the Earl of Arran and his brother, Sir Patrick Hamilton of Kincavell, had slipped through England to France in disguise and without a written permit. In consequence when they foolishly tried to return the same way, Hugh Vaughan, sent expressly by Henry to welcome them, was waiting on the quayside. They were escorted to London, feasted, given great attention and courtesy by the civic worthies, and even received in state by the King himself.

Nevertheless, they were virtually prisoners and knew it. Arran, in fact, was separated from the rest and kept from communicating with them, while guards watched him closely. On one occasion, however, a Scottish doctor gained access to him on some pretext, but Vaughan, at once informed, ejected him with violent words.

Henry wrote to James complaining of the behaviour of his countrymen, and in March an able young clergyman, Thomas Wolsey, was officially despatched to protest. (Wolsey was one day to become a great statesman.) However, James was in truculent mood. There was never anything but fighting on the border, he declared, most of it caused by the English themselves. The way the Earl of Arran had been handled was a breach of the treaty between their two kingdoms, and the English monarch was premature with his complaint. He had not even given Arran's master the chance to punish his subject.

Wolsey conceded four English offences on the border to every one of the Scottish, but advised James that the King would set Arran free if he swore never to return to England. James rejected this proposal, saying that if Arran accepted such an offensive offer he would send him to the gallows the moment he crossed the border. It was not Henry's business to lay down the law to a Scotsman, but his.

Wolsey, though considering him sincere, was less sure of his nobles and populace, hankering after new ties with the French. He did his best to pacify the Scottish King, suggesting that he and Henry should meet. This appealed to James, and in March, he requested a safe-conduct for his envoy, the Bishop of Moray, who, as Wolsey knew, favoured maintaining the treaty.

Moray came to London on the 16th June and remained till the 28th July. Before his return to Scotland the King released the Scots. On the 8th August, Sir Patrick Hamilton swore to see that Arran never returned to England, and on the 13th Arran swore a similar oath in relation to his brother. Wolsey, having drawn an agreeable picture of James for Henry, dissuaded him from treating the Scottish lords too harshly. The compromise by which neither took the oath on his own behalf satisfied all parties, and no more seems to have been said or done on either side.

[8]

Henry now gave up the proposed marriage with Joanna of Castile, and turned his attention once more to Margaret of Angoulême, though with little enthusiasm. He planned to make a great match that would establish his dynasty once and for all. Then, dropping Margaret of Angoulême as he had dropped Joanna, he reconsidered Margaret of Savoy, to him a much more desirable person. An agreeable and able ambassador was to be sent to Maximilian to see what could be done. After consulting Fox and Thomas Lovell, he chose again the almost unknown young man, Thomas Wolsey, one of his own chaplains, a tall, fair-haired clergyman, just over thirty, son of an Ipswich meat purveyor and cattle dealer, ambitious, adaptable, energetic, bold and deferential, a courtier by instinct and a statesman by inclination and outlook, who had already proved himself in Scotland.

Wolsey left Richmond for Gravesend at midday on the 20th July after being fully briefed by the King. He left Gravesend at four, arrived in Dover by barge at daybreak on the 21st, caught the first ship to Calais, and after a crossing that lasted three hours, set off to meet Maximilian at Ghent. Enchanting that mercurial person, he achieved all he had been told to achieve, wasted not a minute, but returning to Calais, arrived in Dover at 10 a.m. on the 22nd, and was back in Richmond by nightfall. This was express diplomacy with a vengeance, and unheard of in those days.

Small wonder that when Henry, on his way to Mass, ran into his chaplain, he was angry, asking why he had not gone on his mission. When he discovered that Wolsey had, in fact, been there and back and been successful, he was astounded and delighted, thanking him for his 'good and speedy exploit'. Before many days had passed the young diplomat found himself Dean of Windsor, and after that, Almoner to the King. He was 'on his way'.

Maximilian told Wolsey he was quite prepared to substitute Margaret of Savoy for Joanna, if that was Henry's wish, but as usual demanded a *quid pro quo*. Henry must lend him 100,000 crowns, for which, of course, he would give adequate security. The King agreed on condition that the betrothal was put in hand immediately and envoys sent to England to arrange it.

The influence of Father Fernandez over Catharine had not been overlooked by those around her, some of whom wrote to her father that she was taking too much notice of her 'light, haughty and scandalous priest', who was causing her to make many errors of conduct, such as refusing on his advice to leave Richmond to meet the King and dismissing the escort sent to take her to him, so that Princess Mary, in attendance on her, was kept waiting for two hours. Instead, Catharine had set off without leave the following day, accompanied by only Fernandez, three maids and a couple of servants.

Henry scolded her severely for this lack of dignity, accusing her of misconduct with her confessor. Meantime the priest was also upsetting De Puebla. The ambassador was having daily to sell gold plate to cover the friar's expenses. Declaring him to be a man 'without learning, looks, manners, competence or credit', De Puebla added that he was the most evil man he had ever known. In a letter to her father Catharine asserted indignantly that 'in the house of the King they would not give meat to anyone, even if he were dying'—a bitter woman's slander.

A rumour now reached London that Joanna had at last agreed to marry—the Sieur de Foix! This was a blow to the King, who, taking it as a sign that she had recovered her sanity, addressed at once to the crazy widow what can be described only as an absurd secondhand loveletter. At his command De Puebla wrote that the King's love was 'marvellously great' and that he had been smitten by her during her visit to Windsor in the previous year, so that her departure from England had saddened him.

Ferdinand immediately dismissed the rumour as nonsense. Joanna, he wrote, was still carting her dead husband's body around with her, and in a condition such that she was totally incapable of giving orders. No one dared cross her for fear of violence, and she had to be handled with the utmost discretion. Henry suspected that the Spaniard was lying, and in consequence the friction between these two great men increased.

[9]

Ferdinand, convinced that De Puebla was under Henry's thumb and revealing too much, summoned him back to Spain, replacing him by the Governor of Membrilla, Gutierre Gomez de Fuensalida, who came with a startling offer, which he tendered in so stiff and irritating a manner that the King took an instant dislike to him. His master, Fuensalida said, would pay the remainder of Catharine's dowry, which he had brought with him, if her betrothal to Henry were confirmed and followed by marriage.

At this juncture, this was not at all what Henry wanted. To delay matters he replied that the dowry must be in gold, not as before, partly in plate, jewels and other possessions. Though annoyed, Ferdinand agreed, with the proviso that his bankers would deposit the money only when the marriage had been celebrated 'for when one has to negotiate with people of little faith and honour, caution is essential'.

This stipulation enraged the King, who replied firmly and coldly that as long as the money was withheld the marriage would not take place. He refused to receive Fuensalida again when that dignified ambassador, much less pliant and far more pompous than either De Puebla or Ayala, cantered over on a mule to the palace gates to soothe the angry monarch. The palace guards took hold of the bridle of his mount, turned him round, and on their master's orders sent him back the way he had come. Henry also wrote that Ferdinand must promise never to ask for the return of the money, and must formally approve the marriage of Charles and Princess Mary. This last, being the very factor that had led Ferdinand to fear expulsion from Castile, was hardly likely to be welcomed. The deliberate insult finally broke the tie between the two Kings.

Catharine was in tears. Life in England had become unendurable to her, she wrote. She had had to dispose of some of her household goods, and unless her father sent her money, she feared the consequences, as she could not go on so for ever.

Beyond question she and her frustrations were thorns in the flesh of both Henry and Ferdinand, and it is not surprising that the wounds festered. Many of her complaints were unjustified. The new ambassador found her largely to blame for her own shortage of money and Henry praiseworthy for his patience with her. Her royal father was, however, furious that she should be, as he thought, shabbily treated at the English Court, but was powerless to bring her back to Spain without Henry's permission. For this reason he could not make war on him, though at one stage he threatened to bring her home forcibly by invading England and punishing the English.

[10]

Money was becoming increasingly important to the King, and he devoted much time to its acquisition. The income from tunnage, poundage and customs duties had been given to him for life, not for a specific period only, and he was not tied down to using it for stated purposes. This increased his net revenues considerably. The estates of the Prince of Wales were made more lucrative by measures not all of them honourable. Money rolled in from the fees received when bishops were appointed; from the royal commission on the minting of gold and silver coins; and from the fines inflicted by magistrates.

Clink-clink-clink! Gold tumbled into the strongboxes from the perquisites of the King on the granting of preferments, from the commission on exchange transactions, from the royal expense accounts presented for payment, from ancient but legal fees and tolls. The new standard weights and measures had, after all, never been sent to the country towns, but were now provided, together with the necessary replicas, which were carried to their respective districts.

Yet despite his acquisitiveness Henry subscribed fully to the

Catholic Church's original belief that to take interest on loans was immoral. In response to his persuasions Parliament passed an Act prohibiting 'usury' or the acceptance of interest. Transgressors were liable to a fine of £100 for each offence. Trial and verdict were both the prerogative of the Crown. As was to be expected, this new law was popular with neither the rich nor the poor, for it was interpreted in many ways, there being no exact definition of 'usury'.

As regards Margaret of Savoy, whom Henry had tried without success to meet in Calais in May, Maximilian was concerned only with getting money out of the English King, and would do nothing until Henry agreed that his offered security was acceptable, and sent him the cash. He at first made no mention of sending envoys to England, but on the 1st October the treaty of betrothal was signed by Margaret at her father-in-law's insistence, and on the 11th he stipulated an agreed sum to be paid by the King if the marriage did not take place. Things were now well in train, and Thomas Wolsey went over once more to arrange for a formal embassy under the Earl of Surrey to be received in Antwerp and a similar party to go to England to ratify the marriage of Prince Charles to Princess Mary.

Wolsey did his best, but for a time made no progress, possibly because Margaret still went on creating obstacles. Maximilian showed himself unwilling to proceed further. In his impatience Henry wrote to Margaret herself, but without result. He was suspected of seeking to control the Netherlands for his own benefit, and although he threw out offers of great reward to those who could promote the match by their influence, he was unsuccessful.

Even at this late stage, however, he would have dropped Margaret like an old shoe if there had been a genuine prospect of gaining Castile through marriage with the mentally infirm Joanna.

However, Wolsey had his way at last. Maximilian received the English delegates first in Antwerp, then at Schonhoven on the 31st November. His own party, sailing to England under Lord Burghes, arrived at Greenwich on the 7th December. Henry, though desperately ill, was able to welcome them, but reproved them for taking so long to complete the treaty.

In the little time that remained to him, Henry used all his skill in negotiation to thwart the schemes of both the French and Ferdinand, his policy being to keep them apart. Indeed, he sought to keep the Spaniard out of all Europe north of the Pyrenees. He was appointed arbitrator of one quarrel, affecting Guelderland, between the Kings of Scotland and France, and undertook with other princes to guarantee a treaty signed at Cambrai.

Throughout his reign, in fact, he opposed Ferdinand whenever he could do so without risk. The King of Aragon, with whom, it was said, he 'had ever a consent even in nature and custom', was often driven to protest at the manner in which he, his daughter and his kingdom's trade were treated by the English. Henry had tried to prevent Ferdinand from joining a proposed coalition of all the great powers of Europe against Venice, but in Cambrai in 1509 the great powers, despite his efforts, agreed to unite against her.

Notwithstanding this, he had many grounds for satisfaction. Indeed, his mood is best expressed by a letter he wrote to the men of London, in which he said: 'This our realm is now environed, and in manner closed in every side with such mighty princes our good sons, friends, confederates and allies, that by the help of our Lord, the same is and perpetually shall be established in rest and peace and wealthy condition.'

Three words in that sentence contain the essence of his policy and preoccupations—'perpetually', 'peace' and 'wealthy'. He meant his dynasty and his kingdom to endure; he wanted peace; and he wanted the kingdom wealthy to consolidate the strength he had built up. He had made allies by marriage and statecraft, so that his defences lay well beyond the shores of England. He had developed his country's commerce so that wealth flowed in, carried in the holds of his new ships. Above all, he had obtained peace at home and abroad, brought the reins of power into his own hands in his own kingdom, reduced crime and ensured social stability, tamed the barons and quelled the unruly. Money, except in rare instances, was no longer false and passed on to the unsuspecting. Highways and bridges were being steadily repaired, maintained and replaced. Towns were being compelled reluctantly to make good all roads within their walls over which vehicles and wagons travelled. This had been achieved in the day-to-day coping with the problems that arose, not by exceptional foresight or systematic planning. These things expressed the fallible, but sound, judgement of a hard-working, careful statesman, who like others before him was limited in vision by his temperament and his times, but had qualities they had lacked.

Even this was not all. He had wiped out the numerous debts of his predecessors and put the finances of the realm on a sound and carefully controlled basis. His royal income had been established and enlarged by accurate accounting, economy and foresight. Revenues from his estates continuously flowed in. He was, in fact, a meticulous and able financier. Everything was set down on paper so that he could see exactly what money had been spent, and how, whether for his private account or on behalf of the State. Like an accountant called in to restore the finances of a company in low water, he was firm in his refusal to let bills accumulate or debtors escape.

As a result, he knew at any moment how he stood. We can almost watch him at work. Nobody of his household could pass off extravagance or waste under loose headings such as 'incidental expenses' or 'petty cash'. What seems like niggardliness compared to the ways of earlier kings was in reality *good business management*. Henry knew how important it was to 'keep out of the red'. Even his most trifling gifts of three or four shillings were recorded.

This was all the more necessary because the kingdom over which he reigned was neither rich nor populous. He had not the wide fields of France nor the productive industrial capacity of Germany and Flanders, nor the overseas wealth of Spain. He could survive only by rigid attention to detail and the best possible use of his resources. It was his duty to ensure that the realm was financially sound. A bankrupt kingdom would be merely a discarded pawn on the European chessboard, and all that that meant in poverty, squalor and misery for his people. Freedom from debt meant influence, security, independence and power for England, her King and his successors.

Best of all, perhaps, he had cleared the Channel of pirates and achieved lasting peace with those inveterate foes, the Scots. He was the undisputed Head of the State and had established what he hoped would be a new and prospering dynasty—based not on the nobles, whom he had reduced to courtiers and messenger boys or decorative figures for ceremonial occasions or uniformed generals for his armies, with no power to dethrone him, but on men he believed wise and conscientious, including even ecclesiastics and statesmen drawn from a totally different and lower class. His aim was what we should call today, perhaps, a 'meritocracy'. Since he did not need money as he had needed it in his early days, he no longer had to placate Parliament, which in fact he had for years ceased to summon.

The Commons were his to a man, for they benefited by the revival of trade and the increase in national wealth and employment he had brought about. There was no risk of a clash with these men and their interests.

The nobles were rapidly giving place in influence and power to the cities and their citizens, a process begun by Edward IV. They had no supreme chieftain of the blood royal, eager for revolt and the upheavals of war, no baronial 'kingmaker' such as the great Warwick. On the other hand townsfolk and peasants created and enjoyed the combined wealth of trade, agriculture and industry. Instead of the arts of war the nobles were learning the delights of peace—art, music and literature—which were coming in on invisible wings from the continent of Europe. Culture was seizing upon the English like an infection. Men of rank worked off their high spirits now in tournaments, feasting and masques. They were expected to attend the Court and present to foreign visitors— whether Erasmus or some other notability—a galaxy of resplendent figures about a dignified and respected monarch reigning unchallenged and supreme. The King cast a cold eye upon them if they did not.

In short, he had created a powerful kingdom with a fine new navy, a growing manufacturing ability and a thriving commerce. His own merchant vessels were bringing wines and dyes from France, and goods from other lands. England was sending out adventurous seamen on voyages of discovery. Under him the realm was beginning a new existence as a prosperous trading state.

Furthermore, the crown was now a symbol of undisputed power and authority. He had gained the esteem and backing of the Church with its immense riches, and with each year his throne received new reverence. It is significant that he was the first English King to be addressed directly as 'Your Majesty' rather than 'Your Grace'. His personal power was so great that he could even veto an Act of Parliament which had passed through all its stages.

His legislature had altered the entire system of monarchal government. The rich had been put in their places, the common people treated with leniency and given a good measure of personal freedom. Of course he was a despot, but a reasonable and capable one, who did not sit too heavily on his kingdom's back. If he meddled in the business of the towns, it was usually with good reason. If he had men here and there listening, watching and reporting to him, it was necessary, for men would never learn wisdom, and a medieval king had to know what was afoot in his realm and elsewhere.

Above all, he had taken a bewildered and broken nation needing a firm hand and put it together again, keeping it strong and healthy when it had recovered. In himself he was not ambitious for conquest. He fostered his country's military and naval power not because he hankered after the territory of other princes, but because a strong defence against marauders and ambitious rivals was essential. He had learned only too well that the acquisition of lands not one's own entailed endless warfare and the grinding down of a kingdom's resources. He was one of the first medieval kings to appreciate long before Shakespeare that the separation of his small island from the great European land mass by a strip of deep water was an invaluable boon. He retained his hold on Calais solely as a bastion, a watch tower, against hostile intrusion.

For the rest he was content with holding down Ireland and containing the Scots. Wales had been his from the start. He knew that the more firmly he bound his people's welfare to his own with a tight and enduring knot, the stronger would both become and the less easy it would be to part them. No other means could be so effective. His greatest achievement in the realm of statecraft was his recognition that he and his subjects were wholly interdependent.

Despite his careful eye on the exchequer, he was not afraid to spend. He believed in giving his people all the ostentatious luxury and show they expected of him. He never shirked paying out money to gain a political or national advantage. He borrowed large amounts, but only for urgent needs, borrowed them early before any lender could doubt his solvency, and paid back everything he borrowed on the appointed date. He made the Queen, who also frequently borrowed, do the same. If he wrote stiff letters to offenders, they usually deserved it. His reign, though not without its brutalities, had no such record of executions and murders as those of Henry VI, Edward IV and Richard III. The ghastly dungeons of the Tower were no longer full to overflowing.

His lands were rented out at reasonable prices. Men preserved game and timber in his forests. Others produced the beef, mutton, salt and fresh fish, corn, poultry, horsemeat and litter for his household needs, as well as ale, wool, cloth and other merchandise. His people were better-trained in war than for many years, regular jousts, hunts and other exercises keeping them fit and giving them practice. He had stopped the bowmakers from putting up the prices of their bows, and although the crossbow was becoming fashionable, he refused to let the longbow be superseded by it, partly for religious reasons, partly because the crossbow was useless in wet weather owing to the loss of tension in the strings.

He could not have done all this had he not been cautious, realistic, sound in judgement and a man of vision, ever looking to the future.

[11]

In February he had been ill again, and this time there were signs that he was suffering from an incurable complaint—phthisis— though his people were told it was 'gout'. At this period he was still toying with the idea of marriage to Margaret of Savoy, and through Wolsey told her that if she would marry Henry he would spend part of every year in Burgundy, and let her return there whenever it could be arranged. Margaret, however, was still no nearer to taking the final step.

Now, as his life shortened, the King experienced an access of religious fervour. He seriously considered participating, together with the French and Portuguese, in a new crusade, and addressed a letter to the Pope urging him to call every Christian prince to a holy war against the Turks. He wrote that he had always aimed at peace, and had never striven after conquests, but although it was repugnant to him to shed Christian blood, he would willingly shed that of unbelievers.

The letter was carried to Rome, where its contents were recited to the College of Cardinals and their Superior. The Pope, while expressing delight with the sentiments of the message, remarked drily that he did not need to be told what was wanted. In his reply to the King, who had sent duplicates of the letter to the potentates of the Holy Roman Empire and others, he suggested that Henry would do well to join with him in settling the quarrel between Maximilian and Louis of France, so that their combined armies might attack the Turks. Consequently, Henry's appeal fizzled out for lack of papal and princely enthusiasm.

He had always been a devout and orthodox churchman, accepting the tenets and disciplines of his faith and devoting much of his wealth to the benefit of its members. Thus, he had houses built for the friars of one Order at Richmond, Greenwich, and Newark, and for those of another at Canterbury and Southampton. The library of the friars at Greenwich was stocked with books given by him. On the site of the former Savoy Palace, then in ruins, he built a hospital for one hundred poor people, and dedicated it to John the Baptist.

During his last months he was planning to put up an even larger one at Bath. He did not pay for all these out of his own purse, but devoted to them the income from church institutions on their last legs and not to be restored. He left £5,000 to the Abbot of Westminster to complete the chapel known as 'King Henry's,' which is said to have been constructed of stone quarried at Huddlestone in Yorkshire and cost £14,000.

By December, 1508, the King, though he had rallied during the summer, was growing steadily weaker. It was obvious that he was failing. He himself was now alarmed and went on pilgrimages to Our Lady of Walsingham and St. Thomas of Canterbury. The marriage of Charles of Castile to Princess Mary was consequently hurried on, and was performed by proxy at Richmond on the 17th, Lord Burghes standing in for Charles. The King attended the ceremony, and watched Lord Burghes take the right hand of the Princess in his own and declare, speaking in French, that he took her for his wedded wife, to which Mary made the usual reply.

Burghes then formally kissed her and encircled her finger with a golden ring. This done, the envoys got down to the business of jointures and settlements. Henry lent Maximilian 50,000 crowns for his new Venetian war. Too wary to lend any sum without security, he received in return a large diamond in an expensive setting, known as 'la riche fleur de lys'. With the completion of this marriage treaty, Henry felt he had made England safe, or as Bacon says, had 'built a wall of brass around the kingdom'. There were great festivities in London at Henry's request, which was contained in a letter to the Mayor. To Ferdinand, however, it was the last straw.

1509 saw the King growing steadily worse. Day after day his health declined. He suffered acute pain in the chest and his breathing became difficult. Venice, now in desperate straits because of the concerted attack upon her, sent ambassadors to ask his help, but he was too ill to receive them. England had not been formally included in the Treaty of Cambrai that initiated the attack upon her, so he was not precluded from sending the ambassadors a message of goodwill. Maximilian also sent an embassy to him on the 20th March. They remained eight days in London without being able to see the King.

By this time the news that he was dying had been transmitted to every Court in Europe. The King himself was aware now that his days were being dealt out one by one like a pack of cards, and made his will on the 30th March.

In it he bade his son be prudent and avoid war. Asking to be laid beside his wife, he remitted all debts below £2 owed to him by those imprisoned in London, and is said to have repented the exactions of his ministers, Empson and Dudley, expressing a wish that their severity might be tempered by his son, though he himself had done nothing to this effect during his lifetime. He now wished the money unfairly extracted to be refunded.

He pardoned all who had broken the law, with the exception of thieves and murderers, and left money to pay for masses for his soul, having already paid for masses said for his recovery. From Prince Henry he extracted a vow to marry Catharine of Aragon.

He is said also to have seriously put forward the suggestion that Henry VI should be canonized, declaring that miracles had been performed at his place of burial, and to this end opened his purse more widely than usual to distribute alms, while leaving funds for the completion of various foundations. He left £2,000 for the construction of good roads and bridges between Windsor, Richmond, Southwark and Canterbury. His conception of a good road was one that enabled two wagons to travel along it side by side. The Pope avoided giving a decision on the point of Henry VI's canonization, holding that the honour would be brought into disrepute if bestowed on a king of known feeble intellect. All Henry could win from Julius was permission for this King's remains to be carried in state from Windsor to Westminster.

The King appointed his mother an executor of his will, her name appearing before all others. Legacies were bequeathed to his Councillors and household staff. His testament is still in the possession of St. Paul's Cathedral.

Pilgrimages were now made to shrines, and prayers for his recovery were offered up.

[12]

Towards the end of his life a great scandal broke. Sir William Capel, Mayor of London, had been fined £20,000 for misdemeanours committed which had not been detected by him. He refused to pay, attacking the character of his judges. In consequence he was sent to the Tower. An alderman, also arraigned, died before his case could be dealt with. A previous Mayor and two of his staff were fined £1,400. Sir Lawrence Aylmer, also a former Mayor, with his two sheriffs refused to pay his fine, and remained in the Tower until in course of time Empson took his place.

Henry lived for a further fortnight, then on the 14th April took the Sacrament and made his final confession. After struggling on desperately for a few more days, lying between life and death, he died at Richmond on the 21st April, 1509, at the age of fifty-two.

CHAPTER SIXTEEN

Funeral of a King

[1]

THE FUNERAL OF Henry VII was a spectacle such as few then living could have beheld. Between his death and the service men were hard at work putting up stands along the route of the cortège, to be occupied by children holding lighted tapers in their hands. In all the counties of England the nobles and esquires, the knights and yeomen, were having mourning robes made, as well as gay new raiment for the coronation that would eventually follow. They handed down their bedsteads to be packed for the journey to London, furbished up their armour, renewed their banners and pennons. The young Prince of Wales quietly took up his quarters at the Tower so that his presence in London should not mitigate the gloom of the people.

On the evening of Tuesday, the 8th May, the King's body was taken from Richmond in solemn and dignified procession by the light of six hundred torches, through Southwark, along the south bank of the Thames and over London Bridge. The cortège passed green parks studded with the great houses of the nobles, and ornate asymmetrical well-windowed houses of rich traders with their bushes and signs hanging outside to show the wares in which they dealt, the mean streets where the brothels and taverns abounded, and the graveyards, forlorn and unkempt, of forgotten paupers.

There came two kings-at-arms and a knight riding on a horse caparisoned in black and bearing the royal standard, followed by bishops, abbots, spiritual lords, representatives of the King's Bench and other courts of law. Intoning their Latin lamentations followed the trudging girdled monks and friars, the canons of the cathedral chapter, and the choir of the King's Chapel. At St.

George's Bar they were met by the Mayor, mounted on a good, well-trained horse, holding his mace and accompanied by one hundred and four mounted commoners. They emerged, all robed in black, from the Great Gateway.

Now, behind them, the observer saw seven black horses drawing the car on which the coffin was placed. Managed by Sir Thomas Brandon, Master of the King's Horse, they wore trappings of black velvet. The car itself carried the conventional wax effigy of the King wearing his crown, dressed in the magnificent robes in which he was accustomed to attend the sessions of Parliament, and holding both the sceptre and the golden orb in fingers stiffened with wire. Over the car stretched a canopy of cloth of gold, the coffin being draped by a pall of black velvet. Beside each of the seven horses walked a knight, while two others, termed 'mourners', sat at the head of the coffin and two at its foot, each holding the royal standard. The Knights of the Garter came next in order of precedence, led by the Duke of Buckingham, and after him five earls and three barons, the temporal lords. Lastly came many gentlemen and yeomen, esquires carrying swords and wearing caps of maintenance, trumpeters and clarioneers.

Through the streets of the city they went, moving at a slow pace. London Wall with its ancient Roman bricks and loose stone core, its many arches and dark openings, sheltered ruffians and pickpockets who, even on this occasion, slunk out to reap a good harvest from honest, unsuspecting citizens. On this sombre evening they circulated among the crowds, together with watermen, carters, seamen of many races, and women at the doorways of mud and wattle houses, watching with griefstricken or impassive faces the procession moving towards the Cathedral of St. Paul's.

The glimmering tapers of the children in the erected stands laid an undulating tapestry of light, soft and yellow, on the heads and shoulders of the marching men. Lamps and candles blossomed in the windows, and the chanting of priests and monks was punctuated by the frequent noisy jolts of the funeral car as it rolled over the stony, irregular ways. There was a slow shuffle of feet as the cortège went by, and everywhere was a chiaroscuro of light and shade. The black bats of shadow went flitting by, the sizzling torches were like red flowers swaying on black stems, and bearded faces, illumined, came suddenly out of the darkness with an effect of prestidigitation.

The streets, narrow, ill-kept, streaming, steaming and stinking, were so many varicose veins, clotted with a mass of men representing the crafts—weavers, shoemakers, labourers, barbers, masons, apprentices—each craft in order of its status, the lowest taking up the first place. London Bridge consequently received first the least honoured of the guilds. Swarthy Italians, bright-eyed Frenchmen, burly Flemings, the men of Florence and Venice, haughty Spaniards, a Hanse merchant or two, all came by either mounted or tramping in their soft cloth, felt or velvet shoes, or even going barefoot, carrying smoking torches after the slowly advancing procession.

Those lining the ways saw foreign potentates, courtiers, sheriffs and aldermen, men of the guilds carrying white roses in their hands, the Yeomen of the Guard, Lord Dacre at their head, and men of the city companies. They saw the Duke of Buckingham and the earls laying their hands on the bier to steady it, while four barons held the golden canopy. They saw a knight, Sir David Owen, representing Wales, carry the King's helmet, its golden crown glinting in the torchlight. They saw Sir Edward Howard, wearing the royal suit of armour, visor open, and holding the King's battleaxe, head reversed and supported by the stirrup. They saw an armed knight, resplendent and stately, carrying the Sword of State. All these things were impressed upon their minds so that in after years they spoke of them to their children in the tones of those who have witnessed marvels.

[2]

Arriving in the cathedral, where the Bishop of London in full canonical dress awaited them, the cortège halted so that the coffin might be 'censed', i.e. perfumed, before being carried by royal guardsmen through the nave. The canopy was reverently laid on the high altar, and after a lament by the Bishop the mourning procession left the cathedral, knights and a herald remaining behind to guard the body as it lay in state throughout the night, illuminated by 'a goodlie curious Light of Nine Branches'. Mass was celebrated thrice next day, and a funeral sermon delivered by John Fisher, Bishop of Rochester.

About 1 p.m., after dinner, the coffin was taken once more in procession to Westminster Abbey, and after being 'censed' a second time by the Abbot, other abbots and monks, it passed through the west door to be received by the Archbishops of Canterbury and York and laid once more in state, 'the most costly and curious light possible to be made by man's hand' being cast upon it from twelve standards. In the darkness of the abbey it must have presented a profoundly moving sight to the beholders.

There it lay for a whole night, guarded as before, then on Thursday, the 10th May, the royal armour, helmet, crown, shield and sword were offered up to four heralds. One of the King's horses, mounted and ridden to the altar by the bareheaded Sir Edward Howard in his suit of armour, was presented as an offering. Dismounting, Howard followed after the Earls of Kent and Essex, approached the Archbishop at the altar, then passed into the sacristy, removed his armour, and returned dressed in black to make his personal offering, after which the rest of the company, in order of precedence, made their own individual offerings.

The Duke of Buckingham and other lords paid respect to their dead sovereign by laying palls on the bier. The Bishop of London now delivered a funeral address at some length, and when his voice ceased to echo from walls and rafters, the effigy of the King was elevated and the choir united in singing the psalm 'Circumdederunt genitus mortis'.

A third censing of the wooden coffin, which was enclosed in a black velvet cloth showing a great white cross, was followed by the removal from it of the royal insignia. The inner receptacle for the body was of lead, and inscribed: 'Hic jacet Rex Hanricus Septimus' (Here lies King Henry VII). The coffin was finally placed in the same vault as that of the Queen. The Archbishop of Canterbury pronounced absolution, throwing down the first handful of earth, being followed in this by the Lord Treasurer and the Lord High Steward.

Then, according to custom, the heralds, breaking their white wands of office, tossed them into the open vault, as did the other officers of the royal household, and removed their 'tabards' or emblazoned jackets, hanging them on the railing about the tomb, crying the old words: 'Le roy Henry VII est mort!' The vault was then sealed and covered by a pall. A solemn pause ensued, after which the heralds resumed their tabards and through the soft murk of the abbey their joyous voices resounded in the traditional phrase: 'Le roy est mort! God send the noble Henry VIII long life!'

The tomb of Henry and his Queen was built by Pietro Torrignano, a Florentine sculptor, who came to England at royal request for the purpose. He began it in 1509 before the King's death, and completed it in 1517 at a total cost of £1,700 for his materials and skill. The King's will gave careful directions as to its character. It was to be in black marble with a nobly chiselled frieze, ornamented with copper gilt medallions. At either end were to be the royal arms supported by cherubs of brass.

[3]

The portrait of Henry in the National Gallery, attributed to Michel Sitium and possibly painted in 1505, is revealing. It shows the calm, ascetic face, the firm lips, of a man accustomed to self-control, as well as a strong chin and long slender fingers. Here one sees a sensitive, thoughtful man with a touch of pawky humour. Little would be required, one opines, to bring a slightly cynical but tolerant smile to that watchful face. The eyes, widely separated, are intelligent and penetrating, betraying experience, but revealing little of the inner man. They are the eyes of one who listens with patience and makes few comments, while meantime intense cerebration goes on. The nose is prominent and straight, the clothing rich, but not extravagant.

In singular contrast to his son, 'bluff King Hal', Henry had the features of a thinker, wise, sceptical, gentle, secretive. Looking at his portrait one feels one could have liked him.

As far as can be gathered, he was not conspicuously handsome. Towards the end of his reign he had become balding, wrinkled and to some extent toothless, which may account, of course, for the firm set of the lips in the painting. Like many other quiet, mild-mannered men, he could be vivacious when amused, and then his whole face would light up. On the other hand, he was quick-tempered and could be both stern and angry. He looked older than he was, but 'young for the sorrowful life he had led'.

One of his achievements had been to open the doors of the realm and allow a few sweet winds to blow through the dark and stuffy alleyways of English life. The Renaissance and the discovery of the New World had opened men's eyes and ears, touched their imaginations. As a nation, the English when he came to the throne were at a low intellectual level except for a small tight circle of scholars, clerics and administrators about the King. Most rural squires and many nobles were virtually illiterate. Indeed, Edward IV and his brother, the Duke of Clarence, were almost alone in having done something during the preceding decades for literature and the arts. Both visited the printing works of Caxton and encouraged the printing of books. Henry's appreciation of the value of printing is exemplified by his swift publication *in print* of Warbeck's confession.

Not until Henry's reign, however, did books come off the presses in quantity, and by the year 1500 there were four hundred of them. The King sought to widen his people's horizons. His own children were more than usually well educated in a manner consistent with their station and future duties. Their training was vastly superior to that of many other princes. He also fostered and rewarded ability and creative powers, encouraged the study of Roman law, the classics and the exposition of the Scriptures. He employed many Italians. (John Baptiste Boerio was one of his physicians.) In particular he was generous to those who wrote good verse or composed ballads he enjoyed. From overseas he brought books for his own and other libraries, and kept scribes hard at work making copies of others.

He himself spoke French with fluency to ambassadors and others, as was understandable in view of his early adventures, and was a fair speaker of Latin. Though not himself a scholar, he respected scholarship. He caused the first paper mill to be erected in Britain.

Erasmus, the great scholar, in England in 1499, found the land far less insular than he had expected. New ideas were surging in and powerfully stirring men's minds. There was a craving for enlightenment and he was even invited to act as tutor to Henry's sons should they be sent on a tour of Italy. He noted, however, that lead tokens were being used as currency.

Henry was no architect, but had excellent taste in architecture. He loved music, and was to some extent unusually liberal in outlook, though in other respects a man of his age. As he grew older, he became warped by desires and fears, held as in a vice by unreason, superstition, the dark beliefs and cruelties of his age. He listened gloomily to the absurd predictions of astrologers and may have executed the Earl of Warwick because one of these foretold peril. He kept up a morbid interest in freaks and monstrosities, especially those of human type. A lonely man, not personally compelling, he knew quite well he had neither the gaiety and charm of Edward IV, the audacity and ruthlessness of Richard III, nor, as it proved, the robust masculinity of Henry VIII, nor the guile and subtlety of Elizabeth I, but undeterred he walked his lonely way, a great, if not conspicuously lovable King.

Bibliography

THE STUDENT WISHING to study for himself the original material on which this book is based cannot do better than consult the *Oxford Bibliography of British History* for 1485–1603, which most city libraries possess. The list below is intended for those without ready access to the volume, or wishing to be guided to some book or books relating to a particular aspect of the reign. It is advisable for them to note that André, a contemporary writer of the period, is a flatterer and not to be absolutely trusted. Hall is vivid, but wrote later, and much of his work is hearsay, though not without value. The various continental state papers of the period give essentially foreign points of view. Lord Bacon was writing many decades later and is not always trustworthy, but he understood the problems of government and the minds of rulers and statesmen, and should be given careful consideration when he discusses the mainsprings of royal policy. Holinshed is terse and sensible within his limitations, but he, too, was not a contemporary. The Rolls of Parliament are the bare records of the Court kept by royal clerks, and are useful for checking facts and dates. Stow is reliable, but it must again be remembered that he was not a first-hand reporter.

Perhaps the most detailed and valuable contemporary account, of which I have made considerable use, is that of Polydore Vergil. The Paston letters are authentic and give a few interesting sidelights. Of the chronicles other than those mentioned I like best *The Great Chronicle of London*. Pollard has, however, compiled an invaluable collection of authentic material for the use of the historian. For incidental information reference to most of the other volumes and pamphlets listed is indispensable.

Acts and Monuments, Vol. iv.

Anglicae Historicae Libri, xxvii. Polydore Vergil (ed. Hay, Royal Hist. Soc.).

Annales de Aragon, v.

Annals of London. J. Stow.

Archaeologia, Vols. iv, xxvii.

Battle of Bosworth Field. W. H. Hutton.

Book of Howth (eds. Brewer and Bullen).

Bull of Pope Innocent VII on the Marriage of Henry VII with Elizabeth of York.

Calendar of Bristol, Ricart (ed. Toulson Smith).

Calendar of Documents relating to Scotland.

Calendar of Spanish Papers, Vol. i and supp. (ed. Bergenroth).

Calendar of Venetian Papers, Vol. i. (ed. Brown).

Cambrian Register of England.

Cambridge Medieval History, Vol. vii.

Cambridge Modern History, Vol. i.

Carew MSS.

Cely Papers.

Christchurch Letters (Camden Soc.).

Chronicle (G. Fabyan).

Chronicle, Greyfriars (Camden Soc.).

Chronicle (G. Hall).

Chronicle (R. Holinshed), iii.

Chronicle of London (J. Stow).

Chronicles of London (ed. C. Kingsford).

Chronicles and Memorials of Great Britain and Ireland during the Middle Ages (ed. W. Campbell), Vols. i and ii.

Chroniques, 1474-1506 (Molinet), Vol. iii (ed. V. A. Buchon).

Collección de Documentos ineditos (Navarrele), xiv.

Collectanea (Leland), Vols. iv and v.

Collection des Voyages des Souverains des Pays Bas (Gachard), Vol. i.

Constitutional History (Stubbs).

Cott. MS. Vitellius, A. xvi.

De Vita abque gestis Henrici Septimi (Bernard André or Andreas) (Memorials of Henry VII, v. Gairdner, Rolls, Series).

Dialogue (Starkey).

England under the Tudors (Busch), Vol. i. (Todd).

English Works of John Fisher (Early English Text Soc.), extr. ser. xxvii.

Erasmus (C. Hollis).

Excerpta Historica, Privy Purse Expenses (ed. Bentley).

Foedera (Rymer), Vols. xii, xiii.

Grandes Chroniques de Bretagne (Bouchard), Vol. iv.

Great Chronicle of London (Thomas and Thornley).

Hakluyt Voyages (ed. 1903), Vol. i.

Henry VII (G. Temperley).

Henry VII (J. Gairdner).

Hibernica (W. Harrow).

History of Epidemics in England, Vol. i, p. 237.

History of England (Fisher), Vol. v.

History of England (Speed).

History of Hinckley (Francis).

History of Kent (Haster).

History of King Henry VII (Bacon) (ed. Lumby).

Hist. MSS. Commission Reports, ix, xi, xii, xv.

History of the Life and Reign of Richard III (J. Gairdner).

History of the Reunion of Brittany and France (Dupuy).

History of Scotland (Pinkerton).

Ireland under the Tudors (Bagwell), Vol. i.

Irish Statutes.

Italian Relation (Camden Soc.).

Kritik von Schanz Jahrbücher (Schafer), Vol. xi, N.F. vii.

Lectures on Medieval and Modern History (Stubbs).

Letter Books (ed. Sharpe).

Letters and Papers relating to the Reigns of Richard III and Henry VII (ed. Gairdner), Vols. i and ii.

Letters of Royal Ladies (ed. Everett Green).

Life of Henry VIII (Herbert).

Mémoires (Comines, P.).

Memorials of Margaret, Countess of Richmond.

Naval Accounts and Inventions (Navy Records Soc.).

Original Letters (Ellis), Vol. i.

Paston Letters, vol. iii.

Percy MSS. Ballad of Bosworth Field (ed. Hales and Furnival).

Pilgrimage of Sir Richard Guildford (Camden Soc.).

Plumpton Correspondence (ed. Stapleton), p. 49.

Privy Purse Expenses of Elizabeth of York (ed. Nicholas).

Records of the Borough of Leicester (ed. Bateson).

Register of Bishop Fox (Camden Soc.).

Reign of Henry VII (Pollard), Vols. i–iii.

Rolls, Parliament (ed. F. Devon), Vol. vi.

Rutland Papers.

Select Cases in the Star Chamber (Felden Soc.), Introduction (Leadam).

Statutes of the Realm (Vol. ii).

Story of Perkin Warbeck (J. Gairdner).

Third Report of the Deputy Keeper of Public Records, Append. ii.

Trans. Royal Hist. Soc., N.S. xvi.

Tree of the Commonwealth (Dudley).

Victoria County History of Buckinghamshire, iv.

Waterford (C. Smith).

Will of Henry VII (Church Quart. Rev.), C. xvi, pp. 244–251.

Year Book of Henry VII (ed. 1585).

York Records (ed. Davies).

Index